INDIGENOUS SOVEREIGNTY IN THE 21ST CENTURY

INDIGENOUS SOVEREIGNTY IN THE 21ST CENTURY

Knowledge for the Indigenous Spring

by

Michael Lerma

FAP BOOKS

FLORIDA ACADEMIC PRESS, INC.

Gainesville, FL

For Mary and Fred Morales. Can't wait to see you again.

Published in the United States of America by
Florida Academic Press, Gainesville, FL, 32635
November 2014

Text and cover by David Greenberg Communications, Inc.
Cover image courtesy of Vernon L. Davis

Library of Congress Cataloging-in-Publication Data

Lerma, Michael.
Indigenous sovereignty in the 21st century : knowledge for the indigenous spring / by Michael Lerma.
pages cm
"FAP BOOKS."
Includes bibliographical references.
ISBN 978-1-890357-49-8
1. Indians of North America--Legal status, laws, etc. 2. Indians of North America--Government relations. I. Title.
KF8390.L47 2014
323.1197'073--dc23

2014042870

Table of Contents

Foreword
Sovereignty

"Sovereignty" is a much misused and misinterpreted term. The word itself comes from the Old French *soverain* or *souverein* and was used in reference to a king or lord who possessed the authority to rule over a particular territory without the benefit of counsel, religious sanction, or the consent of the governed. Various hierarchies of mounted, arms-bearing, property-owning, armored thugs known as knights formed the European feudal system. *Sovereyneté,* which was imposed in 1066 on the English by a feudal *souverein* known as William the Conqueror and hence became an Anglo-French word, came to mean the legal authority of the state. Niccolo Machiavelli, the 16th century political philosopher, thought that the most important concern of a prince was to be well-versed in the military arts presumably to maintain the power of state to protect itself from outside threats and domestic uprisings. Sovereignty, then, is a European concept that is at once hierarchical and coercive.

Through time, the definition of sovereignty has been changed and, sorry to say, misapplied. As this preface is being written the current political climate in the United States is not only toxic but ultimately based on an erroneous understanding of sovereign authority. The Republican/Tea Party/Libertarian/Grover Norquist movement that counts Ayn Rand and Ronald Reagan as its ideological parents does not seem to acknowledge the federal government as having sovereign authority. On the one hand, this movement seems to see the federal government as the enemy, based on the Reagan idea that "government is the problem," and that individual states are sovereignties with the power to nullify federal law. This line of thought appears to ignore the fact that the Civil War ended slavery and limited state sovereignty. The "states' rights" theme is an old adage from the "South Shall Rise Again" attitude that the Republican Party tapped into when developing its Southern Strategy in the late 1960s.

The United States Constitution, the federal government's assumption of the national debt in 1790, and the Civil War should have ended the fantasy that the United States was a simple, loose confederation of sovereign states.

The Tea Party/Grover Norquist anti-taxation wing of the Republican Party appears to base its ideological goals on the notion that the federal government really does not have the power to tax. This idea is, and always has been, part and parcel of sovereignty, along with the ability to coin money, determine citizenship, raise an army, protect its territorial boundaries, establish foreign relations, and promote the economic welfare of the state's citizenry or subjects. This wing also has apparently sided with the libertarian side of the Republican Party that views Ayn Rand's philosophy of the sanctity of individual rights and freedoms. Rand's ideas have bred the notion that each person is a sovereign in and of himself or herself. This philosophy stands incredibly close to anarchism, which, of course, argues that governments inherently and irrationally interfere with individual freedoms.

Given these old and new ideas of what constitutes sovereignty there can be little wonder why scholars of Native American studies are perplexed when the terminology "tribal sovereignty" is brought up. It is a rather difficult concept to take in.

Fortunately, Michael Lerma's study not only clarifies the meaning of sovereignty from a Native perspective, but also provides an intellectual basis for what he calls an "Indigenous Spring." This book is a return to the underlying principle that first supported Native American Studies. Scholarship should not only be sound and based on logic but also be useful. When Native American Studies programs in the universities were first instituted they were populated with scholar/activists like Bea Medicine, Robert K. Thomas, Vine Deloria, Jr., Roger Buffalohead, Rupert Costo, John Roulliard, Henrietta Whiteman, and Elizabeth Cook-Lynn. These scholars sought truth in their research as well as justice for Indian people. Mike Lerma might very well be called a member of the third wave of Indigenous scholar/activists. He pulls no punches and articulates a perspective of Native American/Indigenous individual rights and sovereign powers that is at once powerful, thought-provoking, and rational.

His insights, moreover, are drawn from a conceptual framework particular to Native American Studies. Vine Deloria, Jr. and others developed the theme of Native Knowledge in structuring these programs. Basically Native Knowledge sees the complexity of the world in which we live. Everything is connected and everything is real. Native Knowledge runs against the compartmentalization of knowledge that is the hallmark of the Western European academics. To be a good scholar of Native American Studies is to have a multi-disciplinary understanding of human cultures, political systems and philosophies. One also has to be able to incorporate various theoretical frameworks and raw data into a rational or perhaps lucid whole. It is both art and science.

Lerma's inquiry into Indigenous peoples' sovereign rights in this century refines the idea of sovereignty. Perhaps a better way of putting it is that he gets to the heart of why and how Native Americans and non-Indians seem to talk past each other regarding the concept. Tribal sovereignty is the antithesis of European hierarchical and coercive sovereyneté. It also has little to do with the American/Ayn Rand notion of the sovereign individual. From the Native American perspective it is a rational set of principles based on a group ethos of shared experiences, relationships, and what Native peoples would define as "truth," "the path," "the beauty way," or sometimes, "the red path."

Mike Lerma's study is, as the reader will see, a sound work in Native Knowledge. He does not compartmentalize knowledge, but rather draws from various disciplines theoretically and then adds an Indigenous perspective into the mix. Ultimately, this work is a matrix that contains numerous gemstones of erudition. It offers a much-needed perspective on tribal sovereignty—indeed on the conception of sovereignty—and will stand as a seminal work on the subject for a long time to come.

Dr. Tom Holm
Professor, University of Arizona

Acknowledgement

I continuously acknowledge the contributions of my grandparents, Mary and Fred Morales. They survived so much and I dare not take their gifts to me for granted. And to my mother, Linda. She reminds me to keep my compassion in a harsh world.

To Dr. Tom Holm for more than a decade of encouragement. Florida Academic Press staff, David Greenberg Communications, and Sylvia Sommerville for their immeasurable assistance. Thanks to Laurie Gilbreth for her support. Special thanks to Avery Denny. I acknowledge the contributions of Keren Assaf, Deon Ben, Marcus Cleveland, Stefanie Kunze, Daisy Purdy, Kevin Redmond, Charles Sepulveda, Emily Schnurr, and Carissa Tsosie for critiquing early drafts. I also acknowledge the work of Shonri Begay, Alex Bendle, Monica Burres, David Harmon, Darrell Marks, Tiffany Manygoats, Vanessa Tallman, Sheryle Watchman, and Michelle Yazzie. Perhaps most importantly, I acknowledge caffeine in my coffee!

Nothing is possible without family. To Anna, Michelle, Lizzie, Nannie, and Mikey, I owe tremendous gratitude. Also, David, Isela, Mary, Issa and Baby David. Keep working hard for your place in this world. For Freddie, it's time to go to school.

I, finally, acknowledge all the "invisible Indians." You may not have federal recognition but I can see you.

Introduction
Moving Toward the Indigenous Spring

This book is organized along three themes and into eight chapters. The first section is called Indigenous Sovereignty: Past, Present, Future, Spirit. The second section is on Indigenous sovereignty in the Court of the Colonizer. The third section is on Indigenous resources, colonial wealth, and Indian dependency. While the first theme could be organized along time, it seems more important to frame Aboriginal Title as a fantasy clashing with Indigenous military might. Only after Indigenous nations are subjugated can this normative precept be realized in colonial actor[1] policy. Today, Indigenous nations can confidently state that colonial actors cannot eliminate something they never recognized: the inherent responsibility many Indigenous peoples have to serve their traditional homelands. This is the true essence of Indigenous sovereignty today. It is a clear contradiction and negation of Aboriginal Title. The first three chapters empirically reinforce the section theme of past military power of Indigenous nations, the present subjugation of Indigenous nations, and the future organic tie to Indigenous homelands.

One of the most critical discussions about Indigenous sovereignty has gone missing. Chapter 1, From Savage International Actors to Ingrateful Noble Indians explores what many, apparently, have forgotten about: Indigenous nations were once treated as legitimate international actors because of their military might. Notions of Aboriginal Title cannot be advanced in diplomacy matters. This research will remind readers of Indigenous treaties as they attempted to make relatives of colonial actors (Williams 1999). Indigenous nation behavior later evolved to reflect European norms of war and empire building (Hämäläinen and William P. Clements Center for

1. "Colonial actor" is a phrase used to denote all of the colonial nations that emerged in the Americas today. This phrase replaces the varying nations that colonized the Americas. In an effort to place Indigenous nations at the center of this research, it is easier to use this phrase. For example, Diné (Navajo) people have been interacting with Spain, Mexico, and the United States. Many Indigenous nations share this trait. The phrase "colonial actor" is used in place of naming a colonizing nation, stating a year, and otherwise detracting from more important points.

Southwest Studies 2008; Blackhawk 2006). These incontrovertible histories describe how colonial actors saw Indigenous actors as more powerful and useful alliance partners (Deloria and DeMallie 1999; Deloria and Wilkins 1999). Eventually, international interaction set the stage for the elimination of as many international mechanisms, such as Indigenous war and Indigenous treaty making, once afforded Indigenous actors as fit the interest of the United States (U.S.). This reminder is necessary for several reasons. First, it appears some contemporary scholars and readers may have forgotten that Indigenous actors have played a role in their own demise by behaving in ways not consistent with their pre-contact philosophies. Second, Indigenous peoples have been conditioned to forget about their own history of sovereign power. Third, Indigenous citizens continue to be led by tribal officials who seem bent on exercising "self termination policy" by giving away any remaining vestiges of their sovereign reach. This research intends to highlight concrete and observable issues involved in maintaining and expanding Indigenous sovereignty by centering Indigenous actors as the main variable whenever possible. To truly appreciate this approach, we must now remind scholars about the manner in which the U.S. has "defended" Indigenous sovereignty, which does not center on Indigenous actors as legitimate international actors.

Chapter 2, Wrapping Up Indigenous Nations Within the U.S. Domestic Polity explores how the U.S. will defend Indigenous sovereignty if it serves its goals. The heart of colonial actor policy has, at least implicitly, revolved around notions of Aboriginal Title. At the core of many challenges in maintaining and expanding Indigenous sovereignty are agenda-setting issues. This question first emerged as a debate within the U.S. as a function of states' rights versus federalism. There are at least three eras of U.S. policy based on this fluctuating relationship between state and federal autonomy. The earliest configurations pushed for a more normatively confederated set up where states reserved any level of sovereignty not explicitly contributing to the emerging federal government (Deloria and Wilkins 1999). The U.S. federal government evolved to seize more aspects of state sovereignty contributing to the U.S. Civil War. The Reconstruction era furthered the normative precept to have a federal level of dominance over state sovereignty. Indigenous nations became pawns in this conflict. Indigenous sovereignty was only respected in so far as it furthered the interests of the federal government. The original source of federal power can be traced to Aboriginal Title. The U.S. federal government successfully built a monopoly on extinguishing Aboriginal Title. The monopoly would bolster the U.S. and federalism as a whole. When states respect federal dominance over states' rights, there is no need for the federal government to protect Indigenous sovereignty. These practices of enveloping Indigenous nations into the domestic U.S. polity only more recognizably come onto the radar of federal Indian law and policy scholars as the U.S. sets the agenda of the so-called "domestic dependent nation."

Some disciplinary lines seem to have muddied the waters of our current understanding of Indigenous sovereignty. Chapter 2 also expands on international relations perspectives of Indigenous sovereignty making key assumptions: Indigenous actors were powerful international actors that forced colonial actors to treat with them or be eliminated from the New World as actors all together. The treaty record can be comprehensively explored independent of this research (Deloria and DeMallie 1999). These facts allow contemporary scholars to re-examine the history of federal Indian law and policy not as an instrument to co-exist with "Indian Tribes" but rather as an instrument to eliminate them. Sadly, current scholars tend to only recognize the plight of Indigenous sovereignty as the U.S. Supreme Court begins to sort out its colonial legacy in the early 1820s.

This colonial legacy must work to eliminate some idea of Indigenous sovereignty, and the debate on Indigenous sovereignty has "quietly" raged on since contact. Chapter 3, Indigenous Sovereignty and False Dichotomies provides a three-level view of Indigenous sovereignty based on observable data. *This chapter is special to me personally because I employed the research talents of several undergraduate students.* We link five necessary conditions that are tied to secondary sources. This chapter provides a quick snapshot on what has become so frightening to the U.S. at the federal and state level. Secondly, this chapter also provides a glimpse of the tension many Indigenous leaders face today. There are no easy answers for all policy makers. Being Indigenous originally required a much different relationship with the land. However, Indigenous leaders cannot simply discontinue their resource extraction habits or they would nearly eliminate any remaining aspects of economic development in Indian Country. This chapter does not excuse business as usual, rather, it is required to remind all colonial actors of the nature of Indigenous sovereignty. The origin of sovereignty based on organic attachment to homeland is objectively framed as a major challenge faced by Indigenous leaders today. This could be the first time Indigenous sovereignty, as a viable concept, is discussed in context of the 21st century.

Section I aims to contrast Aboriginal Title with Indigenous sovereignty past, present, and future. For contemporary colonial actors to legitimately exist, they must deliberately deny the ideas expressed in the first three chapters of this book.

Section II, Indigenous Sovereignty in the Court of the Colonizer is the legacy of the U.S., a colonial actor, in its pursuit to sweep Indigenous nations and their sovereignty under the rug. This goal was accomplished through the Court of the Colonizer and meant to provide the farce known as "due process" in ensuring that land appropriation, by extinguishing Aboriginal Title, occurred in a legal manner.

Chapter 4, Normative Assumptions of the Marshall Court outlines how the U.S. first dealt with its precarious tale of land appropriation as epitomized and justified based on Aboriginal Title (Deloria 1974, 85–111). In doing so, the Marshall Court was finally outlining a normative approach to colonization that would grip Indian Country by the throat for the next 150 years. This approach leads to what today we might call the Four Normative Assumptions of the Marshall Court: 1. The European Christian government must remain the more powerful actor, 2. Discovery grants the right to extinguish Aboriginal Title, 3. Indians enjoy the Right of Occupancy at the pleasure of the European sovereign, and 4. Europeans must help the Indian be like the European individual and not like a European state. These normative assumptions have certainly been discussed in previous research but, to my knowledge, they have not been analytically explored as a strategy that deliberately and systematically shifted Indigenous nations from the family of legitimate international actors into the realm of U.S. domestic political mechanisms. These assumptions are the paths that rely heavily on legitimizing Aboriginal Title. The Marshall Court, and subsequent Courts, followed these normative precepts in order to "help" the Indian survive the onslaught of colonization in what many U.S. policy makers believed to be mutually beneficial compromises that just so happened to result in the appropriation of the majority of Indian lands for non-Indian owners. While these normative assumptions sound horrific, the Supreme Court would later work tirelessly to make things even worse for Indigenous actors.

In the aftermath of self-determination emerged the wrath of the Supreme Court and its unofficial judicial termination policy. Chapter 5, The Rehnquist Court and the Canons of Destruction explains how it was actually possible to be even more hostile toward Indigenous sovereignty than Marshall and his colleagues could ever dream. Simultaneously, we also discover that Aboriginal Title gets edited out of the narrative for the sake of being politically correct. Rehnquist came onto the Court and the conservative Right began to re-imagine Indigenous sovereignty as a special right based on affirmative action. The gauntlet against the maintenance and expansion of Indigenous sovereignty relentlessly pursued Indigenous nations as if to signal a new era of perceived "ripeness for conquest." The

Rehnquist Court deserves the utmost credit for turning away from the normative assumptions of the Marshall Court as they re-imagined Indigenous sovereignty as the latest affirmative action ploy meant to appease the left in the pursuit of a politically correct world by virtue of prejudicial determinism.

As Robert Anthony Williams notes in his own research, the nature of legal scholarship is very subjective (Williams 1999, 3–4). The heart of legal scholarship and the subjectivity of all research appears inherent. This, in no way, is meant to disparage the work of Professor Williams so much as to call into question the objectivity of all legal scholarship. (To be certain, this research is NOT legal scholarship.) Hence, the most powerful evidence that legal scholars, such as Rehnquist, are selecting premises based on prejudicial conclusions comes from an analysis of the court cases themselves. Chapter 5 further explores what in social sciences is called selecting on the dependent variable or alternatively as determinism in the court. Rehnquist and his colleagues are required to remain willfully or legitimately ignorant of the Four Normative Assumptions once held sacred by the likes of John Marshall. With little oversight, the Court could certainly act with impunity as it carried out its edict of judicial termination or the Canons of Destruction. This book will outline a set of ideal type cases meant to represent four typologies present in the Rehnquist Court. 1. A case expanding Indigenous sovereignty, 2. A case that leaves Indigenous sovereignty as it was found, 3. A case that diminishes Indigenous sovereignty, and 4. A case that is not clearly expanding, leaving as found, or diminishing Indigenous sovereignty. These ideal type cases outline a set of boundaries for the limits of the Court and lend themselves to a comprehensive and systematic analysis of the Court during the era of judicial termination and the Canons of Destruction.

It makes sense that if there are no voices against the argument for the maintenance and expansion of Indigenous sovereignty then the impact of those in favor loses some level of salience and urgency. Chapter 6, The Rehnquist Legacy 1972–2005 offers more than case study or "anecdotal" evidence that something is awry in the Court. In an effort to simultaneously bolster the fact that there is a systematic effort to terminate Indigenous sovereignty AND demonstrate a level of agenda setting at work, this research will present quantitative evidence of judicial termination. This chapter reinforces the Court's squeamishness in relying on Aboriginal Title philosophy although the outcome is to extinguish Indigenous sovereignty. Qualitative Comparative Analysis is used to explore 45 cases decided during the tenure of William Rehnquist between 1972 and 2005 based on the typology first introduced as ideal types in Chapter 5. Typically, legal scholars have relied upon case study evidence to showcase a pattern of judicial termination only to be rebuked with alternative case study evidence that objections to judicial termination are merely protecting states' rights. Yet, this chapter highlights a systematic effort to diminish Indigenous sovereignty by 1. Promoting states' rights and 2. Ignoring or being ignorant of the Four Normative Assumptions of federal Indian law and policy. Put another way, this chapter goes beyond the case-by-case debate. There are causal mechanisms leading to the extinguishing of remaining vestiges of Indigenous sovereignty in an overt act of judicial termination between 1972 and 2005.

Attacks on Indigenous sovereignty do not end in the Courts. Section III, Indigenous Resources, Colonial Wealth, Indian Dependency discusses how resource extraction in the U.S. has enriched colonial actors. In post-Aboriginal Title America, most of Indian Country is owned by colonial actors and held in trust for the benefit of Indian nations. The basic ability for Indigenous nations to feed themselves was eliminated, forcing them into a state of dependency. The chapters in this section explore economic liberalism as well as the impact of treaty obligations on contemporary tribal leaders. This section focuses on the Trust Doctrine being inconsistent with contemporary aid to Indigenous nations for economic development. Section III will also highlight the co-optation of Indigenous leaders today through Trust Doctrine responsibilities.

Due to many issues raised in Chapter 2, the current state of Indigenous nations remains invisibly tied to contemporary economic development. In the early 20th century, many tribal governments opted to engage in exploitation of their natural resources. Chapter 7, Economic Liberalism and Sustainable Colonization re-addresses the recent economic development efforts of Indigenous nations. Economic liberalism is a phrase not often mentioned in literature on Indigenous economic development in the 21st century. This is an appalling omission that is hopefully rectified here. In the same manner that the U.S. rebuilt Europe after World War II, to serve the U.S. political economy, the U.S. may deserve credit for first carrying out the Marshall Plan in Indian Country. Indigenous nation institutions in terms of culture, politics, and economics are also often ignored by contemporary research purporting to carry out research on rebuilding Indigenous nations. But these are the very institutions that must be eradicated or co-opted by colonial actors in order for the unprecedented wealth extraction and concentration in the Americas, and the U.S., to occur. But this chapter, again, does not focus blame on individuals. Rather, this chapter serves as a blueprint for future tribal leaders who wish to lead themselves into economic prosperity. Yet, perhaps the number one challenge tribal leaders face is avoiding being co-opted by U.S. interests.

In an effort to keep the theme of institutional barriers at the forefront of future strategies for remedy, one of the most egregiously ignored problems is foreign aid. Typically, the phrase "foreign aid" is not analyzed in terms of impact on Indigenous domestic policy. Foreign aid is similar to treaty obligations. The phrase "foreign aid" is deliberately chosen to engender the trust responsibility that the U.S. has with Indigenous nations. Chapter 8, Misplaced Blame? Institutionally Captured Indigenous Leaders explores the intersection of foreign aid from the U.S. and Indigenous domestic policy. The research on the impact that U.S. foreign aid has on aid recipient policy is clear: If your nation receives aid from the U.S., your nation probably has some policies that do not serve recipient citizens. This phenomenon is also present in Indian Country as evidenced by the multitude of domestic Indigenous economic policies that serve U.S. economic interests. This chapter also briefly explores the relationship between democracy and foreign aid. U.S. foreign aid has strings attached and the more autocratic the recipient, the more likely those strings can be observed. This chapter concludes by tying the concentrated nature of tribal government today to the ability for those same governments to dictate policy that does not serve Indigenous nation citizens. An original data set on the size of all tribal governments in the continental U.S. highlights the concentrated nature of tribal governments today. Tribal power was concentrated during the 1930s and 1940s when the U.S., as outlined in Chapter 2, encouraged Indigenous nations to accept Indian Reorganization and write constitutions with very small legislatures. These challenges, though immense, may begin to fall apart if we remember the original racial and ethnic entitlement program known as Aboriginal Title.

Today, "shoot from the hip" states' rights advocates and the conservative Right are sorely misguided by their own inventions of Indigenous sovereignty. The Epilogue—Aboriginal Title: The Original Ethnic and Racial Entitlement explores the misguidedness that many believe to be true about their invention of Indigenous sovereignty in their minds. Many conservative scholars, pundits, and candidates for public office claim they are against any and all forms of racial and ethnic entitlements. I would agree with them. We simply disagree on what the Right imagines and what Marshall and the U.S. Supreme Court can empirically demonstrate. The original and most expansively executed form of ethnic and racial entitlement is the idea of

Aboriginal Title. It was first articulated as legitimate international law by way of the Doctrine of Discovery (Deloria 1974). If any notion of sovereignty deserves our scrutiny, it is the idea of "colonial actor" sovereignty based on the flawed assumption that Indians had a right to occupy their traditional homelands at the pleasure of the European Christian sovereigns. This idea is not limited to the U.S.; but has completely enveloped the entire Western and Southern Hemispheres and justified the most destructive holocaust in human history.

The past, present, and future of Indigenous sovereignty is a matter of empirical and observable reality. This book highlights some of these empirically observable measures of Indigenous sovereignty in treaties, methods of negating sovereignty in the Courts, and economic ploys to extract resources from traditional homelands. The most conservative estimates of Indigenous depopulation are appalling. Indigenous land appropriation is undeniable across the Western and Southern Hemispheres to say the least. Policy makers often ignore treaties based on military alliance. They prefer to focus on treaties signed under duress. Federal Indian law and policy events baited Indigenous leaders with actual redress only to switch the mechanism for redress with policies that wrapped up Indigenous nations within the domestic U.S. polity. Indigenous sovereignty based on creation is unheard of, ignored, or ridiculed. Instead, court cases push the Four Normative Assumptions of the Marshall Court. Later, Rehnquist and company simply ignore these assumptions and eliminated remaining vestiges of Indigenous sovereignty in favor of states' rights activism. Indigenous natural resources are sold for pennies on the dollar to U.S. interests. Tribal leaders cannot afford to turn away these pennies. Many also cannot turn down foreign aid from the U.S. in exchange for policy concessions. These institutional conditions have persisted for hundreds of years. These are all empirical facts that can be supported with primary and secondary source evidence. Some of that evidence is presented here. This does not mean that I personally believe in empirical research only. However, this research does leave theoretical and philosophical analysis to others. Readers are encouraged to make their own philosophical ties to the research here. Again, these writings are meant to promote strategic positioning going forward.

The limited and emerging research on Indigenous nations lacks focus on strategy for maintaining and expanding sovereignty. Many across the spectrum of political ideology remain unsatisfied with policy decisions delivered by the Court. Indigenous leaders may react with indignation to the overt surrender of even more remaining vestiges of sovereignty. States' rights advocates remain conveniently ignorant of any notion of

Indigenous sovereignty. Legal scholars continue to carry out case study research on their favorite cases—be it in favor of states' rights or in favor of the Marshall Court proclamations. Still, few are offering strategies for co-existence on terms that could benefit all parties. Policy recommendations will be offered as a way for various sovereigns to find common ground based on their shared interests. Local and regional economic interests need not hamper Indigenous nation economic development. Ultimately, even the most ardent advocates for Indigenous sovereignty have much to gain by understanding the legacy of not only Marshall but of Rehnquist as well. Our lessons may hide in plain sight masked by disciplinary lines that can be transcended by this innovative, mixed method, and interdisciplinary research approach. Alternatives, such as writing in "plain language" simply would do more to oversimplify a complex set of interacting polities.

Section I
Indigenous Sovereignty: Past, Present, Future, Spirit

The phrase Indigenous sovereignty has been quietly debated since contact with non-Indians in the 15th century. Underestimating the people they interact with is one of the biggest mistakes individuals can make. This was a huge mistake made by early refugees to the Western Hemisphere. Visitors assumed the savages were running wild and free with no thought about yesterday, today, or tomorrow. Section I is a reminder about the complex idea of Indigenous sovereignty as it has evolved through time and space. The idea is only complex because of the dedicated efforts many non-Indigenous elites have carried out to obscure it intentionally or otherwise. Today, many Indigenous individuals have "sipped the Kool-Aid" and they also underestimate their ancestors and their sovereign reach then and now. Section I is a response to Aboriginal Title, an idea that many do not understand, find inconvenient to discuss, or accept as an inevitable consequence of colonization. One consequence of writing back against the American narrative is that responses cannot be organized along time line-based history. Instead, three broad themes are offered. Indigenous sovereignty involves international interaction through mechanisms of diplomacy, economics (trade), and war. The phases of international interaction are contained in Chapter 1.

Time, as an organizing theme, also fails to adequately represent the post-treaty making era in the U.S. Chapter 1 concludes how the U.S. successfully eliminated a multitude of international interaction mechanisms. Many times, these mechanisms never returned. Other times, Indigenous nations were promised U.S. domestic mechanism in exchange for Indigenous nations relinquishing their international mechanisms. Chapter 2 explores the notion that federal Indian law and policy are really the elimination of any remaining international mechanisms for interaction. Chapter 1 is crucial for our contemporary understanding of Indigenous sovereignty. By failing to fully critique contemporary research on federal Indian law and policy, we assume away many aspects of Indigenous sovereignty just as the colonizer wishes Indigenous nations to do. The original manifestation of Indigenous sovereignty is found in Indigenous ceremonies, languages, homelands, and sacred histories.

The future of Indigenous sovereignty is likely found in its past. Chapter 3 advances ties between Indigenous sovereignty and a people's homeland, language, sacred history, and ceremony. By utilizing cutting-edge methods that link case study research with new foci areas, researchers are encouraged to tie their individual stories of Indigenousness to pan-Indigenous notions of sovereignty. These can be based on their homeland, or their language, or their history, or their ceremony insofar as particular Indigenous norms allow sharing. This approach, for the first time, links Indigenous sovereignty to Indigenous creation contained in sacred histories that predate contact with non-Indigenous peoples. The elders and knowledge holders have been saying, all along, that their responsibility for leadership was established during moments of creation, codified in bonds between the creator and the humans, and tied across all other living beings through clan relationships.

(Wilkins 2013, 8–14). By the 1860s the traditional homeland of the Five Civilized Tribes was sufficiently encroached upon and their Aboriginal Title extinguished. Simultaneously, Kit Carson had to go to traditional Navajo homelands and carry out the same Aboriginal Title extinguishment on behalf of the U.S. (Wilkins and Stark 2011, 60–61; Wilkins 2013, 8–14; Getches 2011, 94–98, 113–128). And this story can be retold a few dozen times making the history all the more confusing. Retelling the story using international relations and comparative politics research may better inform the strategic policy platforms behind much of federal Indian law and policy.

While the aim is to re-invigorate the debate on the nature of Indigenous sovereignty, again, there should be more frustration with the current state of research on the topic. Many researchers have written from their own disciplinary lines. Some scholars have, in personal conversation with me, mentioned their research methodology as "political historian" or relying on the "civil liability" measure known as proving points beyond a reasonable doubt. Some scholars have openly suggested that legal research is a process of taking evidence where it is locatable and injecting it into conclusions (Williams 1999, 3–4). These are all laudable approaches but the fact remains clear: Arguments about the nature of Indigenous sovereignty have often not been heard. There are at least two issues inherent in striving to maintain and expand Indigenous sovereignty. First, as many scholars, including Robert Williams and Jeff Corntassel have noted, advocates in Indian Country have either lost or never bothered to show up for the game known as public relations (Corntassel and Witmer 2008, 27–56; Williams 2005, 89–136). Supporters have utterly failed to set or reset the agenda on how Indigenous nations' sovereignty is understood by the non-Indian mainstream world. This failure has spilled over into the second most critical problem. Even Indigenous nations elected officials and advocates for the maintenance and expansion of Indigenous sovereignty seem to be more than willing to give away remaining vestiges of sovereignty as outlined in the Trust Doctrine. These concerns have kept me up at night.

The final straw, as it were, was drawn on February 16, 2014. It was a Sunday afternoon and I was reading Kevin Bruyneel's *The Third Space of Sovereignty* (2007). I had high hopes for the book and figured it would make for a nice and relaxing read for my Sunday afternoon. To be clear, I'm very happy that Bruyneel chose to write his book. It is sorely needed and deserves all the attention it can garner. That said, I was appalled by two discussions that take place in the introduction and the first chapter. The first discussion involves the U.S. Supreme Court case involving the Mille Lacs Band and the second involves the nature of Indigenous sovereignty (Minnesota v. Mille Lacs Band of Chippewa Indians 1999). Regarding the

Mille Lacs Band, there is a very good discussion about how then-Governor Jesse Ventura took exception to the idea that Indians should have the audacity to 1. Survive into the modern times, 2. Claim their fishing rights, and 3. Fish using contemporary boats. (Bruyneel 2007, xiii–xv). Ojibwa Elder Marge Anderson responded to this assertion by reminding all that Mille Lacs did not ask to be colonized. Sovereignty "is not a gift" from the federal government. All of this is true, however, I wish that Anderson had stated so much more. This failure to truly reflect Indigenous sovereignty, a by-product of international relations between the U.S. and Mille Lacs, has colored the otherwise excellent work produced by Bruyneel.

I believe, perhaps incorrectly, that Bruyneel allowed this (and other research) to color his own assumptions on the nature of Indigenous sovereignty. Put differently, while Bruyneel attempted to point out false dichotomies or, as he puts it, the imperial binary, perhaps the imperial binary of Indigenous sovereignty in the international world escaped his purview (Bruyneel 2007, 19). One assumption that seems implicit in the works cited by Bruyneel is that Indigenous sovereignty is somehow special. The idea that Indigenous sovereignty is unique is dangerous. Bruyneel correctly states that Indigenous and colonial actor relations are complicated and goes on to cite other scholars on how this mess got to be what it is today (Bruyneel 2007, 3). Wilkins is offered as evidence of the pre-constitutional and extra-constitutional nature of Indigenous sovereignty. But this question on how this set up makes Indigenous nations somehow special or unique needs scrutiny. It is true that Indigenous nations are unique but the character is not the fault of Indigenous nations.

Deloria and Wilkins probably state the facts best and most accurately:

> "Stripped of the hypocritical veneer given to it by law professors . . . [federal Indian law is] . . . a hodge-podge of personal grudges, ad hoc policies, inconsistent judicial decisions, and a general exercise of ignorance about Indians framed in statutory language" (1999, 33–34).

This premise of confusion, grudges, etc., has not been placed within a context for strategically expanding the sovereignty of the U.S. while diminishing the sovereignty of Indigenous nations. While Deloria and Wilkins warn us not to grant Washington and Jefferson credit for "prophetic powers that would do Nostradamus proud" (1999, ix), we cannot simply ignore the fact that this confusion and grudge-laden canon of law remains obscured. While not a power of prophecy, it is more likely that simple assumptions explored in Chapter 4 are the likely culprits. When jurists have predetermined outcomes about Indigenous nations, it is more believable that policy makers simply worked collectively to make Indians (and their nations) what they wished them to be. In this sense, we are dealing with a self-fulfilling prophecy. This obscurity has worked to the benefit of the myth makers who advocate for the idea of American exceptionalism.

The very real threat of "Indigenous nation exceptionalism" is potentially more dangerous than providing the dialogue about how Indigenous nations actually behaved in both their pre-constitutional and extra-constitutional iterations. Our biggest critics tend to be those who would support the maintenance and expansion of states' rights (Biolsi 2007; United States v. Kagama 1886). This position of promoting states' rights just so happens to involve extinguishing remaining vestiges of Indigenous sovereignty (Biolsi 2007; Getches 2001). It is easy to accuse advocates of states' rights of a whole multitude of crimes against humanity but it is probably best to simply point out their current-day amnesia. Bruyneel says it best when he reminds us that states' rights activists have continuously demanded that Indigenous nations either assimilate with or secede from the U.S. (Bruyneel 2007). This false dichotomy is based on mythical beliefs in manifest destiny. The extent to which Indigenous sovereignty is characterized as "special" or "unique" makes it much more difficult to defend as legitimate. In other words, and more simply stated, doesn't pre-constitutional and extra-constitutional really mean international? We can no longer shy away from this fact: Indigenous sovereignty is international sovereignty even now.

International interaction between Indigenous nations and colonial actors is huge and largely forgotten by states' rights advocates. I now remind all to explore the massive 1,540-page treaty record that only includes current-day U.S. and Canada (Deloria and DeMallie 1999). But exploring this record requires more than searching for treaties that support a predetermined outcome. Scholars should not simply point out treaties that serve my idea that Indigenous nations were once powerful military allies for colonial actors. States' rights activists should not simply point out treaties signed by Indigenous actors under duress either. There is probably a clear critical point in the treaty record reflecting the break between Indigenous actors as alliance partners and Indigenous actors as militarily defeated nations attempting to prevent further ethnic cleansing at the hands of the U.S. This area deserves much more research than can be afforded here. In general, there is evidence that the pre-1812 treaties with the U.S. may be more military alliance based (Deloria and DeMallie 1999, 6–7; Deloria and Wilkins 1999, 5–6). One area that needs more attention is the treaties, prior to 1849, signed in order to regulate commerce (Deloria and Wilkins 1999, 59). As will be argued in Chapter 2, this "footnote" of history deserves much more attention because it seems to be clear evidence of the U.S. systematically wrapping up Indigenous nations within the U.S. political economy.

The other two phases of treaties are, again generally, 1849–1865 establishing land titles, and 1865–1868 establishing peace with plains tribes. The area not mentioned by this research is the so-called "agreements" that ceded more land to the U.S. and allotted lands to individual Indians from about 1871 to 1914 (Deloria and Wilkins 1999, 59). These "clean" breaks in time ignore the colonial actor process of exchanging exclusive rights to extinguish Aboriginal Title via the Louisiana Purchase and the war with Mexico, among other coerced exchanges (such as the Gadsden Purchase). This confusion deserves much more attention because it is the greatest source of misinformation coming from states' rights advocates and tribal leaders today.

Part of the confusion is certainly tied to the way research is conducted and often meant to either justify the U.S. expansion or otherwise attempt to provide a character assassination for Indigenous rights advocates. On their face, these policies were meant to prevent wars on the frontier and bolster the power of the U.S. federal government, not the states, and to regulate trade with tribes so the U.S. could out-compete Spain and France (Deloria and Wilkins 1999, 23). The implicit assumption is that U.S. policy would eventually eclipse Indigenous nations. Obviously, none of this language appears in the treaties. So, on the one hand, the U.S. states will be allies with Indians and, on the other hand, the U.S. finds it expedient to break treaties when they can afford to break them and expand their own sovereign reach. Again, this is nothing mind-boggling but this two-faced approach to treaty making deserves a title: acting all somehow.

There is currently a joke going around in Indian Country (currently probably means since 1492, by the way) that involves a man and a woman in a quasi-unclear relationship. Simply put, we could be together but you are acting all "somehow."[2] In this same way, both Indigenous nations and the U.S. stand to learn from this problem. We could be international actor partners but you are "all somehow." One day you are alliance partners and next time you are breaking the terms. Today, we in Indian Country feel the same way. We could be partners in collaboration to build infrastructure on "the rez" but federal funding is "all somehow." The somehow is that the strings attached ensure that no border-town economy interests are ever threatened by reservation economic development. Hence, building water

2. Originally, this phrase was produced as artwork by Apache Skateboards founder Douglas Miles.

delivery infrastructure in Indian Country could threaten municipalities in states such as Arizona for their "fair share" of water for golf courses and artificial geysers. This is the "all somehow" aspect of contemporary Indigenous and U.S. relations. There is confusion as policy makers on all sides appear ignorant, arrogant, or both, regarding the real understanding of how the partners could work together. We in Indian Country are constantly asked to behave within a frame of false dichotomy. Be sovereign or don't. And, for some odd reason, we seem happy in Indian Country to basically assume the "don't" part and this is very dangerous. Our tribal leaders need to also stop acting all "somehow."

Bruyneel mentions how "simple" definitions do not account for Indigenous sovereignty on pages 23–24 (2007). This is dangerous because the more Indigenous sovereignty appears "all somehow" the more likely tribal leaders are going to give it away. Bruyneel cites Rob Walker's definition as incompatible because it makes "state, power, supreme authority, and legitimacy" synonymous with sovereignty. Bruyneel goes on to state that there must be room to consider "other possibilities" on the definition of Indigenous sovereignty. This type of thinking is probably premature. Again, no one has offered an international relations and comparative politics informed approach to the history of Indigenous and U.S. relations. I'd like to offer this "other possibility" in Chapter 3. For now, and with very little primary and secondary resources to rely on, I see very clearly the definition of sovereignty, as outlined by Walker, alive and well within Indigenous nations. Based on oral accounts and some private discussions with knowledge holders who have had nothing to do with this book, I offer the following. Many Indigenous nations erected what we might call "states" for the purpose of dealing with war or dealing with a drought or some other emergency involving many Indigenous bands within a nation. Once the concern was dealt with, the state was dismantled. There was no need for a permanent state apparatus (Deloria, Pavlik, and Wildcat 2006, 50–56). Power was of a nature involving what we might recognize today in international organizations based on norms of behavior and lacking clear enforcement mechanisms (Goertz 2003, 13–29).

Still, these unclear mechanisms could be very powerful incentives to cooperate with the other actors in the environment. Supreme authority is traced to the multitude of Indigenous creation accounts. Chapter 3 discusses how the people were ordained by a creator to foster a good relationship with mother earth, father sky, and all other people (with wings, hooves, and stingers, etc.) and most generally founded within Peoplehood (Holm, Pearson, and Chavis 2003; Lerma 2012). Following these protocols, and also being internally ordained by your own people to lead, contributed to Indigenous governance legitimacy. There were certainly conflicts across tribes but it was probably not until after 1492, with few exceptions, that we witnessed the genocidal version of inter-tribal warfare. These all point to very clear notions of Indigenous sovereignty that have not been sufficiently addressed in any research until now.

What follows is a re-focus on Indigenous nations as international actors. The once militarily powerful Indigenous nations soon discovered their sacred Wampum Belt treaties meant very little to colonial actors (Williams 1999). Continued interaction with colonial actors taught Indigenous leaders how to behave more like European sovereigns, thus, Indigenous behavior drifted away from Peoplehood-based obligations (Holm, Pearson, and Chavis 2003; Deloria, Pavlik, and Wildcat 2006, 50–56). It probably became more profitable to build into the newly formed interaction-based political economy or what historians might call "trade." The U.S., having descended from a long tradition of political alliance and warfare-based diplomacy, utilized their skills to make expedient alliances with Indigenous actors only to renege when it was in their interest to expand their empires. It is obvious that not all colonial actors practiced this method of empire building. Hence, we enter into a second phase of treaty making that was meant to eliminate Indigenous actors in at least two ways: 1. By way of ethnic cleansing or otherwise confining to geographic areas deemed unattractive by colonial actors and 2. By enveloping Indigenous actors into the U.S. polity via institutional expansion. The expansion usually started with economic institutional expansion (also known as trade and intercourse acts) and later political institutional expansion (also known as federal Indian law and policy). Each era of federal Indian law and policy reflects the later strategy to envelop Indigenous actors economically and politically to function and raise grievances through U.S. domestic mechanisms. Hence, there was a clear transition from international actor to domestic dependent nation and no Indigenous actor ever approved this strategy.

When Indigenous Nations Were International Actors: Sacred Treaties

One of the most neglected, or perhaps rejected, conversations in international relations history is the debate on the nature of Indigenous nations during the time of war and diplomacy. Readers will take note that a continent away, Pope Alexander was declaring a "secure title" to Columbus's discoveries around 1493 (Getches 2011, 48). The reality in the Americas was that Aboriginal Title was the fantasy of popes and kings.

Some interesting research on the nature of the Iroquois Confederacy suggests that the blind spots in political science research have ignored the long peace established via this international actor cooperation. The long peace established by this international organization, today known as the Iroquois Confederacy, should rewrite our understanding of international relations by expanding the longest time of peace between several powerful international actors by at least 50 or as much as 700 years (Crawford 1994, 353)! This is far longer than the oft-cited Concert of Europe lasting only 100 years (Bueno de Mesquita 2014, 489). Hence, our understanding of international relations could be significantly bolstered if only international relations scholars would simply give Indigenous nations the benefit of the doubt. But, this idea is not an academic form of affirmative action. We can be very certain that military men were very clear about the serious danger posed by Indigenous nations. The evidence for their fear is overwhelming.

Typically, international actors have been afforded some interesting characteristics that appear to also be exhibited by Indigenous actors. These tribes and nations all had to operate in a world based on anarchy, as rational unitary actors, in pursuit of power or security or both, and sought to interact within either a bipolar or multipolar international system, wishing to balance power, and mimicking one another's behavior (Waltz 1979; Morgenthau 1948). There probably is less utility in carrying out research that "proves" or demonstrates how Indigenous nations once behaved this way. Besides, not all research will agree and the larger issue is more about perception of Indigenous nations at the point of contact until the U.S. unilaterally ended treaty making in 1871. So long as we can point to some evidence that colonial actors and the U.S. saw Indigenous nations as threats to their security and power base, we have sufficient foundation to proceed with the assumption that Indigenous nations were, in fact, legitimate and dangerous international actors. The evidence that Indigenous nations were feared and sought for alliance purposes comes from the massive, yet incomplete, record of treaties (Deloria and DeMallie 1999). These treaties were not made out of the kindness of colonial actors' hearts. They were originally made out of colonial actor necessity.

It would be illuminating to explore the multitude of treaties and the manner in which international relations scholars have come to view them as instruments of power relations between international actors. Robert Williams does an excellent job in attempting to re-assess the magnitude of treaty relations from the Indigenous point of view in his book *Linking Arms Together* (1999). His main thesis involves the way treaties were probably considered sacred texts that would bind distinct nations forevermore (Williams 1999, 40–61). But that does not mean a whole lot in English. Rather, it sounds nice and happy with little power behind the words. Some exploration of Indigenous philosophy might shed light on the nature of

Indigenous treaties during the earliest contact period. We need to re-imagine a treaty as a sacred document and not a mere contract enforceable only through domestic mechanisms. For our purposes, it would be fine to imagine a treaty that is bound to a traditional homeland, representative of a long sacred history about the origin of a people. Treaties are fostering a relationship with more than one distinct peoples based on a cycle of ceremonial practice, and grounded in very specific Indigenous words and thoughts. These words and thoughts are only expressed during certain times and within specific places, which is probably the ceremonial setting. These ideas have been previously expressed as notions of Peoplehood (Holm, Pearson, and Chavis 2003). There is no reason to assume that this is reserved solely for Indigenous peoples. It remains apparent that Indigenous nations of the early contact period assumed non-Native settlers, as an extension of their respective crowns, had similar ties to their own homelands in the Old World. These diplomacy efforts were made from one human group to another.

Williams goes on to provide a multitude of examples where Indigenous nations actively sought to make a relative out of the new people on their traditional homelands. To fully appreciate this effort, we must examine notions of clan relationship. When clan ties are still intact today, it often represents a cycle of reciprocity. A mother is not only mother to her own children but could also be a mother to the children of her older and younger sisters' children. To the younger sister, a woman's nieces and nephews may owe great respect to the older aunt. This relationship has a multitude of built-in responsibilities that could involve disciplining the child in ways that could potentially trump the biological fathers' reach. In this same manner, Williams provides evidence that Indigenous actors attempted to make a relative of their new neighbors in the earliest moments of contact (Williams 1999, 62–82). The Indigenous actors saw treaties as a way to make an eternal bond with a new people. It is very possible that Indigenous actors truly sought to reach out their hand as a method of allowing the new people from Europe to become refugees in their Indigenous nations. What we might call "adoption" may have been a very serious method of accepting a new clan into the Indigenous nation, marrying them into the other pre-existing clans, and allowing for all to link arms together with responsibilities that would last until the end of time. Navajo philosophy points to the idea that clan relationships are very important and those individuals who ignore their clan-based responsibilities can be reminded about how they are "acting as if they have no relatives" (Austin 2009, 25; Nielsen and Zion 2005, 57). In many ways, there has never been a discussion about how the U.S. has acted as if they have no Indigenous relatives. Understanding the "Trust Doctrine" as a sacred bond among distinct peoples has apparently been lost on many contemporary policy makers (Wilkins and Lomawaima 2001, 64–97). These were the exact barriers Williams notes in a multitude of treaty negotiations.

At some point in early colonial actor relations with Indigenous actors, there was a great deal of respect afforded the ceremonial practice known today as "The Sacred Pipe" ceremony (Williams 1999, 44–47). Primary texts indicated that not only did Indigenous actors take the ceremony seriously enough that they believed it would prevent war, but these types of ceremonies were called upon by colonial actors when they were also fearful that violence would break out. It is telling to remind all of some additional perspective on ceremonial practice. Again, we must really work hard to understand that a Sacred Pipe process was probably tied to an Indigenous traditional homeland. The process must have mentioned the land as the giver of life to all of the humans. Just as no individual should be expected to bring harm to their human mother, why would any human wish to bring harm to their planetary mother? It just seems unthinkable. This learned relationship was best codified through the sacred history of the various Indigenous actors. Elders taught the young about morals for living a good and long life by having their relationship with the land in balance meaning you take only from the earth that which you need and no more or less. These limited extractions from the earth could require songs and prayers in the form of a ceremony in cycle with daily routines such as the rising and setting of the sun. During the extraction process, specific words and language were used that had very little to do with everyday talk. These sacred words, in conjunction with lessons from the elders through the sacred history, in tune with a ceremonial cycle, and directly tied to the landscape itself, were all necessary conditions to ensure that "the people" continued on (Holm, Pearson, and Chavis 2003). Fighting over access to the land signified a serious imbalance in the relations among the peoples. This Peoplehood practice, as exemplified by the Sacred Pipe process, was required to remind all peoples and individuals of these very important tenets of a good life. As an elder once remarked, a ceremonial setting should get the hearts and minds of the participants in sync and toward a common purpose. If all of the people think about the exact same thing at the exact same time, a miracle will occur (Wilson 2008, 69).

It is clearer to discuss the nature of the European philosophy of treaty making and treaty breaking, yet, this discussion has also surprisingly never taken place. This time might be the origin point of Aboriginal Title. Obviously, scholars have written about broken treaties meant to extinguish Aboriginal Title but there has not been an application of contemporary international relations-based strategy applied to our shared history of broken treaties. Sadly, there is always "one guy" who can ruin a good thing for all. The nature of most processes that we might currently recognize today as consensus building or an "Indigenous confederacy" has been regarded as inefficient for decision-making by mainstream scholars. If we are to take the notion seriously that a miracle is required to attain good Indigenous and colonial actor relations, then we are required to get all to think about the exact same thing for a few seconds. When all of the individual participants in a ceremony have such great power to stop the ceremony from working by simply not cooperating, we may better appreciate the fragile nature of not only the ceremony of diplomacy but also the real world impact of diplomacy descending into violent and deadly war. Yet, this is exactly the problem, and the blame falls squarely on colonial actors.

Indigenous actors took their responsibilities to not only care for their own but to also find a place for their newly discovered European brothers and fathers or the agents of colonization. It only needed to be just one individual who regarded these ceremonies as meaningless exercises. The long and drawn-out ceremonial practice of diplomacy was considered a diversion from the "real negotiation" and the more important and seemingly more practical manner of outlining free trade agreements, alliances with tribes, and survival on the frontier (Williams 1999, 81–82). It is quite clear in the minds of many traditional knowledge holders today that if you come to a ceremonial setting with the "wrong attitude," there is no point in carrying out the ceremony at all. A medicine woman can cost a great deal of money to carry out a ceremony and, hence, they may have a financial interest in taking the money and doing the ceremony anyway. However, they seem more likely to turn the money down and save their own energy if the individuals are not willing to contribute to the miracle required to heal and move forward. These "new" and ancient ideas remain obscured when other scholars write about the treaty making process. Instead, most scholarship will focus on the obvious problems of treaty making with Indians.

European Norms of Treaty Making and Treaty Breaking

Making relatives out of former strangers is, again, a delicate matter and the very nature of European-style politics points to clear ulterior motives in the New World. The main motive was to eventually extinguish Aboriginal Title. Allowing us to delve into some comparative politics literature might be illuminating in exploring the expected utility behind the U.S. track record of breaking every treaty it has ever signed with all Indigenous actors in order to extinguish Aboriginal Title (Deloria and DeMallie 1999). The alliance-based nature of pre-1812 treaties was an important instrument for the survival of colonial actors (Deloria and Wilkins 1999, 5). I have often joked that I would one day write an article about the treaties the U.S. did keep with Indians and the manuscript would be a blank page! Fearon offered one of the most powerful examples of using formal models to forecast the likelihood that a negotiated peaceful settlement would eventually break down. He identified three areas that might contribute to the outbreak of renewed war: 1. Private information and the incentive to misrepresent ideal policy preferences, 2. Treaty commitment problems, and 3. Indivisibility issues (Fearon 1995, 381–382). Most students of Indigenous nations must be screaming at the top of their lungs about how these very simple barriers are alive and well in diplomatic relations until about 1812.

As I have continued to ponder these ideas, for perhaps the last 10 years, I have developed in my mind and for classes some drawings that might do a better job of explaining the international interaction of Indigenous and colonial actors. These figures have been created to better explain how extinguishing Aboriginal Title is an overriding goal implemented by decades and centuries of European diplomatic strategy. This work has also been heavily influenced by Bueno De Mesquita. His work attempts to forecast strategic policy preferences of various international actors with respect to discovering a policy space most ideal to one actor and least likely to create violent conflict by other actors threatened by said policy preferences (Bueno de Mesquita 2014). Consider the following illustration (Figure 1.1) of Indigenous and colonial actor interaction and based on Fearon's work (Fearon 1995, 387).

Figure 1.1: The Basics of International Actor Interaction

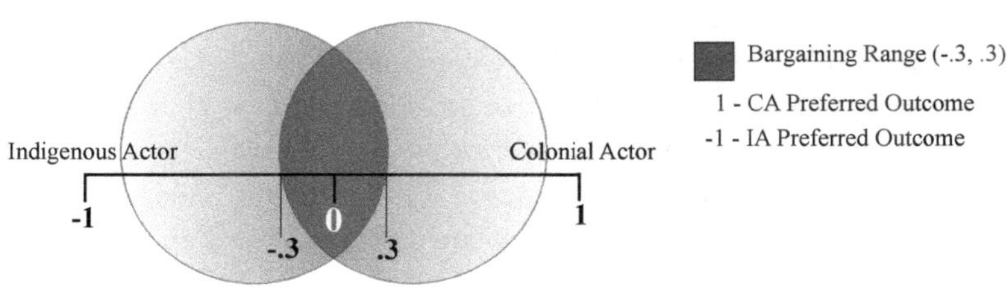

What is in the Peaceful Bargaining Range between -.3 and .3?
- Diplomacy
- Institutional Interaction - Make New Clans or Military Alliance
- Economic Interaction - Free Trade Agreements aka "trade"
- War
    - Cultural War?
    - Political War?

Note that the two polities are beginning to overlap. So long as the space for overlap is sufficiently separate, there should be little in the way of any one nation dominating the interaction process by means of their domestic institutions. Remember that there is no reason to assume that one nation or the other has some inherent belief that they wish to simply envelop the other within their own domestic polity. One of the nations must have set up some specific strategy to envelop the other nation as we see in empire building. It can be convincingly argued that some colonial actors, such as France, may have been slightly more interested in political economy arrangements than in eclipsing Indigenous sovereignty entirely. There is also little early evidence that any Indigenous actor had an interest in eclipsing the refugees from another continent. There is evidence of Indigenous empire building to be noted later. For now, the default policy position should not be assumed as "envelop."

Another way of viewing the level of interaction between two international actors is to focus on specific policy preferences that cannot co-exist. For example, the non-divisibility of land is key to almost every treaty between Indigenous and colonial actors. This is especially true after 1812. Indigenous actors can be relied upon to vehemently oppose extinguishing their Aboriginal Title rights even if they may have not fully understood this idea. While it is difficult to know for sure what the policy preferences of Indigenous actors were, it is a bit easier to decode colonial actor preferences. They clearly wished to extinguish Aboriginal Title. This idea is also present in Figure 1.1.

Note the policy preference continuum ranging from -1 to 1. Each of the whole numbers (1 or -1) represents the ideal policy preferences of a single international actor. Let's allow 1 to be the colonial actor and -1 the Indigenous actor. The "actual" ideal policy preference for each actor really does not matter. What does matter are the gray areas that line up near the 0 point. The line, that I have arbitrarily placed somewhere near the .3 and -.3 is not exactly clear to each actor. This ambiguity is represented by the curves ranging from a space between about -.3 through .3 to 0 space between co-existing policy preferences. This is the nature of Fearon's argument regarding treaty making and treaty breaking (1995, 387).

Indigenous and colonial actor treaties must be re-examined and Fearon's model may be an ideal lens for explaining the expected utility of treaty making and treaty breaking. One assumption to help clarify matters may be that colonial actors clearly preferred an outcome where Aboriginal Title was extinguished. Still, this preference could not be achieved during the military alliance era of treaty making. Our data for how treaties were inconvenient necessities of life comes from the treaties themselves

(Deloria and DeMallie 1999, 6–11). Deloria and DeMallie, not being formally trained in international relations theory, have nonetheless pointed out how these treaties probably amounted to military alliances with much more powerful international actors that we have today called the Tribes. Hence, colonial actor policy preferences at this stage amounted to surviving. Deloria and DeMallie take care to note that these treaties certainly counted as international instruments of interaction, yet they relegate the discussion of their impact in the Old World as moot (1999). Sadly, in the short time between 1999 and the present, the few examples of otherwise quality research that have been written omit this fact of our shared history. How moot is this discussion now? In other words, I now wish to explore the apparent strategy inherent in treating "Indian treaties" as an inferior temporary contract meant to be broken at a time when it is more expedient for colonial actors to maintain and expand their sovereign reach in the "New World" by extinguishing Aboriginal Title.

Military alliances are temporary alliances, at least from the colonial actor point of view. This brings us to Fearon's first lesson about military alliance treaties: They are hampered by the use of private information and the incentive to misrepresent information.[3] Examining a single treaty will help illustrate this point. On May 12, 1781, a treaty was signed between Indigenous actor Chippewa and England. This treaty outlines the transfer of land between Chippewa and a representative of England, France, and Ireland. This land exchange is based on a swap of five thousand pounds and reads a bit like a real estate transaction. Within the treaty language is a mention of a seven-foot-long Wampum Belt that also signifies the exchange (Deloria and DeMallie 1999, 118). But now comes the first major snag in this research: What did the Wampum Belt state? This very limited example represents the potential for private information. Even if we assume away the idea that colonial actors would purposely misrepresent their actual policy preferences, we cannot be sure that the Wampum Belt did not represent the clan-based time immemorial relationship that you do not see in the English language record of the treaty. We could directly

3. While I risk being accused of selecting treaties based on the notion that they represent military alliance as a step toward treaty breaking, an area I comment much more heavily on in the analysis of the Rehnquist Court, I merely wish to point out an example of this larger pattern in the treaty record. It is certainly desirable to carry out a Qualitative Comparative Analysis (QCA) operation such as the one used on the Rehnquist Court cases but this operation may not be possible. The entire treaty record may no longer be assessable unless there are still knowledge holders willing to interpret Wampum Belt treaties and share it with the outside world. Without the Wampum Belt record or other Indigenous records of treaties, any comprehensive treaty interaction analysis is not possible and results are spurious. We may be left to make assumptions and draw conclusions as best we can given our limited record.

tie this interaction record to Figure 1.1 with minor modifications as represented in Figure 1.2.

Figure 1.2: Two Dimensional Figure of the Chippewa Treaty of 1787

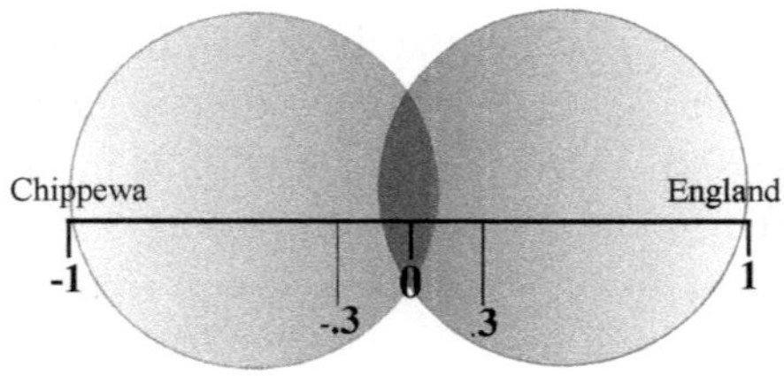

Bargaining Range (-.1, .1)

1 - U.S. Preferred Outcome

-1 - Chippewa Preferred Outcome

Peaceful Bargaining Range - between -1 and 1
- Diplomacy
  - Land Sale
    - Represented by some space in between .1 and -.1
  - The spheres indicate policy preferences
    - The overlap is the negotiated interaction space
      - Anything beyond could lead to war
- Wampum Belt Record
  - The 7 foot long belt is acknowledged in the English language treaty

Figure 1.2 represents a couple of key issues. First is the Chippewa understanding of the treaty. We have to assume, because we don't know, that any space on the policy continuum that goes beyond .3 on the continuum would likely lead to war. This lack of certainty is present in Figure 1.2. Notice how the circle that represents England's policy preference is round. Hence, the linear continuum line could go down to 0. Again, this is merely a representation of the unknown terms contained in the Wampum Belt. What we do know, because we read English, is that there is a clearer record for English intent in the treaty. They had a clear intent to purchase land from the Chippewa for a price of five thousand pounds. This is a manner of extinguishing Aboriginal Title by way of purchase. We can assume, again, that this policy outcome (land purchase) is creeping into a space that is acceptable for the Chippewa but not ideal. If we take the treaty language at face value, which Fearon says we should not do, then we can more clearly draw a line on the policy continuum where the English will accept encroachment or fight. This common trait appears again with another band of Chippewa and England, France, and Ireland yet there is no mention of Wampum Belts (Deloria and DeMallie 1999, 119–122). By the early 1800s, the treaties have taken on a much more unilateral nature.

An unratified treaty between Chippewa and the U.S. indicates an armistice where the Tribes are allowed to go to their hunting grounds and remain there unmolested so long as they behave themselves (Deloria and DeMallie 1999, 1244). Of note is that the colonial actor changed from England to the U.S. A redrawing of the negotiation space is required and presented here as Figure 1.3.

Figure 1.3: Two Dimensional Figure of the Chippewa Treaty of 1813

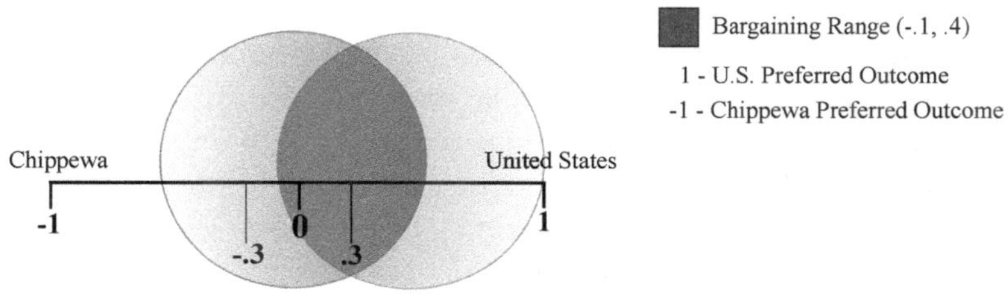

Space for Interaction - Bargain Range
- Diplomacy
    - Land Sale
        - Represented by some space in between -.1 and .4
- Wampum Belt Record
    - Since We Cannot Read the Belt, What are the Policy Preferences of Chippewa? Could it be Greater Than .4? If So, This Leads to War.

Here we return to an unclear negotiation and unclear cause for war space. It may be fair to assume that extinguished Aboriginal Title, perhaps by purchase, is at the heart of the battles. A second issue to note is that the space is creeping in toward ideal policy preferred by the U.S. which I assume is to extinguish Aboriginal Title by purchase or conquest, whichever is cheaper. It remains questionable what the policy preferences of the Chippewa were but we can assume that this treaty would not have been signed had the Chippewa not wished to stop fighting. We are wise to note the other areas Fearon has raised as rationalist explanations for war.

Here we can see a few things going on simultaneously. First, the colonial actor is changing, second the language is getting harsher and filled with more assumptions about the savagery of the Chippewa (but the language does not explicitly state this). Fearon informs us of the prevailing impact of information and misinformation. It probably was not required for the English and then the U.S. to guard their information about their intentions. Language barriers on both sides worked just fine independent of any individual's wish to obscure true motives. But also note how far and away we have moved from any notion or hint of "sacredness" and toward extinguishing Aboriginal Title by purchase or conquest. The second problem involves commitment issues. How can England continue to assume responsibility to any Chippewa band or tribe if they no longer have any impact on the newly independent U.S.? Policy preferences indicate ambiguity in where the space for peaceful settlement ends and where the space for war begins. Another angle on commitment involves the ends each actor seeks. It is quite clear that the U.S. seeks to extinguish Aboriginal Title. It remains a question if Chippewa ever entertained notions of getting beyond squabbles and back to a clan-based relationship with the U.S. This confusion can, more often than not, lead to war. Fearon advises as much when he argues that these very complex and confusing spaces lead to what we might call a comedy of errors when both actors stumble into a space where only violent confrontation can be used to resolve the disagreement.

Fearon's second issue involves commitment problems (Fearon 1995, 381). For many reasons that will not be discussed here, the U.S. has utterly failed to commit to the treaty terms they have agreed to in writing. Our thematic reason for this failure is, again, incontrovertibly tied to policy strategies that would result in the extinguishing of Aboriginal Title by purchase or conquest. Other times, events were beyond the control of the emerging U.S. nation. The U.S. faced many pressures as it emerged from the shadow of England after 1776. Some of these pressures involved preventing fighting on the frontier. The U.S. Supreme Court was well aware of the fact that the deadliest enemies of Indians would be found in close proximity to citizens of the state and out of the reach of federal authority (United States v. Kagama 1886). Part of the pressure was that, in many cases, the federal government was incapable of preventing non-Indians from taking matters into their own hands and carrying out their own versions of "justice." But this really means that non-Indians were defying the federal government, taking Indian lands, and probably committing all other sorts of atrocities in the process. All of these precariously connected occurrences just helped the cause for extinguishing Aboriginal Title.

Other times, the U.S. clearly decided it was expedient to ignore treaty terms, violate the terms, and perhaps sign a new treaty if the Indians chose to object with violence. Whatever the case study evidence suggests, we can be certain that other scholars who wish to explore the treaty record may find all sorts of evidence for opportunities that the U.S. saw as increasing their odds of winning a war if they take the first strike advantage against a tribe (Fearon 1995, 402). First strike advantages, again, lead directly to extinguishing Aboriginal Title by conquest. This interesting facet could further explain treaty breakdowns through the various examples of "preventive war" in which the U.S. would attack first because they believed an Indian attack was imminent (Fearon 1995, 404). A final note of wisdom involves the natural power expansion that can come from taking territory (Fearon 1995, 408). Obviously, as land is acquired, more natural resources can be exploited and used to bolster the power of the U.S. This is yet another potential case study in extinguishing Aboriginal Title by conquest. Secondly, U.S. land acquisition could also bolster strategic military positions and, thus, make them an attractive ally partner to other tribes. Still, the very issue of land indivisibility is also key.

Finally, there are very clear issues with the indivisibility of land. Fearon notes these indivisibility issues and then brushes them aside as "domestic issues" for lack of a better understanding on the nature of organic ties to homelands (Fearon 1995, 382). We stand to be reminded of quantitative research clearly tying the notion of organic ties to traditional homeland with a motivation to put your life on the line to defend such homeland in the Americas (Lerma 2012). This research was directly informed by the idea that the Chippewa probably had a sacred history related to their traditional homeland that was fostered by ceremony and represented by songs and prayers in their language (Holm, Pearson, and Chavis 2003). Organic ties to homeland are the Indigenous-based response to notions of Aboriginal Title rights of occupancy. Hence, it could be unthinkable that any Indigenous actor would dare sell mother earth due to organic ties to their traditional homelands. (This idea would largely be domestic according to Fearon). Yet, we read it with our own eyes that the Chippewa, in this example, agreed to sell land for money. How can that be? We are again reminded to consider the absence of the Wampum Belt from the treaty record as well as the primary document evidence that continued pressure from somewhere, perhaps efforts to extinguish Aboriginal Title, created enough motivation for the Chippewa to violently react to U.S. encroachment. We must also remember the lessons on Linking Arms Together (Williams 1999). It is not at all clear that a land sale was ever an option.

Concluding Remarks

Again, this is a very small section on the exploration of Indigenous treaties as sacred and as military alliances. More importantly, it is a time period where Aboriginal Title extinguishing was not yet possible. Treaties probably hid the fact that they would be used as leverage tools in attempts to extinguish Indigenous sovereignty. My assumption should not stand on its own as the final word on the nature of Indigenous sovereignty today. Scholars who read this are HIGHLY ENCOURAGED to continue this research should it serve your home communities or the communities served within and beyond Indian Country. The main point here is to draw scholars back to this path of Indigenous alliance partners as they were used for their military might only to be cast aside when they were no longer useful to colonial actors. Scholars often abandon these early documents of Indigenous and colonial actor diplomacy after 1871 when the U.S. unilaterally declared that they would no longer make treaties with Indians. There are several problems with this implicit assumption made by most other researchers. First, researchers must understand the origins of the false dichotomies leaders in Indian Country today are asked to choose between. If not now then when? Our future students will continue to make these limited choices tomorrow leading to more loss of Indigenous sovereignty (Bruyneel 2007).

Secondly, the failure of any other scholar to properly examine the strategic approach pursued by the U.S. to envelop Indigenous nations within their domestic polity mechanisms remains obscured and conveniently forgotten by the U.S. today. This is a strategic approach pursued out of convenience on a number of levels. This approach is only useful to federalists who wished to set the foundation for a dominant model placing federalism at the top. Perhaps Indigenous nations were never clearly recognized by federalists in general. Some likely saw Indigenous nations as equal to the U.S. Others were less overt but were forced to recognize the military might of "savage" Indigenous nations. Most federalists seemed to assume that the U.S. would eventually eclipse Indigenous nations and swallow them up within the U.S. polity. Meanwhile, federalists worked to ensure states were inferior to federal domination. Hence, Indigenous sovereignty is perhaps only ever defended and upheld by U.S. domestic institutions if it is clearly also upholding the federalist model as dominant over state sovereignty (Getches 2001). The next chapter will further explicate the policy preference space as U.S. domestic institutions gradually swallow it up.

Chapter 2
Wrapping Up Indigenous Nations Within the U.S. Domestic Polity

The race to wrap up Indigenous nations within the U.S. polity seemed complete and was formalized in 1871 when the U.S. declared that they would now call Treaties "agreements"(Wilkins and Stark 2011, 127; Bruyneel 2007, 27–64). This "domestication" process may seem insulting but it also has a larger subtle meaning involving U.S. domestic institutions. In Chapter 1, readers are reminded of how Indigenous nations served the emerging U.S. as pawns even during times when the U.S. could not survive without them. Yet, few scholars have discussed the strategy to systematically eliminate, piece by piece, international mechanism to solve grievances and replace them with domestic mechanisms housed within the U.S. polity. Not all scholars believe this strategy was deliberate if they believe it exists. To be clear, this research does not vest Washington and Jefferson with "prophetic powers that would do Nostradamus proud" (Deloria and Wilkins 1999, ix). Rather, colonization is hard work requiring constant updating. It requires tremendous genocidal talent to recognize windows of opportunity in order to take advantage of Indigenous nation weaknesses when the climate is right.[4] From a public relations point of view, these false dichotomies or the "imperial binary" could be better understood as an agenda-setting mechanism where the U.S. not only framed the issues but also prevented alternative issues from being raised (Bruyneel 2007, 6–7; Lukes 1974, 16–20). During these agenda-setting opportunities, reneging on treaty obligations was ideal since the old treaty clause could then be replaced with the latest false dichotomy.

Declaring that all future interactions with Indigenous nations would formally shift from international mechanisms (treaty negotiations) to domestic U.S. mechanisms is more than a mere footnote in 19th century CSPAN. Rather, the question must be raised about whether ending treaty making constitutes a deliberate act to never again think of Indigenous nations as

4. This research does not rely on United Nations conventions or declarations of "approved" genocide.

legitimate international actors. This premise could rewrite the history of federal Indian law and policy by focusing on how there was little if any recourse for addressing grievances besides those institutions created by the U.S. What are typically listed as "Indian Rights" including voting, standing in the courts, and the like may be re-interpreted as domestic mechanisms for due process with little promise or guarantee of justice. Hence, federal Indian law and policy may be a series of false dichotomies allowing for U.S. domestic mechanisms to functionally creep into Indian Country (Bruyneel 2007, 65–122). False dichotomies foster the integration of Indian Country into what would become the global political economy based on notions of U.S. dominated economic liberalism (Richardson 2001). Advocates for the maintenance and expansion of Indigenous sovereignty must transcend false dichotomies. We must link, as is done in Chapter 7, the lessons of rebuilding Western Europe in the aftermath of World War II to the original destruction and rebuilding of Indian Country to serve the U.S. political economy. Our focus is admittedly narrow and scholars are strongly encouraged to learn from development literature as explanations for contemporary economic development, or the lack thereof, in Indian Country today. This aside, federal Indian law and policy is merely the foundation for contemporary colonization based on economic resource extraction.

A final crucial note: We may find a great deal of utility in understanding the Marshall Court as very much key players in setting up the current relationship between the federal government and states in the U.S. today. One of the pawns in this set up is the manner in which many vestiges of Indigenous sovereignty are only defended if they happen to also bolster federalism trumping states' rights. This chapter will also point out, where appropriate, how the states' rights and federalism dichotomy played out as the main dependent variable in nearly all Supreme Court cases (Getches 2001). The Court is most likely to defend Indigenous sovereignty when defense would also further admonish states that attempted to thwart federalism creeping into state jurisdictions. In other words, only those aspects of Indigenous sovereignty that also serve the interest of the federal government are defended. All other aspects of Indigenous sovereignty are subject to extinguishing. This chapter will first argue that federal Indian law and policy is merely a means to entrench Indigenous nations within the U.S. domestic polity. Second, we revisit the origin of "reservations" and remind all that these were not gifts from colonial actors. Third, we expand on the post-reservation and post-Aboriginal Title erosions of sovereignty in Indian Country. These sections are integrally tied to all phases of federal Indian law and policy although this chapter will not comprehensively outline all facets of these eras.

Federal Indian Law and Policy: a means to envelop Indigenous Nations into the Domestic U.S. Polity

Federal Indian law and policy is designed to eliminate Indigenous sovereignty as much as possible. This idea might seem simultaneously intuitive and counter-intuitive. Some will argue or believe that Indigenous sovereignty does not exist anymore. As such, that federal Indian law and policy is designed to eliminate Indigenous sovereignty makes perfect sense. However, many, including myself, will argue that Indigenous sovereignty does still exist but in diminished capacity and varying from Indigenous nation to Indigenous nation. Figure 2.1 explains Indigenous sovereignty in flux.

Figure 2.1: "Domestication" of Indigenous Nations

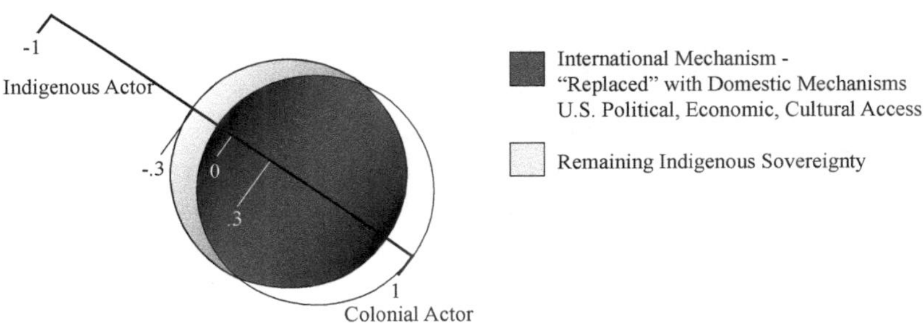

Space for Interaction - (Bargain Range - Most is in U.S. ideal space)
- Access to U.S. Institutions
  - Access is limited based on race
    - Economic Institutional Access
      - Only Some Jobs
    - Political Access
      - Voting
      - "Due Process"
    - Cultural Access
      - Manifest Destiny, Fourth of July, Fight in U.S. Wars

In order to comprehensively discuss Indigenous sovereignty, 566 examples of Figure 2.1 would need to be drawn. This is limited to the U.S. alone and their recognition of 566 Indigenous nations (*Department of Interior* 2014). Since space is limited, Figure 2.1 is generally drawn to represent a pattern of sovereign diminishment. In similar fashion to figures offered in Chapter 1, Indigenous institutions of self governance were systematically eliminated and replaced, sometimes, with U.S. domestic mechanisms. Admittedly, this is a complex process that does not lend itself to dichotomous thinking. Figure 2.1 is meant to depict incremental chipping away, and perhaps restoration, of Indigenous sovereignty over time.

In order to accept this idea, one must entertain viewpoints about functional creep and norms of nation-based interaction. Professor James Anaya of the University of Arizona would lecture in his class on Indigenous Human Rights about the idea that bureaucracy has a tendency to creep away from its original intent. It is probably best to use this idea to frame federal Indian law and policy today. But the idea is much more complicated. There are 8 eras in federal Indian law and policy implying 8 potential creeping zones:

1. Treaty Making Era
2. Removal Era
3. Reservation Era
4. Allotment Era
5. Reorganization Era
6. Termination Era
7. Self Determination Era
8. Forced Federalism Era

Complicating matters are a number of issues. First, readers may find it odd that years are omitted for each era. This is deliberate. We cannot use time as an organizing theme. Research organized by time (years) has created confusion in contemporary research on federal Indian law and policy. For example, we can look at removal of the Five Civilized Tribes in the 1830s. However, we must revisit this removal process in the 1860s if we wish to explore Navajo Nation removal. Hence, time does not work to explain our main themes very well.

A second complicating factor is that using a theme like functional creep is vague. There are a number of individual facets of federal Indian law and policy that cannot be fully captured in text. Even if scholars around the world agreed to write these individual stories down as case studies centered around the 566 Indigenous nations in the U.S. alone, who would have the time or energy to read these stories? Yet, there is a theme alive and well in all of the eras mentioned. Instead of time, creep is a better organizing theme because it will highlight how each era was attempted in specific regions while not applied in others. Although vague, creep might be less vague and more exact than organizing based on time. The Five Civilized Tribes removal example indicates this idea. History teaches us that the U.S. Courts began to allow hair-splitting policy into their domestic polity as evidenced by the Marshall Trilogy. In the end, the Courts could not decide that Cherokee was an international nation and they could also not agree that it was not a nation at all. Consequently, the Court resolved to call Cherokee a "domestic dependent nation." This is the fuzzy space in between the Treaty Making and Removal eras. Ultimately, the idea that Cherokee Nation was a domestic dependent nation and that Georgia state law did not apply in Cherokee Nation, resulted in creeping toward removal of Cherokees on the "Trail of Tears." (Wilkins and Stark 2011, 125–128). This chapter will explore some of the main creeping points in federal Indian law and policy while focusing on the envelopment of Indigenous nations within the domestic U.S. polity.

The end of treaty making in 1871 is often noted as a relatively minor detail in the history of federal Indian law and policy. While there are various explanations for why treaty making was unilaterally ended by the U.S. in 1871, it is important to bring them all together under one paragraph now. There have been at least four, probably more, common explanations for ending treaty making. 1. The U.S. Congress had a fight about ratification, 2. It was assumed that tribes must be forced to assimilate and ending treaty making was a tool to make this happen, 3. Ultimately, the goal of the U.S. was to solidify the federal branches as the superior wing in extinguishing Aboriginal Title, and 4. Intrinsically linked to 3., there were several unclear land titles that needed to be settled in a manner that provided a federal monopoly over making up land titles. Chapter 1 explores the process for the U.S. having the opportunity to extinguish treaty making in 1871. This section will explore the strategy inherent in bolstering U.S. sovereignty and trumping Indigenous sovereignty by eliminating as many international mechanisms for Indigenous diplomacy as possible. The notion of creep makes this area very fuzzy and "schizophrenic" (Williams 2005, 149–160). These mechanisms may have been replaced with a U.S. domestic institution for hearing grievances but there is no strategic advantage for the U.S. to offer new domestic mechanism unless the U.S. public was paying attention or this new mechanism bolstered U.S. interests in trumping states' rights with federalism.

To be clear, none of the above explanations are, by themselves, incorrect. They simply do not focus enough attention on the inherent benefit the U.S. has in ensuring treaty making was no longer a policy option. The most common explanation for the end of treaty making involves the debate in U.S. Congress over treaties and the appropriation of budget funding to meet treaty obligations. Prior to 1871, the U.S. made treaties with international actors in the same way that any nation made treaties. Nations would often negotiate some non-violent interaction method. Diplomacy is cheaper than war. The costs of war are highly unpredictable. It is nearly impossible to "calculate" the cost of lost lives if war were to break out. Rational leaders should curb the costs of disagreements where possible. Hence, in very crass terms, it is cheaper to negotiate than to fight. This might be the military man's perspective on war. Obviously, U.S. policy makers also understood this type of thinking. So, notwithstanding the ideas mentioned in Chapter 1, when nations could be relied upon to agree on information, agree that it was cheaper to keep the deal rather than renege, and agree land was divisible, it is theoretically possible to have peace lasting until the end of time (Fearon 1995). As the U.S. became more bureaucratically complex, these kinds of straightforward ideas grew more convoluted. In other words, functional creep allowed policy makers to question the "cheaper to negotiate" wisdom. Many remain astonished that the U.S. negotiated over 372 treaties with Indigenous nations (Wilkins 2013, 59). This does not include other colonial actor treaties with Indigenous nations nor the multitude of treaties that were never ratified by the U.S., which can be reviewed independent of this research (Deloria and DeMallie 1999). The thousands of treaties between Indigenous nations and colonial actors is evidence that it was cheaper to negotiate than to fight, at least in the short term.

The military men who made treaties had to eventually run their negotiated peace policies by the U.S. government including a president and an ever expanding legislature. The bicameral legislature, due to checks and balances, had to oversee one another. By 1871, the treaty making process may have become routine and perhaps mundane. Typically, a military official would negotiate the treaty with Indigenous nations although there are surely exceptions to this statement. However a treaty was negotiated, it eventually found its way to the U.S. Senate. Upon arrival in the Senate, we can only imagine the 372-plus sets of conditions that would have colored the ratification process. Perhaps the Senate was extra conservative that year or perhaps it was extra liberal. What is certain is that treaties with Indigenous nations were often complex and repetitive. But imagine the Senate ratifying 372 treaties between about 1778 and 1871. In a period of about 84 years, there were 372 treaties ratified and many more discussed but not ratified. This is, on average, about 4 treaties per year. Making treaties with Indians must have become a tiresome and routine process in Congress.

After the Senate ratified a treaty, the House was expected to find money to pay for the treaty obligations. At some point, the House began to resent this "after the fact" process. Frequency must have also played a role; again, 372 opportunities in 84 years for the House to grow tired of rubber stamping Senate expenditures. They wished to be included in all of the treaties, perhaps, because of the frequency of treaty making with Indigenous nations but also because of the expense (Wilkins 2013, 59). Still, another issue creeping during this time was the clear notion that Indigenous nations needed to go away. Their "heathen behavior" in terms of criminal prosecution of their own citizens and non-Indian people was utilized as a public relations threat to civilization. But this idea of wrapping up Indigenous sovereignty within the U.S. polity could only happen after Indigenous nation powers were militarily diminished enough that they could not fight to go beyond their prescribed reservations. Again, the second explanation for the end of treaty making simultaneously crept forward.

Some policy makers in the period of 1840–1871 were appalled by the idea that the U.S. would lower itself to Indigenous nations as an equal treaty negotiation partner. Again, the reality of military men on the ground may have escaped some policy makers who felt like negotiating with Indians was a philosophical misdeed. This idea might be akin to "negotiating with terrorists." Many zealots would never negotiate with a terrorist organization for fear that this negotiation process might lend some legitimacy to the organization itself. Today, some U.S. policy makers also find it distasteful to sit down and negotiate with rogue states such as North Korea or Iran. This idea was likely on the minds of some policy makers who wanted to simply end treaty making with Indians because they were never "real nations" in the first place. This is more functional creep. Evidence for this idea of ending treaty making is not directly available. Instead, it is accessible if we make some assumptions. By the 1860s the U.S. was growing more concerned over the domestic affairs of Indigenous nations. Again, context is key. Imagine today if the U.S. decided that a foreign nation, such as Mexico, was no longer carrying out law and order according to U.S. standards and that the U.S. ought to intervene by installing its own criminal justice system in Mexico. This only makes sense, however, for the Mexican states that border the U.S. For me, this is exactly what the U.S. was debating in the mid to late 1860s. U.S. criminal jurisdiction crept into Indian Country that bordered U.S. ambition to extinguish Aboriginal Title. This debate was clearly centered on the notion of obliterating Indigenous sovereignty.

By the mid-1850s the U.S. was beginning to think about a pan-Indigenous civilization policy. It would be most expedient for the U.S. should they broadly insert themselves into all Indigenous domestic affairs in order to civilize the Indians. This process became focused on criminal jurisdiction but, more broadly, allowed for the erosion of Indigenous sovereignty (Wilkins 1997). This collective strategy to take criminal jurisdiction in Indian Country is one example where Figure 2.1 can be generalized. All Indigenous nations were targeted for their supposedly lackluster criminal justice outcomes. This story, or myth, has been retold in Ex Parte Crow Dog where Indigenous justice does not live up to the U.S. standard. There was once an altercation between two Brule Sioux and one of them lost his life. The survivor was incarcerated by U.S. authorities in the region and sentenced to execution (Ex Parte Crow Dog 1884). All of this is going on without any notion of U.S. criminal jurisdiction to intervene in what amounted to an internal domestic matter for the Brule Sioux people. The Court opinion states that the U.S.

does not have jurisdiction over a crime where one Indian harms another Indian of the same tribe. International treaties do not deliver such jurisdiction to the U.S. Secondly, a post-treaty making agreement also does not provide jurisdiction. There was too much history of treating Indigenous sovereigns as nations and the Court was uncomfortable assuming these international instruments away. The Court concluded that U.S. Congress would need to clearly express an intent to violate Indigenous sovereignty (Ex Parte Crow Dog 1884). Congress would need to unilaterally declare that, from some specific date forward, Indigenous sovereignty over their own methods of crime and punishment was being voided and replaced with U.S. methods. Again, negating domestic Indigenous sovereignty and replacing it with U.S. mechanisms in the name of civilizing the savages can justify this violation. Criminal jurisdiction, then, crept into Indian Country blurring the line between treaty making and some other and unclear era of eliminating aspects of Indigenous sovereignty.

Independent of the Crow Dog opinion, U.S. federal and state officials were well informed that the Brule Sioux incident was dealt with in a traditional Brule manner. After the violent interaction between the two individuals took place, a tribal council met to discuss the matter. Brule peacemakers agreed that restitution must take place. Since Crow Dog committed a violation of Brule norms by taking the life of Spotted Tail, peacemakers determined that Crow Dog's family would pay restitution to Spotted Tail's family. The Brule peacemakers, perhaps with the consent of Crow Dog's family, arranged restitution in the amount of "$600, eight horses, and one blanket" (Getches 2011, 153–158). Some assumptions about this arrangement may be necessary. I will assume, and I may be corrected later, that the peacemakers were more interested in arranging a restoration of balance to their people. Hence, restitution may not be the correct word. When the two men fought, one lost his life. This created a major imbalance in their tribal world and put the tribes very being at risk. Elders probably recognized this as a path toward chaos. Perhaps both families would have resorted to more violence. Alternatively, perhaps both families would have worked tirelessly to sacrifice their own being in order to restore balance to the Spotted Tail family. This is also a moment where chaos could emerge as both families could harm themselves in giving too much to restore balance. Relying on Peoplehood might also help make this exchange clearer (Holm, Pearson, and Chavis 2003). If horses are sacred to the Brule Sioux, perhaps medicine people had to carry out ceremonies for these eight horses. This could be a very time and energy consuming process. While not understandable from the primary or secondary documents on the event, it seems clear to me, albeit with no evidence, that this restoration of balance to the Brule people was quite tasking for all involved. This so-called "restitution" probably involved the unification of these two families for generations. Exchanges were likely never to be exclusively friendly. This story could be exponentially expanded if a historian or a descendent of the Brule Sioux people were willing to carry out independent research on the account. Then again, it may be inappropriate to delve further based on Brule Sioux norms.

Still, federal representatives utilized this event as a method to obtain public support from non-Indian U.S. citizens to extend criminal jurisdiction over Indian Country. Again, this functional creep was meant to further erode Indigenous sovereignty as the opportunity either arose, was facilitated, or both. Many scholars have, correctly, tied these events to the eventual manufacture of "plenary power" or the idea that the U.S. could unilaterally violate (abrogate) treaties with Indigenous nations (Wilkins 1997). Interestingly, the U.S. probably does not need to seek congressional or judicial approval for it to violate international law. As a side note, it is intriguing that the U.S. had this debate with itself over further eroding Indigenous sovereignty, thus, lending credence to the idea that these Indigenous nations must have mattered even more so than the invasion of Iraq in 2003. Again, these seemingly unconnected events need to be reanalyzed as a collective creeping tide meant to drown out Indigenous sovereignty.

U.S. policy makers were already imagining ideas about further eroding Indigenous homelands and relegating the survivors of this ethnic cleansing to reservations even as they quietly imposed their criminal jurisdiction on Indian Country. Yet, once this concentration was accomplished, it would not be enough to merely allow Indigenous peoples to govern themselves with no oversight. Rather, it was decided that Indigenous nations, on reservations, would also need to be subjected to U.S. criminal jurisdiction which basically means that the traditional Indigenous methods of carrying out their own crime and punishment would be negated in favor of imposed norms of crime and punishment from the outside. It was clear, in the minds of U.S. policy makers, that "providing" Indians with law and order, based on the assumption that Indians had no law and order, would further the yearning to civilize Indians (Wilkins 1997). This is willful blindness to the fact that Indigenous nations, specifically the Brule Sioux, had their own methods of dealing with crimes as salient as murder. Indigenous nations could not receive credit for their methods of dealing with murder even if the facts about Brule peacemakers were clear to Bureau of Indian Affairs officials (Ex Parte Crow Dog 1884, 157–158). Rather, it was advantageous for the U.S. to portray Indigenous nations as savages without any understanding of the U.S. ideas about crime and punishment for creep to occur. Again, the line was blurring between treaty making and treaty breaking. Figure 2.1 can visualize this blur or creep. Where is the line between Indigenous sovereignty and U.S. imposition?

The conclusion of Ex Parte Crow Dog makes plenty of assumptions about Indigenous ignorance to U.S. ideas about justice:

> [The U.S. Courts] tries [Indians], not by their peers, nor by the customs of their people, nor the law of their land, but by *superiors of a different race,* according to the law of a social state of which they have *an imperfect conception,* and which is opposed to the traditions of their history, to the habits of their lives, to the *strongest prejudices of their savage nature;* one which measures *the red man's revenge by the maxims of the white man's morality* (Ex Parte Crow Dog 1884).

I have added italics to the original text to emphasize what could amount to a public relations campaign meant to foster an environment with the U.S. public supportive of eroding this aspect of Indigenous sovereignty. Figure 2.1 and criminal jurisdiction amount to a shell game. Where is Indigenous sovereignty? Is it in Indigenous institutions or U.S. institutions or on the line in between them? The policy was quicker than the practice and Indigenous leadership, diminished in their capacity to protect themselves due to war and broken treaties, may have taken the Trust Doctrine too seriously.

Ex Parte Crow Dog concludes that the U.S. does not have the authority to claim what it wants; criminal jurisdiction over Indians. The case opinion goes on to beg the U.S. Congress to proclaim its criminal jurisdiction over Indian Country or the part of the continental U.S. that they could more or less claim they held title over. In other words, the U.S. Congress was given the task of legislating its criminal jurisdiction over land that had its Aboriginal Title extinguished. This process was unilaterally carried out by way of the Major Crimes Act of 1885. This seemingly massive extinguishing of Indigenous sovereignty was carried out as a rider attached to a general appropriations act. The U.S. declared that federal prosecutors would try any of seven crimes that took place in Indian Country including the following: 1. Murder, 2. Manslaughter, 3. Rape, 4. Assault with intent to kill, 5. Arson, 6. Burglary, and 7. Larceny (Wilkins 1997). These events led to another challenge in the Courts which has also come to creep into the only mechanism for addressing violations of Indigenous sovereignty after the U.S. reneged on treaty obligations.

The U.S. has continuously exhibited a pattern in working to eclipse Indigenous sovereignty by 1. Extinguishing Aboriginal Title, 2. Holding the extinguished title in trust for use by Indians, and 3. Proceeding to erode the domestic realm of Indigenous notions of justice. Each of these activities could potentially be animated in Figure 2.1. Subsequent policy changes would push Indigenous institutions further within the U.S. domestic polity. When the Courts still had some sense of dignity, they concluded that they could not decide to take criminal jurisdiction in Indian Country. Be clear, Indian Country means that Aboriginal Title is extinguished and now owned by the U.S. This ownership is held in trust for the Tribes. Even after the justices authoring Crow Dog begged Congress to take criminal jurisdiction, and after Congress does so nearly 18 months later, the challenges still remain. How can one international actor truly and unilaterally violate the sovereignty of Indigenous nations? When a similar situation emerged in California and two Indians from Hoopa found themselves indicted under the Major Crimes Act for murder, they responded by arguing that Congress did not have the ability to assume they could negate Indigenous sovereignty. This case is known as U.S. v. Kagama.

The Kagama opinion retells the common narrative of Indigenous conquest that, by now, should be understood as a complete myth. The typical excuse is that this convoluted story of extra and pre-constitutional anomalies must be dealt with in a manner that happens to promote U.S. sovereignty first and foremost as well as federalism over states' rights. 1. Aboriginal Title is extinguished, 2. Tribes wished to sell land to the U.S. and a treaty was the only way to make it happen, and 3. Indigenous peoples end up not within the U.S. and not completely independent from the U.S. Yet, the assumption is that these remaining vestiges of Indigenous sovereignty will magically disappear in time leading to the assumption that the U.S. federal government must work to assist dependent Indigenous nations. This ward/guardian relationship must, therefore, assume a paternalistic relationship in which the U.S. can unilaterally decide what is best for Indigenous nations. As a consequence, it appears clear to the justices that Kagama must allow the U.S. to unilaterally eclipse Indigenous sovereignty at will if they believe it will help their ward known as Indigenous nations (United States v. Kagama 1886; Getches 2011, 158–160). So the stage is set. The U.S. can carry on its agenda of eliminating as much Indigenous sovereignty as is in the best interest of Indigenous nations. Simultaneously, many other policies are also creeping into the narrative. The very definition of "reservation" is also in flux.

Re-Defining Reservations: we GAVE you?

By 1871, several policy implementations set the stage for the U.S. to wrap up Indigenous nations within their own domestic polity. In many ways, there are three metrics and privileged access points to consider. At the heart of Aboriginal Title is access to institutions. Some of these institutions are cultural, some are political, and some are economic. While these institutions do not neatly divide, they provide a general framework for better understanding the systematic elimination of Indigenous institutions along themes of culture, politics, and economics. As will be noted in Section III, these institutional access points have contributed to the most invasive era of wealth theft and monopolization in world history. For now, it is important to remember that the U.S. is promoting a culture of manifest destiny. Hence, the U.S. must carry out a propaganda campaign involving Indigenous nations. The main policy edicts moving away from international interaction to domestic dependency is part of that public relations myth. Indigenous nations must be too dumb and savage to fully comprehend and understand the intricacies of European style governing. They cannot carry out law and order, they cannot be relied upon to be equal diplomacy partners, and they must be looked after because of their pathetic nature. U.S. policy makers, then, were creating their own U.S. culture and being gatekeepers to this culture. Only the most "civilized" Indian individuals could gain access to American culture so long as they behaved themselves. Some of these famous individuals include Charles Eastman and Carlos Montezuma (Fixico 2003). U.S. policy makers compared themselves to the Brule Sioux traditional method (culture) and deemed it inferior. As such, it is better to bring in individual Indians as criminals too. Perhaps executing one or two will teach the rest about civilization. While individual Indians are gaining very limited access to U.S. culture and the "American dream," it is also a matter of messaging.

At some point in the American historical narrative, the idea that Indians were "given" reservations became convenient. This idea is certainly an area worth researching in great detail but, for now, we need only acknowledge that powerful actors in the U.S. Supreme Court were relying on these myths of giving reservations away as a form of affirmative action. The idea that reservations were gifts from the benevolent, powerful, and altruistic U.S. nation was most recently expressed in 1955. Note how this functional creep of 17th and 18th century ideas must be relied on in the 1950s. In Tee-Hit-Ton, the U.S. federal government was dealing with one of the final examples of Aboriginal Title through Russia, the Tlingit people, and the Tee-Hit-Ton clan within Tlingit society. As usual, the narrative of Tee-Hit-Ton, and Tlingit people more generally, was that Russia, as a European and Christian sovereign, discovered the traditional Tlingit homeland. By 1867, the U.S. purchased this traditional homeland claim from Russia. This means that the Tlingit, and Tee-Hit-Ton, all transferred to the U.S. as a claim on an unextinguished Aboriginal Title. We may cautiously tie this to time. Between

1867 and 1955 the Aboriginal Title of Tee-Hit-Ton remained intact as "discovered" but not extinguished. The U.S., in 1955, had to extinguish Aboriginal Title by purchase or conquest. The Tee-Hit-Ton opinion clearly states that neither a treaty between Russia and the U.S. in 1867 nor the exchange of money between Russia and the U.S. for Alaska was sufficient to extinguish Aboriginal Title. Aboriginal Title, being an instrument of international law, would need to be explicitly extinguished in this court case (Tee-Hit-Ton Indians v. United States 1955). Perhaps the most informative comments are in the conclusion of this case.

By 1955, it was clear in the imaginations of the justices that conquest was an inevitable and unavoidable "fact" of Indian interaction. Besides, it was cheaper in 1955 to declare conquest than pay Indians for their land. How would the Tlingit protest anyway? As a consequence of these sad ideas, many non-Indian policy makers felt it necessary to make "gifts" to the remaining Indians. One of these gifts was, apparently, establishing reservations for their use. These reservations were based, supposedly, on the altruistic nature of policy makers. In making a reservation, the U.S. would extinguish Aboriginal Title to a people's traditional homelands. This was going to "help" Indians. With the title gone, the U.S. then owned the land all together. They then would reserve a small portion of the traditional homeland for use by Indians. Again, Indians are incapable of owning their own traditional homelands, or diminished portions of those homelands in spite of the fact that Indigenous peoples did not destroy their homelands from time immemorial until about 1492. Notions of civilizing the savages so that they could one day enjoy very carefully monitored access to U.S. culture should heavily guide their homeland use. Eventually, these gifts of reservations would disappear as individual Indians abandoned their traditional ways and became selfish individual landowners (not communal tribal occupiers). At some point, perhaps, this civilizing process would further allow very closely monitored access to the U.S. political economy and other institutions, ideally, through voting or low-wage jobs. This narrative, again, is a myth created in the minds of U.S. policy makers. The Tee-Hit-Ton conclusion is strikingly reminiscent of this myth:

> Every American schoolboy knows that the savage tribes of this continent were deprived of their ancestral ranges by force and that, even when the Indians ceded millions of acres by treaty in return for blankets, food and trinkets, it was not a sale but the conquerors' will that deprived them of their land (Tee-Hit-Ton Indians v. United States 1955; Getches 2011, 259–266).

Note how this passage must legitimately or willfully ignore all of the reality noted in Chapter 1. Specifically, this kind of revisionist history denies any notion of international interaction all together. According to Tee-Hit-Ton, no treaty was ever sacred nor based on a military alliance with very powerful Indigenous nations. Just ask any schoolboy.

Currently, many may incorrectly believe that the notion of Indigenous savagery is a relic of 18th and 19th century assumptions. Sadly, it is alive and well in mid-20th century policy. Hence, this chapter becomes all the more necessary to reset the agenda. A cursory reminder of ideas first noted in Chapter 1 should revise this notion about what every schoolboy apparently knows. The amnesia inherent in forgetting about treaties recorded on Wampum Belts may be excusable. We cannot conclude that non-Indigenous peoples ever really understood those treaties. In fact, it may be debatable that many descendants of those Indigenous peoples who created Wampum Belts really understand them now. Yet, it is quite clear that colonial actors and the U.S. are very knowledgeable about military alliance treaties. Had it not been for these treaties, there would be no colonial actor nations in the Americas. Instead, every schoolboy is merely taught to regurgitate the narrative about treaties, based on duress, employed to extinguish Aboriginal Title. The treaty record, again, can be analyzed and reviewed independent of this research (Deloria and DeMallie 1999). Were all 372-plus treaties really about trinkets, blankets, and food? These tough questions always emerge when there are no schoolboys around to provide answers since they know so much about their mythical nation.

Got Land? Thank An Indian!

Extinguishing Aboriginal Title is hard work! Genocide does not carry itself out. Contrary to more myths, the Indians did not end up being a doomed race destined to disappear. Indigenous nations and their citizens wound up being far more resilient than any non-Indians ever imagined (Holm 2005; Holm, Pearson, and Chavis 2003). Indigenous nations and specific individual leaders were very keen on the schemes carried out in their "interest" by the U.S. government. Accounts about fighting further encroachment do a good job of detailing Indigenous heroes of various eras (Holm 2005; Fixico 2013). When non-Indians needed land, they first pushed Indians west or massacred them if they refused to leave. The reservation and assimilation era of federal Indian law and policy was a land grab diminishing Indian land holdings, or extinguishing Aboriginal Title on a wholesale scale. While time might be the typical organizing theme, again, I believe that this theme is unnatural and confusing due to the schizophrenic nature of federal Indian law and policy. So while I could point out that about 90 million acres of Aboriginal Title land was extinguished, issued a paper title, and handed over to non-Indian owners, this idea cannot be contained in time (Wilkins and Stark 2011, 128).

As Tee-Hit-Ton showcases, these strategies happened as late as 1955 and perhaps as early as Spain establishing Santa Fe. This means, we cannot contain the story to the U.S. either! But these land cessions cannot be mere land grabs by a conquering and unstoppable colonial force. Hence, it is important to remind readers about Aboriginal Title and the Trust Doctrine.

The reason that every schoolboy is ignorant of the origin of his own nation is because most have never heard of the Trust Doctrine. It is debatable if citizens of Indian Country understand this idea either. The Trust Doctrine was once a clear assumption about Indigenous and U.S. interaction in light of the massive treaty record between Indigenous nations and colonial actors including the U.S. While the Trust Doctrine is related to treaties, it is likely unrelated to sacred treaties. Rather, the Trust Doctrine was conceived out of the military alliance era of treaty making AND the land cession treaty era of diplomacy. Treaty negotiations are, at their core, a give-and-take discussion created to avoid violence. When the U.S. and an Indigenous nation were no longer interested in shedding blood, they agreed to come to the table and negotiate a peace. The early alliance treaties were based on a militarily powerful Indigenous nation in the region that could enforce norms of behavior. As a weaker actor, a colonial actor, such as England, was forced to negotiate a land space accommodation. So an Indigenous nation would allow English colonists to live on some land. The Indigenous nation would, therefore, reserve their other land holdings. Indigenous nations were reserving their sovereign reach over their traditional homelands. This is the origin of the Trust Doctrine. Although it has never been applied in a two-way fashion, we can assume that colonists were the first recipients of this doctrine. Colonists, in obtaining some land from powerful Indigenous nations were at the mercy of these actors for their lives. Indigenous nations agreed to act as a guardian for colonists by providing food and protection from other Indigenous nations that might not like the colonists being alive. Colonists were the original dependent groups. This set up crept, just as has been explained in Chapter 1. After a series of treaties, violence, negotiations, new treaties, and reneging, Indigenous nations became less powerful and eventually were eclipsed by American military might due primarily to land acquisitions.

As Indigenous nations were systematically harmed by the destruction of their political economies (recall economic institutions), disarmed, and held hostage on lands they reserved for themselves in treaty negotiations, the Trust Doctrine came to represent something much different than my own analysis in the previous paragraph. Indian reservations are reservations of diminished sections of traditional homelands. An example of this idea might help illuminate the process. Many accounts detail the story of colonization between colonial actors and Navajo Nation (Austin 2009; Benally 2006; Bighorse, Bighorse, and Bennett 1990; Denetdale 2007, 2008, 2011; Iverson and Denetdale 2005; Lerma 2010; Porter 2005; Wilkins 2013; Yazzie et al. 2011). Some research has been written about the origin of *Diné* people within their homeland known as *Diné Bikéyah* (Benally 2006). According to noted scholar and practicing Medicine Man Avery Denny, Navajo people were ordained to live within four sacred mountains by a series of holy people. If we were to ask John Marshall about this, maybe he would surmise that Navajos had a right to occupy their traditional homelands within their four sacred mountains as ordained by the holy people. At least three sovereigns attempted to extinguish Navajo Aboriginal Title but two failed. Around 1860, Kit Carson carried out a scorched earth policy war against all Navajos on their homeland. Carson destroyed any ability for Navajo people to feed themselves by obliterating cattle and corn fields. About 8,000 Navajo people surrendered and ended up walking some 400–600 miles away from their traditional homelands to "a reservation" known as Bosque Redondo at Fort Sumner, New Mexico. Navajos call this event *Hwéeldi*. It is debatable that all Navajos that were caught or surrendered actually understood that they would be force marched beyond their traditional homeland within the sacred mountains. Another 8,000 Navajos, led by War Way leaders, stayed on the homeland and continued the war with Carson. Logically, had Navajo leaders actually reserved Bosque Redondo, then they would not have carried on the fight on the traditional Navajo homeland. Hence, the story continues on.

By 1868, the U.S. realized the reservation at Bosque Redondo was a failure. Navajos at Bosque Redondo could not live there without massive U.S. supplements. Additionally, oral accounts suggest that Navajo leaders chose to join the long walk in order to accompany the Navajo citizens (Bighorse, Bighorse, and Bennett 1990). Joining the walk may not have been a surrender so much as a measure to try and mitigate loss of life during the walk itself. Meanwhile, other War Way leaders continued to fight the U.S. military within the sacred mountains. For a variety of reasons, including the continued battle on Navajo homelands, the U.S. released the incarcerated Navajos at Bosque Redondo and they walked back to their traditional homelands. Again, Navajo leaders probably joined the walk to Bosque Redondo to ensure that a return would be as safe as possible. Oral accounts state that many people walking back from Bosque Redondo began to weep, sing, and pray at the sight of *Tsoodził* also known as Mount Taylor or the southern sacred mountain. This sight was probably only possible so long as the war against Carson continued within those sacred mountains.

The Navajo Treaty of 1868 codified the return to traditional homelands. This treaty memorialized how Navajo leaders, 12 in all, reserved a diminished portion of their traditional homeland in exchange for ceding the remaining land to the U.S. (Navajo Treaty of 1868). For the record, Denny contends that these leaders actually believed they retained all of their homeland within the sacred mountains. For our purposes, I'll assume the treaty reservation was a legitimate exchange. Let's, again, be very clear about what this means. A post-1868 treaty recorded the extinguishing of Navajo Aboriginal Title by conquest. All of the homelands within the sacred mountains were once discovered by three sovereigns. Spain originally made a claim to *Diné Bikéyah*. They "discovered" *Diné Bikéyah* and then had to purchase, conquer, or take the land if it was abandoned (Getches 2011, 31). Spain failed to carry out this edict across many areas within the sacred mountains. As a counterexample, Spain did successfully carry out this process in Santa Fe, New Mexico.

When Mexico emerged from the failed Spanish colony, they assumed the right to extinguish Navajo Aboriginal Title. In other words, international law of the era declared Aboriginal Title trumped any ideas that a creator ordained Indigenous peoples to act as stewards over their traditional homelands. Obviously, there were no international law scholars or policy makers during that time who had any clue about Indigenous philosophy or spirituality. By 1846, the U.S. was taking this right to extinguish Aboriginal Title through war with Mexico. The treaty of Guadalupe Hidalgo recorded a transfer of rights to extinguish Navajo Aboriginal Title to the U.S. It was not until 1868 that Carson and the U.S. could finally take *Diné Bikéyah* and extinguish Navajo Aboriginal Title. The Trust Doctrine, then, means that Navajo leaders only surrendered specific areas within their *Diné* sovereign reach mentioned in the Treaty of 1868. Article II of the treaty is a delineation of not only the land base that would be the reservation of traditional homelands, but also a surrender of lands not listed in Article II. At the heart of the Trust Doctrine is the idea that the U.S. obtains full title to all of *Diné Bikéyah*, that the U.S. holds the land title demarcated in the treaty in trust for use by Navajo people, and has the option to utilize the land ceded by Navajo leaders to the U.S. But there is more to the relationship.

The Navajo Treaty of 1868 notes many other exchanges for ending the war and setting aside some land for nearly exclusive Navajo use. These conditions include compulsory education for Navajo youth, buildings, provisions for the return of Navajos incarcerated at Bosque Redondo, but most importantly an article on supplementing the decimated Navajo political economy with seeds, agriculture, and other food-based provisions (Navajo Treaty of 1868). These types of accommodations are rarely acknowledged as payment for taking Indigenous lands by the U.S. Instead, these ideas are merely discussed as charity that Indians should be thankful for receiving. Hopefully it is clear that no one gave Navajo Nation anything except for the Holy Ones also known as *Diyin Dine'e*.

The Trust Doctrine was never charity. These types of discussions diminish the lives lost in order to maintain any level of existence by many Indigenous leaders. One of the most visible and unknown articles in the Navajo Treaty of 1868 deserves much more attention here. It highlights just one example about the Trust Doctrine:

> If bad men among the whites, or among other people subject to the authority of the United States, shall commit any wrong upon the person or property of the Indians, the United States will, upon proof made to the agent and forwarded to the Commissioner of Indian Affairs at Washington city, proceed at once to cause the offender to be arrested and punished according to the laws of the United States, and also to reimburse the injured persons for the loss sustained (Navajo Treaty of 1868).

This "bad men clause" is typical of many treaties. Others ought to investigate just how many of the 372 ratified treaties contain this clause. Reading the bad men clause with contemporary misconceptions of "protection" in mind does not capture the correct meaning. Rather, using an international frame, scholars going forward must re-examine many of these bad men clauses for what they are. In many ways, this bad men clause should be understood as the Navajo agreeing to cease war-making activities. This idea, consistent with the Trust Doctrine, suggests that Navajos would surrender their ability to make war and, in exchange, they would rely on the U.S. military for protection in lieu of protecting themselves. This is a quid pro quo exchange: The U.S. gets land and, in exchange, they both agree to stop war. Navajos retain land and, in exchange, can rely on a peaceful future. Many on all sides including Indigenous peoples, today, have forgotten these Trust Doctrine responsibilities.

Hopefully this representative case study serves as a useful explanation of reservation formation. No one gave Indians anything. They fought and died for the remaining tidbits of traditional homelands that remain today. In some cases, unlike the Navajo example, removal was successful and many tribes currently govern from their post-removal locations, particularly, in Oklahoma. The Navajo example is very rare because after the Treaty of 1868 was signed, a series of Executive Orders actually expanded Navajo Nation into the largest reservation in the U.S. For nearly all other Indigenous nations surrounded by the continental U.S., even these diminished portions of traditional homelands were not enough to satisfy non-Indian demand for their traditional homelands.

When the "Reservation" is Not Enough: How Much Is Too Much?

Extinguishing Aboriginal Title and creating reservations was a monumental task, again, not limited by time and better understood as a re-occurring theme or nightmare for Indigenous nations. There was still a massive amount of land in Indigenous hands. Trust Responsibility for individual Indians, not Indigenous nations, became twisted up in notions of Richard H. Pratt's famous tale on Indian education: Saving the Man by Killing the Indian. As a consequence, many policy makers ignored ideas about responsibility and demanded that more Indian land be opened up for non-Indian purchase. Figure 2.2 is an advertisement announcing the sale of Indian land with "perfect title" meaning that Aboriginal Title was already extinguished.

Figure 2.2: Advertising for Sale of Indian Land circa 1910.

These advocates for the Individual American (White) appropriation of land were based on ideas that Indians were wasteful or not using the land correctly. Many of the advocates for taking more Indian land were typically of the states' rights persuasion. In similar fashion that the Tea Party suggests that the U.S. federal government has overstepped its reach and trampled individual liberties, so too were states' rights advocates crying foul about federal policy makers more interested in attempting to honor the responsibility they had to Indians. This is the probable high point of states' rights versus federalism debates that dragged Indigenous nations along for the ride. I say this reluctantly because, again, time is not the most useful theme for organizing these ideas. This is a good "escape clause" for contemporary states' rights advocates who wish to have a "clean and friendly" debate about the greatest holocaust in human history. It was, apparently, never about race. Rather, it was the idea that the federal government was overreaching and drunk on power. For this to be true, of course, all must be willfully or legitimately unaware of Aboriginal Title. All must ignore the posters advertising land with "perfect title." But with this major plot hole aside, this places many Indigenous individuals in a strange position: They, and I, find ourselves in agreement on this idea. The federal government ought to stay out of our business as we try to recover from their latest schemes. The problem is that many residents of the states, the closest neighbors to Indians, were also the most likely to be violent toward Indians.

Documentation on the massively confusing nature of state, federal, and tribal polities can be explored independent of this research (Biolsi 2007; Getches 2001; Johnson 1972). Suffice it to say, it is clear that activities can be equally and legitimately legal and simultaneously illegal depending on which regime of laws you consult. Again, this raises serious questions about whether states' rights advocates are willfully or legitimately ignorant about many facets of federal Indian law and policy as both positions are plausible. Interestingly, we find that Indigenous rights tend to be defended insofar as they simultaneously maintain and bolster the superiority of federalism over state sovereignty. Readers might surmise that this relationship posits clear binary opposition of nearly all states' rights advocates squarely against Indigenous nations for seemingly legitimate reasons depending on which body of law one consults!

When states violate Indigenous sovereignty and there is no clear threat to federalism, these threats are often ignored. Again, functional creep explains this better than other methods. These patterns probably emerged only after many international mechanisms for defending Indigenous sovereignty were eliminated. This latest strategy was only more expedient after reservations were largely established, Aboriginal Title extinguished, and Indigenous nations incapable of mounting violent attacks in defense of traditional homelands and against encroachment. After these approaches were employed, the strategy could further creep into notions of criminal jurisdiction. The U.S. Supreme Court was quite clear on this idea when they proclaimed that the states are where Indians will find their deadliest enemies (United States v. Kagama 1886). Therefore, in paternalistic fashion, the U.S. government intervened to simultaneously take criminal jurisdiction over Indians in Indian Country (also known as post-Aboriginal Title extinguished land) and prosecute non-Indians in federal court should they violate U.S. laws. This intrusion into Indian Country simultaneously deprived states of the privilege of choosing when to prosecute crimes by non-Indian state citizens perpetrated against Indian victims, if they are prosecuted at all. This also bolstered federalism trumping state criminal jurisdiction over state borders. Prosecuting crimes, or not, is one thing. Taking more land, however, was quite another and the federal government was more than willing to provide a bureaucratic path to taking more Indian land so long as they were the ones making the policy first.

By the early 1830s, and remember the problem of time, there were approximately 213 reservations. These were again lands that had been reserved by various Indigenous nations in their long drawn-out interactions with the U.S. in terms of violence, negotiation, treaty signing, treaty breaking, more violence, more negotiations, more temporary peace. This process continued until Aboriginal Title was extinguished, reservations were held in trust by the federal government (not states), and Indigenous nations could no longer defend or feed themselves creating dependency. Once again more creep is on the way. By the 1930s, just 100 years later, about 113 reservations underwent allotment. Many readers, but not all, will recognize that allotment is the arbitrary diminishing of Indigenous land holdings or another example of functional creep. Remember, reservations in the 1830s, more or less, were already extinguished Aboriginal Title lands and held in trust by the U.S. The U.S. decided that it was in the interest of Indians to actually have less land.

In order to wind up with less land in Indian hands, typically an Indian census would take place where Indians would go to the Indian agent or the Fort and be listed on the census roll. The roll was then used to divide up land into 160-acre parcels or less depending on whether the Indian named on the roll had a family or was single. After the tally was made, the land was divided up among the individuals. Whatever was left over was put up for sale to non-Indians and advertised as in Figure 2.2. During this policy era, nearly 90 million acres passed into non-Indian owner hands (Wilkins and Stark 2011, 128). This created a patchwork of mixed jurisdictions in which one 160 parcel could be Indian Country while the neighboring parcel would be owned by non-Indians and subject to state laws. South Dakota was particularly impacted by this process. The map in Figure 2.3 indicates pre and post allotment land holdings placing the Deadliest Enemies as next door neighbors to Indian individuals.

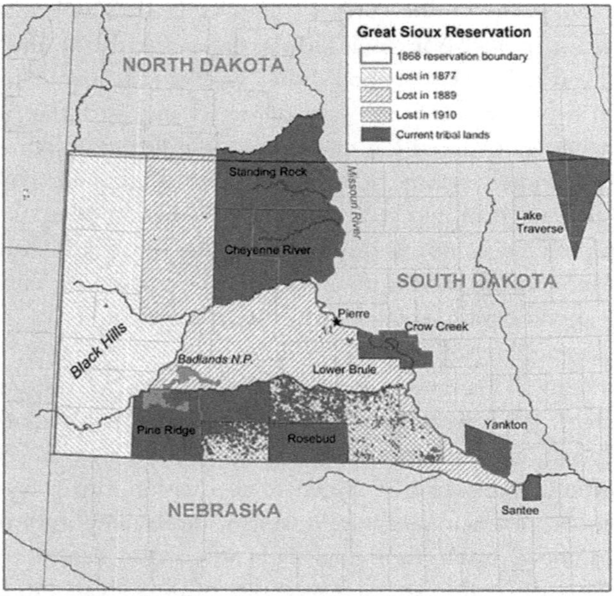

Figure 2.3: Allotted Lands in South Dakota. The "checker board" region has created tremendous havoc in terms of jurisdiction.

This "checker boarding" led to a whole host of complicating matters including a jurisdictional vacuum in which it was very unclear who would prosecute which crimes. Jurisdiction, then, all depended on the racial identity of the perpetrator. As readers can appreciate, I won't have the ability to capture all of the explicit and implicit creeps that have occurred.

President Theodore Roosevelt is famously quoted for saying that allotment is a "mighty pulverizing engine breaking up the tribal mass" (Wilkins and Stark 2011, 128). This is certainly true. The devastated Indigenous nation conditions were documented in the Merriam Report. This, more so than not, is due to the destruction of Indigenous political economies and the policy platform that all Indian nations should simply vanish (Holm 2005), along with all of the functional creep. Interestingly, some texts tend to point to a notion of white liberal guilt or otherwise liberalism itself as a mechanism to improve Indigenous peoples' lives. One solution was constitutional reforms in Indian Country through the Indian Reorganization Act of 1934 or IRA. There is debate about whether IRA was a boilerplate mechanism for writing Indian constitutions or if there was a major level of nuance and customization applied to each nation (Bruyneel 2007; Champagne 2007; Cornell and Kalt 2000; Fixico 1998, 2012, 2013; Fletcher 2011; General federation of women's clubs. Public welfare Department [from old catalog] and Smith 1928; Getches 2011; Holm 2005; Jorgensen 2007; Lemont 2006). My own suspicion is that some type of technological advance prompted resource extraction companies to "discover" Indian Country all over again. There are too many convenient consequences of IRA to ignore. Namely, it just so happened that after IRA, the Secretary of the Interior had much more veto power over tribal government activity. Too many times it turned out that tribal resources were sold for pennies on the dollar, and too many times were strangleholds over Indigenous political economies strengthened (Fixico 2013, 151–164). These ideas will be explored further in Section III and Chapter 8. For now, we only need understand that post allotment colonization takes on more functional creep toward economics.

Regardless of the success of corporations in obtaining cheap natural resources for under fair market value, with lax environmental protections for mother earth and with lax protections for workers, some policy makers still believed that Indigenous nations should not exist at all. Some tribes that exhibited a "gusto" attitude toward individual values (selfishness) and a willingness to stop acting like a tribe were terminated. This idea was linked to an "emancipation" similar to the way Lincoln once supposedly freed the slaves (Getches 2011, 200–215). Termination resulted in major setbacks for tribes that were no longer protected by the Trust Doctrine although many would question what protections, if any, were ever honored. Additionally, many individual Indians were paid to relocate to urban areas such as Minneapolis, St. Paul, Oakland, and Los Angeles to disappear into the urban sprawl. Some have credited this concentration of "urban Indians" in cities, along with a common cause in termination to rally against, as leading to a pan-Indigenous movement that worked to repeal termination.

By 1975, Self-Determination was ushered in due, in no small part, to the promotion of self-governing policies lauded, at least in speeches, by President Richard Nixon. Some note Nixon as a friend to the Indian (Champagne 2010, 138). Others question his true motives (Forbes 1981). Ideally, Indigenous nations were the ones closest to the action and there was no need for policy makers to sign off on every single activity in Indian Country. Some have likened Self-Determination to having the federal government act as an advisor to Indigenous nations working to govern themselves. Indigenous nations began to either contract out services, such as education, to states, or perhaps carry out needed services, such as Indigenous policing. By 1987, gaming began to come on the scene creating more creep. The Cabazon Case concluded that Indian gaming could take place if states were also engaged in gaming (California et al. v. Cabazon Band of Mission Indians et al. 1987). Just one year later, Congress passed the Indian Gaming and Regulatory Act or IGRA (*Indian Gaming Regulatory Act* 1988). IGRA was purportedly designed to ensure that gaming nations would be the sole or main benefactors of gaming in order to foster economic development. Many have seen IGRA as the gateway to even further erosions in Indigenous sovereignty by forcing Indigenous nations to create compacts in which they guarantee a percentage of their revenue to state governments. These ideas are more fully engaged in other research arguing that gaming has led to a new era of federal Indian law and policy. Self-Determination may be over and replaced with Forced Federalism. A creep toward diminished Indigenous sovereignty in the wake of gaming enterprises makes sense. State legislatures have worked overtime to quietly wage war on economic windfalls in Indian Country. Many gaming operations are, today, depicted as potentially violent and activist, a form of dependency and welfare, or an emerging economic contender to be crushed (Corntassel and Witmer 2008). Given these schizophrenic attitudes towards Indigenous nations, one can only guess where the policy will creep next.

Concluding Remarks

The themes inherent in federal Indian law and policy are seemingly clear. There cannot be any notion of real economic development because such activity would threaten the regional economic hegemons in non-Indian state and local areas. Obviously, this is not always true and some Indigenous economies have crept toward "accidentally" flourishing. The history of federal Indian law and policy cannot ever be a manual for how to survive colonization. Once, Robert Williams asked his class "what is criminal law?" Some law students gave a simple and short answer that I do not recall. He asked, "What is civil procedure?" and then asked "what is tort law?" The answers came quickly and seemed simple. Then Williams asked a doozie . . . "what is federal Indian law?" The class was silent. Williams admitted that it was kind of like the TV show, *Seinfield* . . . it is a body of law about everything so, essentially, it might be about nothing. While this may seem like an insensitive joke, the obvious tie in is that Indigenous peoples have long taken more holistic approaches to their responsibilities to their families, their relations across species, and to their relations with mother earth and father sky as well as relations with the spirit world. Indigenous sovereignty, as explained through federal Indian law and policy is a losing game that should be avoided, if possible, but acknowledged and defended when necessary. Sadly, it used to be that Indigenous peoples knew that federal Indian law and policy had very little to do with Indigenous sovereignty. Indigenous accounts of sovereignty are best understood in terms of ceremony, language, homelands, and sacred histories. Indigenous sovereignty, in reality, has nothing to do with Aboriginal Title. As Williams joked, maybe Indigenous sovereignty is about everything because it is so holistic.

Chapter 3
Indigenous Sovereignty and False Dichotomies

By: Shonri Begay, Monica Burres, Michael Lerma, Tiffany Manygoats, Darrell Marks, Maka Monture, and Vanessa Tallman

On March 19, 2014, I woke up early in the morning and reviewed exercise 3 submissions for the Applied Indigenous Studies Research Methods class. About three weeks before, I asked the class if they wanted to contribute to this book by collectively writing a chapter. As usual, they all kind of looked down in their laps or toward the floor. A few seconds passed and some heads began to nod in agreement. That day in class we collectively drew a concept of Indigenous sovereignty on the white board based on a sentence in Kevin Bruyneel's depiction of what Indigenous sovereignty is not (Bruyneel 2007, 19–24). I took a picture of the drawing on the board and hastily redrew the concept on a computer, made hard copies, and handed it out in class. I told the students to mark it up with criticisms or suggestions. I even suggested they leave their names off the mark ups in case they were worried about hurting my feelings. I teased them for a couple of weeks about how I had not received any feedback. This drawing would become Figure 3.2. I think my co-authors deserve a great deal of credit for their hard work. But I don't think I taught them anything new. They already think in two or three dimensions.

I have always believed that concept building is a good exercise that all researchers with interest in working in Indian Country should learn. At the risk of essentializing, all Indigenous peoples think in two or three dimensions. The big question is whether they have ever been encouraged to think that way in academic settings. I'd like to believe I encourage this type of thinking. I'd like to think this chapter is evidence of encouraging behavior. In research methods class, I ask the students to play with a concept of something related to Indian Country. What is a federal Indian law case? What is a chief? In our case, we played with the idea of Indigenous sovereignty. There are three levels to a concept. The top level is called the "basic" level and indicates a name. The next lower row is called "secondary" level and represents necessary and/or sufficient conditions of the concept. Each of these conditions should operate on a continuum line where the extreme points make it either the perfect condition at one end or the absence of the condition or total negation at the other end. Under each condition should be data to support or debunk that the condition exists (Goertz 2006). I asked my co-authors to turn in exercise 3 providing evidence that each of the necessary conditions for Indigenous sovereignty exists today in the 21st century. Each student was arbitrarily assigned a single condition and each was asked not to consult one another about their thoughts on the evidence supporting the existence of a single condition. The research from these students will appear in this chapter in support of the existence of Indigenous sovereignty in the 21st century.

I wish it was enough to simply leave this chapter on Indigenous sovereignty at that. While I would greatly enjoy students taking center stage in this chapter, I do need to explore how we wound up in a contemporary world that denies Indigenous sovereignty even exists. Hence, we need to explore the false dichotomies of Indigenous nations being "with us" or "against us." Second, there must be an understanding of Indigenous Peoplehood-based sovereignty. We will mention how contemporary Indigenous scholars criticize the Westphalian model of sovereignty questioning its applicability to Indigenous nations past and present.[5] We then explore the tensions inherent in contemporary economic liberalism in Indian Country when tribal leaders attempt to both honor their relationship to their homeland AND provide jobs and revenue for their nations. Next comes the student-created concept of Indigenous sovereignty along with evidence that each of the conditions Bruyneel claims does not work for Indian Country actually does exist.

False Dichotomies and Pre-American Sovereigns

We have already explored false dichotomies of Indigenous policy positions in Chapter 2. It is worth mentioning that these false dichotomies have also been called the imperial binary by others and identify them as no-win situations forced on Indigenous policy makers (Bruyneel 2007, 8). In short, be reminded that many of the policies advanced by the U.S. involved a "heads I win, tails you lose" type of wager which is not winnable by Indigenous actors. The extent to which we see our options as being inevitable and that we are better off making a choice now before it is too late is the inherent tension of the false dichotomy sales pitch. It's the deal of a lifetime, it is fleeting, and it will make your life better. None of these promises ever come true. Sadly, some of our own Indigenous youth also believe the hype falsely stating that Indigenous nations do not have sovereignty today.

5. See Bueno de Mesquita for a definition of the state system based on the Treaty of Westphalia. (Deloria 2014)

Hence, this chapter is required! It must not only be tied to Indigenous creation but it is almost equally important that young Indigenous scholars attending Northern Arizona University drive this chapter.

There is a general pattern of attachment to Indigenous homelands that transcends anything else ever explored in the Western Hemisphere. In the 20th century, only Indigenous peoples are willing to give up their lives to mount an attack on colonial actors (Lerma 2012). What are these Indians fighting for? Did they not get the memo that they were conquered? Myths of conquest are much more fanciful than anything written by your favorite fiction author. This interesting social science fiction often starts with tales about "the eve of conquest" based on a few selected tales of battles and defeats. But the reality is that we are still here and we remain attached to our homelands. It is even probable that we remain attached after a removal act such as the Cherokee Trail of Tears, *Hwéeldi* (the Navajo Long Walk), or La Paz (the Hualapai removal). How can this be? Could all the anthropologists be wrong? Maybe we are much more than a group of savages running around naked in a wild forest waiting to be saved by colonial actors. Just maybe our Indigenous philosophies deserve more attention.

Peoplehood: A Pre-Contact Concept of Indigenous Sovereignty

The idea of Peoplehood is offered here as a way of grounding some sense of an original or pre-contact version of Indigenous sovereignty. This idea was originally presented as a form of Indigenous higher education (Holm, Pearson, and Chavis 2003). Holm hypothesized this idea with Robert K. Thomas and Vine Deloria at the University of Arizona during the 1980s and 1990s. They all knew that there were some common traits within all communities. I once naively stated that you had to be Indigenous to be attached to land but Holm disagreed. He reminded me that Germans are tied to their Deutschland and that if we go far back enough in their history, they too had an organic attachment to their homeland. Germans say their attachment is called "Heimat." It was only because of a severed tie to their homelands and a lack of ties to the Americas that colonialism could actually exist. Colonial actors, then, are only tied to the Americas insofar as they can extract a resource or value from the Americas. Hence, a European version of sovereignty may be based on a mechanistic attachment to lands because of economic extraction or military strategic positioning. I won't deny that this attraction also works with Indigenous nations past and present. But I will argue that the ties are simultaneously organic and mechanistic.

Holm carried out research on the Hopi and Navajo land dispute arguing that both Indigenous actors had simultaneous organic and mechanistic ties to the same traditional homeland or Joint Use Area (Holm 1989). The organic side of Indigenous sovereignty is expressed in Figure 3.1 on the notion of Indigenous sovereignty. Indigenous scholars hate essentializing about Indians but I'm about to do just that anyway. All Indigenous peoples are tied to their homelands and waters through their ceremonies, their sacred histories, and their specific languages. This is the original source of Indigenous sovereignty. Our sacred histories often discuss the emergence of the people onto mother earth. We say "on" because we are not "in" anything. Being "in" the U.S. might be a social science fiction. Being "on" mother earth is a reality. We are beholden to our mother for our survival and growth as humans. Our creation accounts are our sacred histories. Our sacred histories also contain our ceremonies. There are instructions on how to carry out ceremonies and what time of the year to carry them out. These ceremonies are required to maintain a good relationship with our mother earth. Our sacred histories and our ceremonies contain specific words in our languages that are only stated or sung during the ceremonial process. These powerful words evoke our dependence on mother earth and our contribution back to her.

Without these histories, ceremonies, and languages, we would not be able to sustain ourselves on mother earth. This is our organic attachment to our traditional homelands and waters. This is our original Indigenous sovereignty. We do not "own" our homelands, rather, we are ordained to watch over our homelands as best we can. If we take these creation stories seriously, then we have a proven track record of existence since time immemorial until now. We have existed all this time without destroying mother earth. That claim falls to the hands of colonial actors, corporations, and their crony elite Indigenous leaders who serve up resources on a silver platter.

Figure 3.1: Three Level View of Indigenous Sovereignty based on Peoplehood

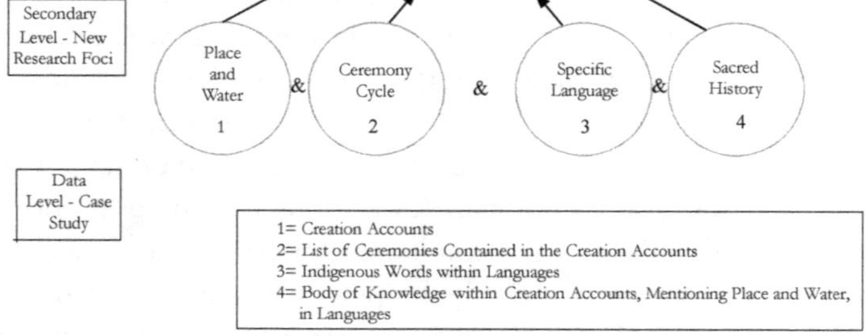

The Pitfalls of Western Conceptions of Sovereignty in Indigenous Nations Today

Just as European societies lost their organic attachments to their homelands, we Indigenous peoples are seriously at risk of losing our own organic attachments to our homelands. We have experienced several crises of leadership. When we were forced to fight wars, we prayed, and our prayers often went unanswered. Had our creator abandoned us? When we were removed we did the same and hypothesized that maybe we were doing things the wrong way. When we were trapped on the reservations we wondered if our traditional Indigenous leaders had made serious errors. We witnessed crises of legitimacy and a vacuum formed in our home communities. Maybe the colonial actor way of doing things was the right way. Maybe we needed to abandon our organic ties and create mechanistic ties. Maybe we needed to modernize and exploit mother earth. This was the path that many tribal leaders took long ago. I don't say this to insult them but to point out that their decisions may not be as misguided as others might assume. They did the best they could under serious duress and we have them to thank for having any homelands to return to at all. Their responsibilities continue to be immense and their continued path along the imperial binary is frightening. It is not so easy to simply abandon the imperial binary. It is not so easy to forget that our current ties to traditional homelands are both mechanistic and organic.

We have been reminded by contemporary Indigenous scholars that it may be worthwhile to simply abandon the colonial actor model of sovereignty. Alfred warns of the pitfalls of adopting Western notions of sovereignty (2009, 80–81). Alfred is suggesting a throwback to Peoplehood based on one specific ceremony as a potential model for other tribes to assemble their own Indigenous way of governing. This approach would be much more practicable had he engaged with Peoplehood as a way to ground an Indigenous structure into a contemporary setting:

> The lack of any coherent strategy to solve [injustices and abuses of power] suggests that Native people need to go beyond the divisive electoral politics and Western-style institutions recommended by most scholars and develop solutions for themselves from within their own cultural frameworks, reuniting themselves as individuals with their collectivity. (Alfred 2009, 29)

This research is attempting to take Alfred's suggestions seriously by advancing a Peoplehood-based mechanism for getting beyond the imperial binary of our contemporary world. Hence, we must move past internal Indigenous institutions based on colonial actor resource extraction needs.

Obviously this is much easier said (written) than done. There is far too much disagreement on what counts as the "correct" creation account or sacred history. Secondly, there is far too much abuse among Indigenous leaders today claiming they are being "traditional" when they are actually preserving their own job or at least their own policy platform.

We are also wise to deal with our own inherent mistake of repackaging Western notions of sovereignty into our own internally developed mechanisms for governance today in Indian Country. Moreton-Robinson has many warnings about Indigenous actors adopting Western notions of sovereignty without first exploring what assumptions get adopted in the process. The literature on Australian critical Indigenous sovereignty and whiteness deserves our attention as we do not wish to haphazardly adopt even more race-based hierarchy into our communities (Moreton-Robinson 2006, 384). Her research is also indicative of a neglected story on the impact of liberalism on depictions of Indigenous human rights (Richardson 2001; Moreton-Robinson 2006, 385). Sadly, this criticism has yet to be written in terms of contemporary Indigenous political economies, a form of our contemporary Indigenous sovereignty concerns. Many of the issues raised in Richardson are not at all on the radar of contemporary Indigenous political economy scholars (Jorgensen 2007; Lemont 2006). Richardson, and many other scholars on economic liberalism, outline some notion of liberal assumptions in the international world (2001). These assumptions involve the maintenance and expansion of power of all nations but neglect Indigenous actors.

Economic liberalism holds that states are rational unitary actors in the international sense. So the U.S. acts as a unit to ensure, among many things, that Indigenous nations are eliminated as threats to their sovereign reach. International politics are hierarchical and Indigenous nations, while once powerful, don't even get mentioned in contemporary international politics discussions. This hierarchy implies the presence of an actor that can enforce norms of conduct between states. As a consequence, Indigenous actors are being forced to behave in ways that are conducive to the U.S. political economy through corporate resource extraction companies among other influences. Cooperation, not war, is the natural state of affairs between states. Hence, it would be more instructive to view Indigenous political economies the way development literature treats third world political economies in relation to powerful states around the world. In short, both Indigenous actors and third world countries play a similar role by providing cheap resources to their feeder and dominant hegemonic powers. Finally, the distribution of power is not as important as distribution of shared interests. Hence, the interests of the U.S. trump our interests in Indian Country. Our resources are purchased for under fair market value, in ways that destroy the environment exposing Indigenous workers to health hazards. We will return to this discussion in Section III, hopefully encouraging others to continue this research. This could stop the cycle of embedding contemporary Indigenous political economies into the larger U.S. interests.

Contemporary Sovereignty Concept

However we address our contemporary tensions between pre-contact sovereignty and post-contact adoptions of European norms of sovereignty, it would still be instructive to explore how these varying ideas have merged into our definitions today. Figure 3.2 is a concept of Indigenous sovereignty based on Bruyneel (2007, 19–24). It should be clear that Bruyneel's definition is something I believe appropriately defines Indigenous sovereignty today but only if we re-examine the limited evidence offered in Chapter 1. Bruyneel cites Rob Walker's definition of sovereignty as incompatible because it makes "state, power, supreme authority, and legitimacy" synonymous with sovereignty (2007, 23). There is much more evidence supporting what Bruyneel believes are misconstrued notions of Indigenous sovereignty. I'll now renew my warning that any context that frames Indigenous sovereignty as a unique entity distinct from Westphalian definitions of sovereignty runs the risk of doing more damage than good. Perhaps Bruyneel meant to limit his definition of Indigenous sovereignty to pre-contact times. If so, then my critique is not warranted. Regardless, we must acknowledge past Indigenous actors transgressions as well as Indigenous creation to arrive at how Figure 3.2 works today.

Figure 3.2: Three Level View of Contemporary Indigenous Sovereignty

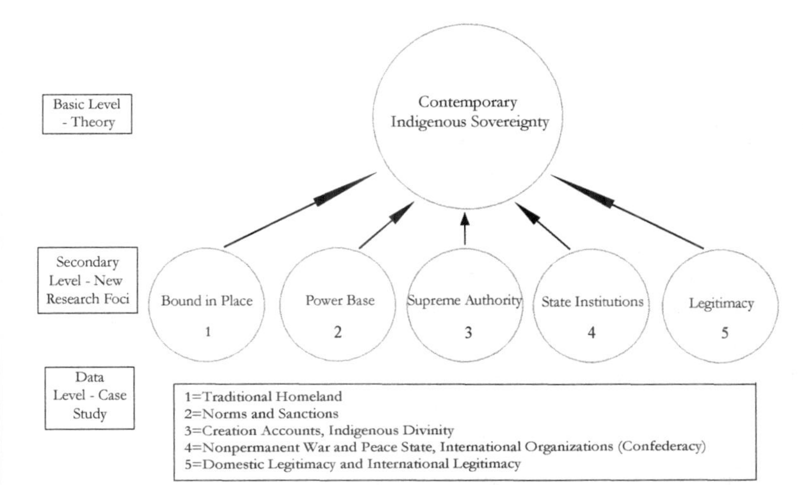

Each of the conditions for Indigenous sovereignty in the 21st century is quite evident but only if one is not hostile to the idea in the first place. Again, perhaps contemporary Indigenous sovereignty is based on "state, power, supreme authority, and legitimacy" (Bruyneel 2007, 23). We are bound in place through Peoplehood and our traditional homelands. As well we are bound to our finite resources and we exploit them just like other colonial actors do. Our power base, then and now, is based on norms of behavior coupled with sanctions for violating such norms. The traditional mechanisms involved creating a sense of embeddedness and responsibility probably within clan relationships among other mechanisms. These mechanisms are often underestimated because they tended to lack coercive enforcement mechanisms. Readers are encouraged to explore how these norms might operate in international organizations today (Goertz 2003). Our supreme authority can come from at least two places. One is the notion of Peoplehood. Within Peoplehood are ideas that the creator has generally endowed humans with abilities that imply responsibilities, through clan relations, to all peoples on the earth. All peoples include other tribes, winged people, hooved people, insect people, plant people, and so on. We even have responsibilities to maintain our own individual health since we cannot help others if we ourselves are not healthy and in balance. Today we have colonially inspired tribal governments built, primarily, to allow for resource extraction and cobbled together to function as interdependent nations alongside the U.S. Again, our interdependence is clear if we explore our relations to one another (Indigenous actor to Indigenous actor) as well as Indigenous nation to colonial actors, including the U.S.

Our Indigenous state institutions may not have been permanent fixtures of the landscape once upon a time. Our confederacies and temporary state institutions were used to weather crises of peace (famine) as well as crises of war. Once the calamity was neutralized, our institutions could be put away until needed again (Deloria, Pavlik, and Wildcat 2006, 50–56). We only learned about permanent state institutions sometime after Reorganization in 1934 when we were encouraged by the U.S. to set up institutions that could sign off on land leases and resource extraction operations (Getches 2011, 187–199). Finally, our legitimacy for leading domestically (within Indian Country) and internationally (beyond Indian Country) came from our individual understanding of local governance and beyond. Before contact, our leadership qualities were revered and leaders were not expected to amass wealth. Certainly some Indigenous nations strayed from these norms and built empires but these are more deviations than the norm. Sadly, there is no one that can be cited to "prove" this reality. After we became so-called "domestic dependent nations" we were often ordered to build up our nations, in the aftermath of destruction through war and all of the other activities detailed in Chapters 1 and 2, in the image of our colonial masters. We had our crises of domestic leadership and allowed an Indigenous elite to emerge at home. We adopted coercive measures of leadership and relied on governments based on distrust of leaders. We fractured our communities and learned how to spread rumors for our own individual ambitions. We in Indian Country might be the best kept secret, wealthy dictators that serve our masters because it serves our own individual well-being to maintain a status quo. We self-colonize based on our institutions of permanent governance. Each of these necessary conditions in Figure 3.2 can be supported with primary and secondary evidence.

Observations of Indigenous Sovereignty in the 21st Century

This section of Chapter 3 is primarily written by the co-authors listed at the beginning. These examples tend to lean toward Navajo examples because of Northern Arizona University's or NAU's proximity to Navajo Nation. NAU is within a short drive to *Dook'o'osłiid,* or the third sacred mountain and Western barrier of the traditional Navajo Homeland also known as *Diné Bikéyah*. Contrary to some translations, I do not hold the notion that this phrase *Diné Bikéyah* means "Navajo reservation." It means the traditional homeland within the sacred mountains. I gave the students limited guidance on how they should frame their research. I wanted them to be free to offer what they could find in the line of supporting their reasoning. Unlike other teachers they may have had in secondary and post-secondary schools, I highly encourage independent thinking . . . perhaps to a fault. Each student was assigned to carry out research on one condition listed in Figure 3.2. Here is a list of condition assignments:

- Bound In Place – Begay
- Power Base – Burres
- Supreme Authority – Marks and Manygoats
- Institutions – Monture and Tallman
- Legitimacy - no students assigned

The students chose to focus almost exclusively on Indigenous-based depictions of these conditions. I do not see a necessity in criticizing this decision. I will disclose that focusing solely on Indigenous accounts is biased. Scholars can study for themselves how contemporary tribal governments have negatively adopted what I might call self-colonization mechanisms for governance (Getches 2011, 140–243). This process, of course, was heavily coerced through the means outlined in Chapter 2. Hence, we focus on the

Indigenous point of view as it is necessary for the maintenance and expansion of Indigenous sovereignty in the 21st century.

Bound In Place (Begay)

The concept of Indigenous sovereignty is conditional on Indigenous Peoples' connection to place, a power base, a supreme authority, a state institution, and legitimacy as expressed by Rob Walker (Bruyneel 2007, 23). The conditions of a concept must be supported by observations. This section will support the condition that Indigenous nations are bound to a place, in the context of *Diné* ties to homeland.

The Navajo Nation is a sovereign Indigenous nation that exemplifies a strong tie to traditional homeland. The traditional region and its unique features act as a foundation for all that is *Diné*. In his book, *Foundation of Navajo Culture*, Wilson Aronilth, Jr. combines the identities of the *Diné* culture and *Diné* homeland. He states, "These sacred mountains are our thinking, our knowledge, and our ways of life" (1991, 30). Geological landmarks stand today where events from the *Diné* creation accounts have played out.

The creation account of the *Diné* centers on land naturally delineated by four sacred mountains. The mountains were planted in the sacred soil, imbued with religious identity and purpose for *Diné* people. In Aronilth's book, he explains that spirits traveled to reside within the mountains to see to the blessings, needs, and wants of the *Diné* people. Interactive and powerful, the mountains live in *Diné* oral accounts as members of the family. Existing as shields, representatives, givers, and safe-keepers, the mountains act and cause things to happen. For instance, *Diné* jewelry, according to Mr. Aronilth, is inspired by the precious jewels on the sacred mountains. We "adorn ourselves just as they do" (1991, 31-32). *Diné* people carry the land wherever they go, if not physically, in the form of such things as corn pollen, then internally in the orientation of themselves and their relationships.

In contemporary times, the Navajo Nation is on traditional land, spanning across the Four Corners region, mostly in northeastern Arizona and northwestern New Mexico. Many families continue to live close to the land, farming and ranching. Navajo Nation derives a significant part of its economy out of environmental resource extraction. The sovereign nation of the *Diné* people has a clear relationship to a land base. The spiritual connections might be considered organic since it is tied to place, ceremony, sacred history, and language. The mechanistic ties to the homeland also exist through sheep herding, oil extraction, and the power to tax visitors and citizens. The ties to the Navajo homeland are certainly complex. Navajo people, and the contemporary Navajo government, are bound to their homeland.

Power Base (Burres)

The power base of the Navajo Nation is based on the norms and sanctions of *Diné* governance. These norms are based on a traditional checks and balances system that includes emphasis on kinship or clan. Within the Navajo culture, kinship and traditional governance go hand-in-hand in the form of chapter houses. Chapter houses are the local version of leadership on Navajo Nation today. There are 110 chapters, each tasked with governing at the local community level (Wilkins 2013, 149–160). Within chapter houses, elders always want to know the youth attending meetings. Elders wish to understand youth relationships. Elders encourage community participation in the most respectful manner. Of course, these are only some of the aspects of kinship within the average Navajo chapter house community.

Many chapter houses today maintain the same traditions as they did long ago, including promoting infrastructure as well as economic development and community development to benefitting the community and "safeguarding the environment" (Tiis Tsoh Sikaad chapter 2013). This is certainly not a coercive form of power. But it is a power base. No one is ordered around. Rather, individuals are highly encouraged by the community to behave according to Navajo protocols when building a home, a community park, or contributing to youth education among other tasks. The Navajo power base remains at the chapter level. It can be a powerful incentive to behave according to traditional norms.

Supreme Authority (Manygoats and Marks)

Supreme authority can be tied to the creation accounts that Native Americans used to settle their disagreements. In the early years, before Western customs came to be one of the primary ways of going about life, there were creation accounts transmitted through oral traditions with a multitude of versions for various situations. Native Americans traditionally followed the creation accounts their ancestors passed down from generations before, which were a form of guidance for different conditions. Creation accounts are the source of Supreme Authority over traditional homelands. It just so happened that many creation accounts revered preservation and taking what was needed. Creation accounts, almost universally, frowned upon exploitation and monopolization of resources.

The right to self-govern was given to Indigenous peoples by the gods who created the universe. For one particular tribe, the Navajo, self-governance rights came into being through their creation account, "Emergence." The Emergence is the ascension of *Diné* into the present physical world. The Emergence takes place through a series of events that lead the people (insects, animals, etc.) through several worlds of existence and conditions. It was during these events that the gods of the Navajo provided and bestowed their values and laws to the Navajo people, thus imposing a correct conduct and right of manner. This is the origin of Supreme Authority. Humans were told that they had the power to destroy the world through carelessness. They were also taught how to prevent this destruction by following Navajo teachings. This is their Supreme Authority over the land.

The recognition of this Supreme Authority lends validity to Navajo nation, and its right to claim Indigenous sovereignty, because they have had a right of self-governance as was birthed in their Creation. "Begochiddy now created Kay-des-tizhi (Wound in a Rainbow), who is both man and woman. Begochiddy said: 'I made the law, and there shall be no other'" (*Navajo Creation Myth* 1980). The gods of the Navajo created laws that the people were to abide by and adhere to, along with a code of conduct. The animals also taught the people how to plant, what to plant and how to exist amongst nature, as asked by their deities. "The Holy People made a song and prayer to let plants grow. Then the people planted their own food" (Carey 2011). The traditional Navajo people still conduct themselves in this manner today. They carry on the songs and prayers that were passed on to them by the gods or the animals of the world. It is their Supreme Authority to know the songs and prayers and pass them on to younger generations when they are mature enough to handle the responsibility. Preserving the earth is a huge responsibility and not given away lightly.

It was believed that in the Navajo culture that First Man and First Woman were not humans and, instead, nature figures. Navajos typically originated in the Four Corners area including southeastern Utah, northeastern Arizona and northwestern New Mexico (Begay and Maryboy 1998). Navajos are very big on the land being spiritual and sacred, which means that they would treat the land with respect. The origins of the Navajos is very important because it is a valuable place that makes the people who they are, in this sense, they are able to adapt and raise their culture and traditions on the lands. Hence, they have supreme authority of land use but this use is not extractive or coercive.

Another major part of why the lands within the Four Corners are important is because, as noted in the bound by place section, it lies within the four sacred mountains. One of the most important things for Navajos is to stay within the four sacred mountains. It is believed that if an individual wants to travel beyond the four sacred mountains, then they would first have to have a ceremony conducted. The four sacred mountains are in all four directions; east, south, west, and north. In the east region, the sacred mountain is known as *Sisnajini* or Blanca Peak in Colorado. The east sacred mountain is represented in a white color; the reason for the color white is that it is what direction the Navajo people pray to in the morning. The blue sacred mountain is located south and it is known as *Tsoodził,* or Mount Taylor, located in Grants, New Mexico. The yellow mountain is known as *Dook'o'oosłiid,* or San Francisco Peaks, located in Flagstaff, Arizona. The fourth mountain is black and it is known as *Dibé Nitsaa* or Mount Hesperus, also in Colorado. Each of these mountains represents sacred meanings and are very important to the Navajo people (Aronilth Jr. 1991). These mountains, fastened to the earth, are the Supreme Authority over the land. They are sought for strength and guidance during tough times.

Tlingit Leadership Institutions (Monture)

State institutions are one of the necessary conditions of Indigenous sovereignty. Several of the subcategories of state institutions in Indigenous communities include traditional norms of enforcement, local government, and education, among others. While these state institutions vary from tribe to tribe, oral tradition and documentation point to the existence of norms for the traditional education of future clan leaders in the society of the Tlingit people of Southeast Alaska. Clearly understanding the mechanics of traditional Tlingit leadership training is important for examining how methods implemented in the past would be effective in training future leaders in Tlingit society today.

The concepts of Tlingit traditional leadership training begin with bloodline. Honorific titles are granted at birth (De Laguna 1972, 450), given that the child is born to a family that falls under the bloodline of a high caste. The Tlingit people were very conscious of social rank in society. The children born into high caste families are the first to be considered for future leadership, especially the nephew of the existing chief of a clan. There are other paths to leadership as well. Some youths prove themselves to be worthy in battle and experience. They end up being eligible for a leadership position. Furthermore, within each clan there are more houses or lineages, each of which has their own chief or "master of the house" (*hit sati*), or "one who stands at the head" (*cadi*; *hani*). These lesser chiefs formerly acted as council members for the head chief. During the time of training, between such groups there was often rivalry and jockeying for position (De Laguna 1972, 462).

Youth could gain additional respect and position through exceptional skills in hunting, public relations, and battle. At a young age, a male would be sent to live with his maternal uncle to learn the "makings of a man." These trainings included the traditional ceremony of submerging one's body in the ocean water inducing an early stage of hypothermia and fainting. Hunting for deer and consuming the raw heart was also ceremonial and educational. These processes likely taught young men how to persevere under stressful conditions. Most importantly, individuals were encouraged to admit to personal mistakes in public. These trainings were designed to teach several traits that were crucial to a leader: humility, honor for all life (human and non-human), mental fortitude, and physical endurance.

Through these intensive trainings, combined with selflessness in the defense of one's village, "a wealthy and ambitious man or youth, with the backing of his relatives, could elevate his own position and that of his family" and could become eligible for a leadership position (De Laguna 1972, 464). Furthermore, "the higher the rank of the individual and the greater the consequent responsibilities, the more stress was set upon wisdom, judgment, and education." These elements were absolutely necessary for a leadership position in the Tlingit society (De Laguna 1972, 465).

Navajo Institutions of Traditional Leadership (Tallman)

The Navajo word for leader or leadership is often associated with individuals who have certain governmental and decision-making authorities such as, the current Navajo Nation President. The Navajo word for leaders is *Naat'áanii***.** According to "Navajo ways," the concept and exercise of *Naat'áanii* is taught, which include certain Navajo rituals and ceremonies that prepare and enable one to become a *Naat'áanii* (Benally 2006). Contemporary Navajo government has changed their behavior to mirror the Anglo-American concepts of political order. Although, it was introduced to serve the needs of non-Navajo political and economic interests, the *Diné* shaped and transformed their 1920s era governing institutions into a body uniquely their own. The Navajo government continues to evolve as it deals with serving a community that remains based in Navajo culture. Today the Navajo Nation Council and the Chapter community government utilize established institutions fundamental to Navajo society (Wilkins 2013).

Legitimacy

Once, the Navajo leaders were legitimate leaders. These *Naat'áanii* were revered and looked to for guidance. They were responsible for a specific region, had ties to the holy people, had good relations with medicine people, and specialized in either peace way (healing) or war (protection) ceremonies (Wilkins 2013, 3–8). Navajo legitimacy was seen as a problem for the U.S. Many U.S. officials complained that the *Naat'áanii* were too powerful and they prevented the Indian agents from doing their job

(Bailey and Bailey 1999, 27–36). One "solution" was to educate Navajo children in boarding schools. This way they could learn the ways of "civilization" and forget about their traditional beliefs (Lomawaima 1994; Lomawaima and McCarty 2006). This "solution" was furthered when many *Naat'áanii* began to pass on in the 1890s. This was the opportunity to replace the old guard of traditional leadership with "modern" Navajos educated in boarding schools, fluent in English, and perhaps open to, or fully embracing, Christianity (Bailey and Bailey 1999). Hence, the traits that made leaders "legitimate" were evolving through time in order to embrace a Western model of leadership.

From the 1920s until today, the Navajo Nation has experienced many ebbs and flows in terms of governing institutions. It is more or less assumed that contemporary leaders have some level of legitimacy to lead. This does not mean that these leaders are unquestioned or not criticized. Some of these governing institutions include chapter governance (Wilkins 2013, 149–160), the birth and evolution of the Navajo Tribal Council (17–23), and the emergence of the Navajo Nation Council (24–31). As these evolutions took place, the extractive nature of Navajo government today has followed patterns first pioneered by European style institutions. The Navajo executive branch (Wilkins 2013, 133–140) and a court system (141–148) seem to support this creep toward non-Navajo norms of leadership. However, this does not mean that contemporary Navajo governance is completely non-Navajo. In fact, there was a movement in the early 1990s to bring in Fundamental Laws of the *Diné* in order to restore balance to contemporary life (Austin 2009; Bobroff 2004–2005; Council 2002; Nielsen and Zion 2005). Institutional legitimacy remains a force, however the source of that legitimacy can certainly be questioned.

Concluding Remarks

It is my hope that this chapter accomplishes several goals. It should showcase the accurate and neglected discussion of contemporary Indigenous sovereignty from a conceptual point of view and in at least two dimensions. Obviously Indigenous nations have adopted some, but not all, of the baggage of Westphalian depictions of sovereignty. Indigenous nations must own this adoption and, if they wish, make overt policy decision to divest themselves of this adoption. We must also not kid ourselves about how massively expensive this process could be for many Indigenous nations. For some, it may be impossible.

Secondly, I wish to showcase the excellent research capabilities of young advocates for the maintenance and expansion of Indigenous sovereignty. Many in Indian Country may be fearful that their children are coming home for their jobs. I would say the fear is correct. Some tribal leaders correctly wish to outsource their jobs to their youth. Others cling to their jobs and the status quo. These leaders need to go. But I also wish to practice what I criticize as a problem with old (modern) ideas and old ways. I say modern because these are ways learned in the Western educational system. Rather than talk about allowing a space for the youth, I have attempted to make a space for the youth here and now. This should give the youth motivation to know that they have the answers. Neither tribal leaders nor I will always have answers. We need the youth to be engaged and I have hopefully opened up a window into the world of writing and policy analysis. I hope, one day they will take my job.

Overall, we have a very serious chasm between our Indigenous ideas about sovereignty and the way domestic U.S. mechanisms and some tribal leaders treat our homelands. One of the most pervasive opponents to our very existence has been the U.S. Supreme Court. While I have attempted to be clear about my assumptions throughout, the same cannot be said about the Supreme Court. Some scholars have hinted about the negative perspective the Court takes with Indians, many have gone straight to race as an explanatory factor. I don't deny that race is a factor. However, many in the current struggle for Indigenous sovereign reach have also relied on this factor and it tends to fall on deaf ears. Our struggle to co-exist with colonial actors brings in factors much broader than race. We have to also remind our opponents about misguided assumptions that have been lost in the conversation. We have many things to assume about ourselves but we must also recognize and negate what others assume about our Indigenous nations. The root cause of ignorance, while salient, is not as important as pointing out the outcome of ignorance to the policy makers with the most control over our Indigenous sovereign reach.

Section II
Indigenous Sovereignty in the Court of the Colonizer

The practices of Indigenous nation interaction with colonial actors have revolved around misunderstanding and then negating their organic relationship with traditional homelands. This systematic process, particularly with the U.S., is similar to other experiences carried out by colonial actors against their genocidal targets. By the time interaction practices became unilaterally dictated by the U.S., it was now possible to hear objections within a single U.S. colonial venue. Domestic U.S. institutions might be generally understood as access to the president, access to Congress, and access to the courts. It would be inconvenient for the U.S. to allow further international interaction with Indigenous nations. The U.S. could imagine no alternative than to negate the Indigenous voice as best they could. Readings of the early documents on the U.S. and its founding reflect the normative notion that Indians must be contained as a domestic problem. The Court of the Colonizer, in this case the U.S. Supreme Court, was the only instrument available to adjudicate disputes with Indigenous nations after international mechanisms were successfully eliminated. This section explains the various strategies employed to demographically eliminate Indigenous individuals when acts of war and violence were not successful.

Section II outlines the colonial philosophy and legacy of the Courts and their stance in opposition to Indigenous sovereignty. For a long time, the Courts were the only venues that could oversee violations of Indigenous sovereignty within the U.S. domestic polity. From about 1821 to the present, various facets of federal Indian law and policy were decided in the Court of the Colonizer. While the Court represents itself as an impartial adjudicator of justice, this idea is a farce. Sometimes the idea of impartiality may be accidental. In what might be an accident of ethno-centric assumptions, Chapter 4 explores the Four Normative Assumptions of the Marshall Court. These assumptions revolve around bringing the international law of Aboriginal Title into the U.S. domestic polity. By adopting this idea, Marshall and company ensured that federal Indian law and policy would bolster federalism over states' rights by ensuring the federal government a monopoly on extinguishing Aboriginal Title. Neither states nor Indigenous nations could legally sell their land to individual non-Indians. These ideas also evolved into the Canons of Construction which attempted to treat Indian individuals fairly so long as those treatments were consistent with Aboriginal Title.

Marshall and many future justices laid a foundation for Aboriginal Title in the Courts. The Rehnquist Court decimated the Canons of Construction in the late 20th century by substituting Indigenous sovereignty for a state's rights. Chapter 5 explains the Canons of Destruction in which nearly every precedent set by the Marshall Court was either mistakenly or deliberately ignored in favor of promoting states' rights. This era is the birth of states' rights arguments as a clean and "race free" rhetoric employed in ways that just so happened to diminish Indigenous sovereignty. At this point in time, Aboriginal Title is no longer a viable foundation for theories of colonization. Instead, Rehnquist and company employ "racism by ellipses" when they still rely on the spirit of Aboriginal Title even if they take out all of the language about savages, superiority and the like. Three cases are explored in which Indigenous sovereignty is diminished, expanded, and left as found. These cases lead to a new focus area in between the case studies and the theory of diminishing Indigenous sovereignty. In Chapter 6, quantitative research is presented which finds that in 45 cases heard by the Rehnquist Court, about 90% of the outcomes diminish sovereignty covering about 68% of the cases in an original data set constructed exclusively for this chapter. Section II is not so much a call to quit the game. Rather, it is a call to explore new strategies for maintaining and expanding Indigenous sovereignty in the 21st century. This section makes the case that playing in the Court of the Colonizer can never result in a loss for the colonial actor.

Chapter 4
Normative Assumptions of the Marshall Court

We have so far reviewed some evidence for sovereignty based on Indigenous creation along with the tensions this idea has faced. Somewhere along the way many scholars and tribal leaders neglected our "domestication." While it is not clear what some other scholars have meant when they say that Indigenous peoples have been domesticated; I don't mean to say we were wild and now we are tame. Rather, I mean to say that we have had our Indigenous nations wrapped up into domestic U.S. mechanisms as explained in Chapter 2. This idea of being wrapped up within the U.S. polity did not have to be a negative consequence. There is no reason to assume that we must always remain international actors. Still, we have to remember our international status because it is our history. We must remind the U.S. and other colonial actors about our international status and Indigenous shared histories based in creation as well as being the focus for colonization. Colonial actors must be reminded that they are only the wealthiest nations on earth because we made it so. We are here despite colonial actor attempts to fully and completely commit genocide. Colonial actors are here in spite of our audacity to survive genocide.

John Marshall is complicit in the attempts to wrap up Indigenous nations within the U.S. polity. Somewhere along the way it appears many individuals have forgotten why Indigenous nations sought justice in what Walter Echohawk calls the Courts of the Conqueror (2010). Yet, this idea of conquest is still in contradiction to what was outlined in Chapters 1 and 2. Perhaps this is a semantics concern but it seems more appropriate to call the U.S. Supreme Court a court of the colonizer. I now reject the ideas that Indigenous nations were ever conquered. But, whatever we end up calling the courts is irrelevant. We still remain, at times, forgetful about the nature of why we Indigenous nations go to courts of the colonizers in the first place. In our histories of false dichotomies and functional creeps, some of these outlined in Chapter 2, we are often coerced into choosing between two bad choices. Go to war or sign a treaty. Sign a treaty to cede land or continue a war. Be exterminated or walk 400 miles to another land and that will be your reservation. And as this process continues on, the false dichotomy choices have inherently allowed our grievances to have their due process requirement carried out in colonial actor domestic institutions such as the courts. This process crept up on Indigenous nations boxing us into corners we may feel powerless to escape. It is so bad that we often forget how these boxes we wish to escape may be boxes we have learned to see as "benefits" and "rights."

Once upon a time, we Indian individuals had no say in the direction of the U.S. governmental policy at the federal or the state level. We could not vote, we could not run for elected office in the U.S. government, and we could not obtain employment or majority control over any economic institution. It was even a struggle for Indian individuals to gain "standing" in the U.S. court system (United States ex rel. Standing Bear v. Crook 1879). Yet, this supposed victory was what I would call one of the steps that would end up eclipsing other aspects of Indigenous sovereignty. This chapter will outline what a "weakest link" argument is all about. Next, I will apply the weakest link approach to Four Normative Assumptions that are present in the Marshall Court and specifically in the M'Intosh case (Johnson and Graham's Lessee v. William M'Intosh 1823). These assumptions appear to have been obscured by Marshall during the authoring of the opinion or perhaps obscured by what Fixico has called the use of the First Dimension of this cases history. He states, "The First Dimension is like a door or window, and it is basically the linear mainstream's interpretation or perspective on American Indian history" (Fixico 2003, 8). Hence, a linear history of M'Intosh may have also obscured the Four Normative Assumptions that work more to bolster federalism over states' rights than they preserve or respect Indigenous sovereignty. This research will go beyond a one-way door into the logic behind M'Intosh exposing how the weakest link argument is the best explanation for how this, and many other cases operate.

To begin, it is necessary to understand something about a "weakest link" argument. This argument is not objectively bad. Weakest link is a comparative analysis tool developed by sociologists in making cross case research possible (Ragin 2008, 114). What does that mean exactly? It means that 1. We should not compare apples with oranges and 2. We can compare these two distinct entities because they do have traits in common: they are both fruit. These two fruits have some things in common such as both having seeds within their core and both having peelings. But which is "better"? That's a subjective question. The extent to which we objectively call our judgments "subjective" is the extent to which we attempt to be clear about our preferences. This is no problem if we are clear about which of the traits we prefer and why. So a weakest link argument about fruit would involve us understanding which of these two fruits would spoil first. It would be important to know which spoiled first because if the apple spoils first it could also spread to the orange. Hence, we are trying to not simply say "I like oranges better." We are more concerned with how much time we have until our fruits spoil and we go hungry. The best way to calculate this time is to observe the two fruits until one begins to decay. This might be an example of a good application of weakest link thinking.

In comparative research, it is ideal to have some statement on the measurement of the units you wish to understand. Weakest link thinking has been applied in research on democracies that work together for a common cause. When two nations work together, they are sometimes called a dyad. Let's say you wish to understand some measure of democracy within a single dyad. The weakest link argument states that the dyad can only be as democratic as the one country with the lowest level of democratic institutions present in their government. Hence, the dyad is only as democratic as the weakest member (Goertz 2006, 114). I have made some simplifying assumptions here as I explain weakest link arguments. This explanation on democratic dyads is meant to show how the argument can work in an objective way. We can replace the idea being discussed with anything. We have discussed two fruits and we have discussed two democracies. At the core of these comparisons are degrees of membership in a club. In very technical terms, we are looking for traits that make a case qualify as a member of a club. Each of the traits we explore will provide some level of support for membership in a club. The trait with the least supportable evidence is the level to which we should consider the case a member (Ragin 2008, 114). All of this talk of comparative research techniques does more to bolster credit for well thought out arguments in the Marshall Court and this credit is certainly not warranted.

At the core of any weakest link argument are traits for membership (conditions) and traits for results we can observe (outcome). I'm about to argue that there are four conditions present in the Marshall Court. They are listed in Table 1. They are 1. The European Christian Government Must Remain the More Powerful Actor, 2. Discovery Grants the Right to Extinguish Aboriginal Title, 3. Indians Enjoy the Right of Occupancy at the Pleasure of the European Sovereign, and 4. Europeans Must Help the Indian be like the European Individual.

Table 4.1: The Four Normative Assumptions of the Marshall Court
1. The European Christian Government Must Remain the More Powerful Actor 2. Discovery Grants the Right to Extinguish Aboriginal Title 3. Indians Enjoy the Right of Occupancy at the Pleasure of the European Sovereign 4. Europeans Must Help the Indian be like the European Individual

Going forward, we must begin to acknowledge these assumptions as conditions that Indigenous peoples have no control over. Since 1492, we have had little choice in how these conditions were invented out of thin air. States' rights activists must also be made to understand these facts. At every turn of U.S. court rulings, these Four Normative Assumptions were at the heart of any argument for the maintenance and expansion of colonial actor sovereignty. While this research here may only focus on the U.S. case for using these conditions to justify taking Indigenous homelands, this model could also be applied to all colonial actors around the world. These conditions were used in the same manner that weakest link arguments are used in research now. The courts relied on dichotomous thinking to justify their land appropriation tactics. If only one of the four assumptions was at all remotely detectable by the courts, then it must be a foregone conclusion that Aboriginal Title was gone before we knew anything about it.

Figure 4.1 is a Set Theory depiction of the Four Normative Assumptions of the Marshall Court (Ragin 2008, 13). There are two important issues to note. First, this figure may be quite inconvenient for Court scholars because it highlights the fragility of reasoning in the Marshall Court. Any one of the Four Normative Assumptions is enough to trump Indigenous rights to their own homeland. Any of the assumptions is enough to extinguish Aboriginal Title. A second point to take away here is how each condition is ill-defined by the Marshall Court. These are supposedly "black and white" conditions that only require a yes or no response. You are a colonial actor or not. You are an Indian or not. It is evidence of importing a hierarchy based on race. Hierarchy importation is tied to contemporary colonial actor development in what became Latin America (Mahoney 2010). The type of research carried out in Latin America would certainly prove the same point in the U.S. and Canada. Had it not been for the Indigenous-based relations with land, there would have been no resources for colonial actors to monopolize and exploit today. This attachment to homeland, based on Peoplehood, is the source of all colonial actor wealth today. Peoplehood holds that a people are tied to their homelands because of ceremony, language, and sacred history (Holm, Pearson, and Chavis 2003). These ties to homeland are very powerful even today (Lerma 2012). It would be instructive to understand where these ideas came from and how they were imported into U.S. domestic law.

Figure 4.1: Weakest Link in the Marshall Court

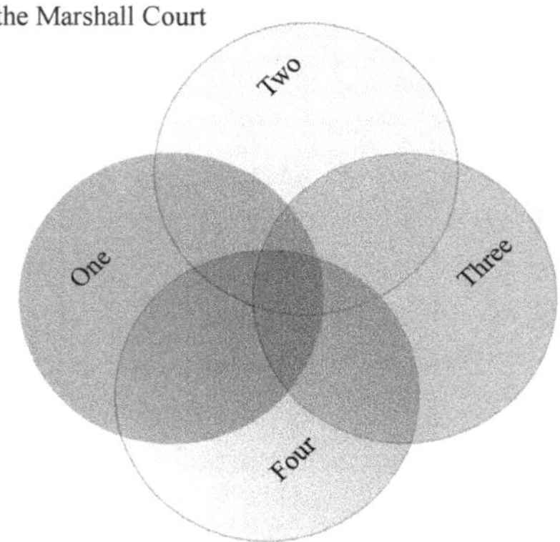

Weakest Link Arguments:

1 - The European Christian Government Must Remain the More Powerful Actor

OR

2 - Discovery Grants the Right to Extinguish Indian Title

OR

3 - Indians Enjoy Right of Occupancy at the Pleasure of the European Sovereign

OR

4 - Europeans Must Help the Indian be Like the European Individual

The Four Normative Assumptions are hiding in plain sight today in the U.S. and probably throughout the world where colonization has taken place. Chapter 1 discusses the international relations events leading to disarming Indigenous nations through treaties followed by reneging on treaties. Chapter 2 explores how domestic U.S. mechanisms came to creep into and replace international mechanisms once available to Indigenous nations through coerced negotiations. This chapter explores the normative nature of the court decisions. It really is the only tie that links colonial actor policy from first contact to the Marshall Court to states' rights activists today. Even so-called "friends" of the Indian have been guilty of holding some of these assumptions close to heart in misguided efforts to help Indians. Nevertheless, the Marshall Court faced an opportunity to incorporate these Four Normative Assumptions into the body of domestic U.S. law when they heard the Johnson v. M'Intosh case in 1821. While this story has been told countless times, there appears to have been no other research that takes the initiative to point out how the case is 1. Linked to a weakest link argument, 2. Linked to the most massive land theft in the history of the world, and 3. Linked to the greatest wealth monopolization in the history of the world. Even now I feel like I have understated the impact of the Four Normative Assumptions of the Marshall Court.

Re-Analyzing M'Intosh from an Indigenous Point of View

The Four Normative Assumptions for federal Indian law can also be expressed using short titles: 1. U.S. domination, 2. Exclusive acquisition, 3. Aboriginal Title, and 4. Indian civilization, and they are largely unrealistic myths that serve more to legitimize domestic mechanisms of U.S. governance over Indigenous homelands than anything else. Here I wish to explore Johnson v. M'Intosh as a normative case meant to bolster the myth of the U.S. nationhood. As such, it is necessary for M'Intosh to be premised on a set of stereotypes that serve as or supplement the reality of U.S./Indian relations at the time the case was being decided. Sometimes a case is one in which the court aims to legitimize its colonial past, its hypocritical, inconsistent, contradictory, etc., application of some rule, and/or its current economic and political domination over Indians more generally. (Wrapping Indigenous nations within U.S. domestic polities such as economic and political institutions, again, actualized this normative goal. The evidence for this strategy is outlined in Chapter 2). Other times, a case is used to legitimately attempt improving the Indian condition. Sometimes, the good intention approach is merely a cloak meant to obscure a more sinister motive or interest. Other times, it appears the good intentions were genuine. Interestingly enough, every single court case has carried with it unintended negative consequences which ultimately harmed the Indian condition regardless of the intent of the Supreme Court. Research on these Four Normative Assumptions could be carried out on every case ever heard by the Supreme Court, however, this breadth of analysis is beyond the scope of this research.[6] Such harm is painfully evident if we understand the driving force the Four Normative Assumptions contain when federal Indian law is constructed.

M'Intosh, Normative Assumptions, and What History?

The M'Intosh case serves as an excellent example on how the Four Normative Assumptions operate in weakest link form. In a logical argument, sets of premises are offered. Premises relevant to a solution should accurately represent policy issues. The interpretation of these premises and their implications

6. Some tips on how this research might be carried out can be located in Chapter 6.

are weighed in a conclusion and, after careful consideration, an outcome is offered as a solution to the problem first encountered. Yet we have been examining a set of underlying assumptions that have substituted for the role that logic should play in decision-making. Let us first highlight the impact that history has on the outcome of M'Intosh. Next, we will explore the manner in which the Four Normative Assumptions of federal Indian law have impacted the uses of history in this case. Finally, we revisit the question of normative conditions being applied to decide the case, and the outcome that is in the best interest of the U.S. at that time. These considerations will be tied back to the actual outcome of the M'Intosh case.

M'Intosh deals with giving and receiving title to land as well as the obligation courts have to recognize such title transfers. Specifically, can an Indian convey a title to a private party and can the private party receive title? More importantly, will policy makers recognize these title transfers? If the answer is yes, then the matter of court obligation to recognize such title transfers becomes the issue. The rule is that discovery of Indian land by European colonizers gave them an exclusive right to acquire the title by extinguishing the Aboriginal rights to occupy their traditional homeland. Such a right excludes the private party from receiving the title from Indians directly. With M'Intosh, the private party and Indian land title transfer occurred prior to U.S. independence. The title of discovery, however, can be traced back to the British sovereign. Heads colonial actors win, tails Indigenous nations lose. If this quick tale spins your head, I would not worry so much. I would, instead, be concerned if this psychotic twisting is logical to you. This is just another example of functional creep that is more deeply addressed in Chapter 2.

Following the Twisted Logic of Aboriginal Title: The Original Ethnic Entitlement

At the source of this "schizophrenic" history is the idea that colonial actors gave themselves the right to extinguish Indigenous rights to occupy their traditional homelands. This is also known as Aboriginal Title (Williams 2005, 149–160). This story of creative non-fiction or social science fiction can be explored through the case or through contemporary legal research (Robertson 2005). Most importantly, our analysis here will further illuminate the reference, implicitly or otherwise, of the Four Normative Assumptions in the Marshall Court. Why is this important? The future Courts would also rely on these assumptions until around 1986 when Rehnquist began ignoring these assumptions all together. The turn away from the Four Normative Assumptions is detailed in Chapter 6. Beyond the M'Intosh case and contemporary research, the actual facts of the events below are really nothing more than a fiction and this makes it difficult to find citations!

What follows might be a play-by-play call of the events discussed in M'Intosh. Perhaps this is what some Indigenous leaders in 1821 might say if they turned on their version of 19th century CSPAN. They'd see this type of exchange: Sometime between contact and establishing British colonies, England declared an exclusive right to extinguish Aboriginal Title over lands that ended up being the original 13 colonies or states of the U.S. Upon losing the Revolutionary War, the British discovery right was assumed by the U.S. The discovery of territory grants the discovering sovereign the exclusive right to bargain for the acquisition of land. The exclusive right to bargain for acquisition is settled by looking at the history of colonial interaction. The competition to bargain over the territory went on between France and the U.S. The question of exclusive right to bargain was settled in the 1763 Treaty of Paris. As such, if France were to attempt to acquire land during the post-1763 treaty agreement, such an act would supposedly violate U.S. sovereignty. The M'Intosh case is essentially about two non-Indians having title to a common tract of land. All of this right to extinguish discussion is very important because the case could have decided that Indians COULD sell land to non-Indian individuals. But, SPOILER ALERT, it turns out that only the U.S., at the federal level, has the right to bargain for acquisition of the territory that the private party now claims title to via purchase from Indians.

M'Intosh was forced to consider the right of Indians to convey title. This discussion leads to the Second Normative Assumption: Discovery Grants the European Sovereign the Right to Extinguish Aboriginal Title. Based on the Doctrine of Discovery, the U.S. sovereign has a clear title to all Indian lands even before it extinguishes Aboriginal Title! How can this be? While the Indian right of occupancy exists, the right may be terminated at the pleasure of the European sovereign. This is the Third Normative Assumption. As such, Aboriginal Title may be extinguished by purchase or conquest. In short, Indian right of occupancy, or Aboriginal Title, does not include the right to convey land to private individuals. Rather, Indian rights of occupancy only allow for Indian conveyance of land to the European sovereign within the boundaries set forth in the treaty of Paris. Alternatively, and as the case is for the particular lands in dispute, the lands can be taken by force or conquest. Since conquest was the manner in which the U.S. extinguished some portions of Aboriginal Title, only those rights that are not in conflict with the European sovereign remain in place. This idea points to the First Normative Assumption: The European Christian

Government Must Remain the More Powerful Actor. The right of Indian conveyance is in conflict with U.S. interests and, therefore cannot be honored. Along with conquest comes the requirement to honor conquest title in the court of the colonizer.

In M'Intosh, the Court concludes that a private party may not obtain land from an Indian if the European sovereign discovers the land first. Second, an Indian can only convey Aboriginal Title to land not taken by conquest. Third, when an Indian has not lost Aboriginal Title due to conquest, the Indian can only convey Aboriginal Title to an appropriate European sovereign. Logically, although not stated, it should follow that an Indian may transfer Aboriginal Title to a non-sovereign only after the sovereign surrenders the exclusive right to bargain and acquire territory. Finally, the court will only recognize the exclusive European sovereign's right to acquire by conquest or purchase.

The Under-Examined Consequences of Aboriginal Title—What Exactly Did You Just Buy?

This twisted logic leads to interesting and often neglected consequences. What does it mean to say that someone like Thomas Jefferson doubled the size of the U.S. with the Louisiana Purchase (Bueno de Mesquita 2014, 490)? The question is equally intriguing when discussing the Mexican/American War between 1846 and 1848 as well as the various methods used to acquire what is now known as the Pacific Northwest. We are likely aware of the U.S. metanarrative about winning wars and purchasing land but all of the above and subsequent twisted logic requires a second look at the nature of land acquisition. Probably the two most famous supposed land acquisitions are the Louisiana Purchase and the Mexican/American War. But if the logic of M'Intosh is applied in these other instances, does it mean that what was actually purchased was the exclusive right to extinguish Aboriginal Title?

In the Louisiana Purchase example, it appears that the U.S. purchased an exclusive right to extinguish Aboriginal Title in the region from the French. No Indians were needed to seal this deal. Apparently France was the first Christian nation to discover what became the Louisiana Purchase area. As a result, according to the M'Intosh version of how this international law should work, France had to do some more work, or not. France had to exercise their right to exclusively extinguish the Indians' rights to occupy the land that would later become the Louisiana Purchase. This is a reference to the Second and Third Normative Assumptions of the Marshall Court. Recall that France could buy, conquer, or otherwise extinguish that Aboriginal Title or right of occupancy at their pleasure as outlined in assumption three. The work of genocide is apparently never easy or automatic. This, obviously, places a different interpretation on what Jefferson actually did purchase.

Given this revealing exercise in logic, the U.S. instead purchased an exclusive right to extinguish Aboriginal Title, but they had to actually do the dirty work of ethnic cleansing by purchase or conquest. This same logic should also apply to the spoils of the Mexican/American War as well as the Gadsden Purchase. Both of these "transactions" involved what we now call the American Southwest. Prior to 1846, first Spain and then Mexico claimed the exclusive right to extinguish Aboriginal Title in the region. Again, this logic is based on applying M'Intosh. It is also another example of the second and third Normative Assumptions of the Marshall Court. Recall that a very similar story is also recounted as the British claim was taken over by the U.S. and so went the exclusivity clause. When the U.S. invaded Mexico in 1846, the fight was on for the right to ethnically cleanse the region. Just two years later, the U.S. declared victory and the right to extinguish Aboriginal Title was transferred to the U.S., apparently, through the Treaty of Guadalupe Hidalgo. This is another example of Assumption Two and Three. A few years later, the U.S. purchased land that would become southern Arizona in the Gadsden Purchase. Obviously this is rather twisted and precarious logic to try and follow yet this may have been the way the courts would have settled claims in these regions had they ever been challenged in the Courts! Regardless, history and reality often have little to do with extinguishing Aboriginal Title.

Given the outcome, there are a few places where history has either been superficially revisited or ignored altogether. A controversial assessment of compensation for the discovery of the Americas appears to trade Christianity and civilization for the Americas, not just the U.S. (Getches 2011, 65). This is the Fourth Normative Assumption of the Marshall Court: Europeans Must Help the Indian be Like the European Individual. Note that this is not about "tribes" or Indigenous nations but help for the individual to be an individual! To avoid conflict among the "superior" Christian nations, it was decided that the sovereigns must settle among themselves how the Americas should be divided. The bargaining completed, the justices assume that with no other civilized group around, the exclusive right to acquire land belonged to the U.S. alone. Implicit in this argument is the fact that only those actors that had a relevant purpose in bargaining were present to strike the deal. Indigenous actors had no part to play in dividing the Americas. By virtue of the discovery and the exclusive right to acquire as obtained by agreement among the other discoverers, it is also implied that the Indigenous actors were irrelevant actors. Their supposed discovery automatically made them less than sovereign overseers of the territory due to the fact that they were not Christian nations. Readers should contrast this 1821 fantasy with Chapter 1. The source of the less than equal relations between Indians and the British had to do with the English common law stating that a King had the right to conquer infidels. Unfortunately, Indians proved to be "rebellious," "fierce," and preoccupied with "making war" as well as deriving their livelihood "from the forest" meaning that European laws were inconsistent, and threatened by Indian society. Based on such a history, it was unthinkable to allow the land to remain a "wild forest" (Getches 2011, 68). Again, one of the Four Normative Assumptions would always work to justify taking Indigenous homelands while pretending Indigenous sovereignty was a fictional entity.

Marshall, States' Rights, and Federalism: Indians are Along for the Ride

There are plenty of scholars who discuss how the Supreme Court prefers to uphold states' rights while they ignore the ramifications that these normative assumptions have on Indigenous sovereignty (Getches 2001). States' rights trumping federalism was first discussed here in Chapter 2. This discussion has focused more on the way the Courts ignore precedent in the canon of federal Indian law than on issues raised throughout this book. But, to what extent has Marshall and company used the Marshall Trilogy to lay a foundation for federalism trumping states' rights? To what extent does Marshall deserve credit for this strategy? While this is a debate for other historians and political scientists, the basics of American history is that you have a period of uncertainty. Would the U.S. be a decentralized democracy with states trumping federal reach without the Marshall trilogy? What can be said for sure is that states' rights advocates believe and tell the tale as if it is settled, just as much as federalist advocates do the same but the tensions remain (Brinkley 2010). For our purposes, let's assume that the Marshall Court deliberately attempted to lay a foundation for federalists to rely upon in the future. If this is so, then it seems clear that Indigenous sovereignty should only be defended to the extent that it also bolsters or maintains federalism over states' rights. These two important facets are clear in the M'Intosh case.

The notion that international actors wished to acquire and extinguish Aboriginal Title is also clear. There is something to be said about the "non-case" of how states play a role here. This is another methodological tool in which scholars could objectively discuss what counts as a case that is important enough to explore (Ragin and Becker 1992). But, for our purposes, it is also instructive to understand what Marshall believed was NOT a case for concern. What role did states play in extinguishing Aboriginal Title?

There is some evidence of these debates where states are said to keep the U.S. federal government advised of their exploits (Deloria and Wilkins 1999, 13–20). These seemingly uninteresting relics of history books deserve much more attention. Part of the M'Intosh opinion is to ensure, through implicit assumption and omission, that the discussion on the role that states played in extinguishing Aboriginal Title remains an unstated and accepted norm of practice. The Cherokee Cases do a much better job of making this point and readers are encouraged to explore them independent of this research (Getches 2011, 105 and 113). Specifically, Cherokee v. Georgia held that Georgia state law does NOT apply to Cherokee homelands (Getches 2011, 105–113). This trend makes sense from the perspective of the U.S. federalist advocates. The more federalists can set the norm for a super-ordinate federal system that trumps state law, the more likely the norm will come to be accepted and followed. This area of research certainly deserves more attention. Could it be that every single case heard in the Supreme Court on federal Indian law ALWAYS supports federalism over states' rights? This is a good question that is beyond the scope of this current research. And while the answer remains hidden in plain sight in the existing literature, it will not be illuminated unless future scholars go into the books in search of the answer to this question.

But before we start thanking Marshall and company for their apparent contributions to Indigenous sovereignty, we must remember that these aspects of sovereignty are likely only ever respected and upheld when they also happen to serve the interests of the U.S. and federalism. We can point to cases where Indigenous sovereignty is trumped only when it also happens to bolster federalism over states' rights. One of the most famous examples of this outcome is how residents of states tend to be the deadliest enemies of Indigenous nations. Here we find Indigenous sovereignty defended but it just so happens to also uphold federalism over states' rights (Biolsi 2007). This is another example of interest convergence working to benefit a marginalized people (Bell 1987, 62). Some have linked this idea to the U.S. Supreme Court and federal Indian law (Williams 2005, xxxv). Today we have the benefit of discussing the Four Normative Assumptions in the Marshall Court and we also have the tools to carry out comprehensive and systematic research on the body of federal Indian law (Ragin 2008). We may also discover that our history of compromise with the U.S. may be nothing more than a discussion where we openly agree to fall within a frame outlined by the Four Normative Assumptions in what Bruyneel has called the imperial binary (Bruyneel 2007). At the very least, all people invested in policies of subjugation deserve to understand how pervasive ethnic entitlement policies (Aboriginal Title) have come to dominate almost all areas of contemporary sovereignty. They operate very resiliently now in the 21st century.

The Four Normative Assumptions: Weakest Link Prevails

The Four Normative Assumptions have differing and uneven sections within M'Intosh so we will look at each separately. Recall that the issue involves the ability of an Indian to convey a title to a private party, the ability of a private party to receive title conveyance from an Indian, and the court obligation to recognize such title transfers. The distinction drawn between an Indian and a private party hints at the first normative assumption of U.S. domination. More importantly, it is clear from the way the issue is framed that the second assumption, exclusive acquisition of Aboriginal Title, is at the heart of the case. Falling to the background are notions of Indian occupancy and civilizing the Indian largely because these assumptions cannot take precedent over the first two. Note here that we can see a priority ranking is also at work concerning the Four Normative Assumptions. The rule, however, almost exclusively focuses on Aboriginal Title and the underlying assumption of exclusive acquisition rights.

In many ways, the second normative assumption is the rule relied upon to arrive at the outcome. By virtue of its discovery, Indian lands can be exclusively acquired by the U.S. to the exclusion of individual private parties. At least one other assumption still plays a role. The U.S. is still allowed to dominate both the Aboriginal Title and the private party transfer, yet occupancy and civilization are hardly at issue for this particular case. The rule is also used to drive the analysis into a restating of the rule as the outcome, making the reasoning for U.S. domination and exclusive acquisition rights a complex, but nonetheless circular argument. Each step of tracing the title relies on the Aboriginal Title, meaning that U.S. domination and exclusive acquisition rights drive the entire opinion. Discovery, negotiations among civilized nations, exclusive acquisition, and right of occupancy all push the agenda of U.S. domination and exclusive acquisition rights. It is unnecessary to re-articulate the same reasoning that appears in the outcome because it will read much the same as it has for the analysis. The conditions and outcome will produce another circular argument.

The condition under which the Supreme Court is visiting the question raised in M'Intosh involves the need for the U.S. to legitimize its own sovereignty. As such, it is clear to see that the best interest of expanding and solidifying U.S. sovereignty is to find that Indians cannot transfer title to private parties, private parties cannot receive title from Indians, and that the U.S. courts have an obligation to recognize only title that has traveled through Aboriginal Title institutions. Of course, the outcome arrived at was the most beneficial to the U.S. Removing the normative assumptions and then reanalyzing would result in a different outcome. Interestingly, the first two assumptions need to be negated for the outcome to change in the

M'Intosh case. Yet, even if only those two are negated, it is still likely that Aboriginal Title and the need to civilize the Indian would result in the invalidation of the Indian/private party title transfer. As time went on, many of these normative assumptions were criticized as racist forcing the Supreme Court to utilize another strategy to retain self-interested outcomes. This has become known as racism by ellipses.

Concluding Remarks

The complex legal history of colonizing the U.S. has often been assumed away as matter of fact. While there is certainly room for argument that not all of the normative assumptions of colonization have been documented or that perhaps one of the included assumptions is not correct, there is certainly less debate about the impact that these assumptions had on Indian Country. Alternatively, it would be great for those who have never considered these aspects of U.S. history to actually have the discussion! Yet, for all of the credit Marshall and his Court receive for their work on the three most impactful cases on federal Indian law, the Marshall Court is certainly not an advocate for Indigenous rights. As Robert Williams states in his own work on legal research as well as more broadly about legal scholarship in general:

> . . . legal scholars tend to pursue a much different type of research paradigm from that of our colleagues in the humanities or social sciences. We practice the strong belief that legal scholarship should be actively directed toward the resolution of contemporary policy issues. (Williams 1999, 3–4)

Professor Williams is an excellent representative of his field. His statement, as I understand it from a social science point of view, suggests that legal research has some problems with selecting on the dependent variable. Actively directing research toward the resolution of inconvenient consequences of colonization sounds tricky. It appears that legal scholars actively seek to support conclusions they wish to support which might mean that they ignore premises that do not support their conclusions. This becomes a much bigger issue as we turn our attention toward problems in the Rehnquist Court when they carry out their own form of judicial termination via the Canons of Destruction.

Chapter 5
The Rehnquist Court and the Canons of Destruction

We have explored the Four Normative Assumptions of the Marshall Court and how these assumptions are more in line with U.S. interests than anything else. It used to be that most scholars, even policy makers holding the Four Normative Assumptions close to their hearts, were aware of the coerced and disingenuous nature of most treaties written between the U.S. and Indigenous nations after 1812 (Getches 2011, 128). Chapter 1 reminds us of the three cut points in treaty making history where Indigenous actors tried to make clans of refugees from Europe (Williams 1999). Next, Indigenous actors took on European norms of behavior and were recognized as powerful international actors (Deloria and Wilkins 1999). Finally, in the post-1812 era, it was clearer that the U.S. had emerged as a more powerful international actor forcing tribes to sign treaties under duress and mostly involving land cessions to the U.S. (Getches 2011, 128). Again, these time line themes creep away if we go beyond the current northeast in the U.S. The times go away if we examine the southwest and the Pacific Northwest but the themes remain. Our mainstream U.S. history may not even mention any of these tidbits, but when something from this history is recalled, it is usually the last part. Rather, most casual readers only "remember" war and conquest. Most casual observers only think they remember a treaty as a gift to a few remaining savages.

For a time, the mythical history in the minds of legal scholars and jurists must have nagged them as they continued to extinguish Aboriginal Title. As is typical in shaping norms, the U.S. domestic mechanisms for dealing with Indians came to creep in practice. It no longer became digestible that Indians should be overtly cleansed from the land now claimed by the U.S. Scholars began to assemble a list of reasons why Indigenous nations deserved some latitude when it came to dealing with the U.S. after 1812:

- Treaties exclusively deal with removal
- "Chiefs" that sign the treaties often do not represent the removed tribe

- Language was a barrier in negotiations
- The "young" U.S. was more concerned with building an empire than honoring treaty terms
- The U.S. army continued wars against tribes even after treaties were signed
- The Doctrine of Discovery was a limited rationalization for taking land
- Treaties did a bad job of codifying ALL rights reserved by tribes (Getches 2011, 128–130)

It became clear to all involved, even on the U.S. side, that all of these factors contributed to a less than ideal outcome. To be fair, it is clear that many U.S. policy makers were surprised that Indians continued to exist at all. Our audacity to survive in the face of genocidal conditions proved impossible to ignore.

In order to correct the issues raised above, or at least acknowledge that they produced a less than livable condition for most tribes, a norm known as the Canons of Construction emerged showcasing three practices:

1. [A]mbiguous [treaty] expressions must be resolved in favor of the Indian parties concerned
2. Indian treaties must be interpreted as the Indians themselves would have understood them
3. Indian treaties must be liberally construed in favor of the Indians (Getches 2011, 130)

Many policy makers, including jurists in multiple levels of the U.S. court system as well as members of Congress, used these Canons of Construction. It is noteworthy that ambiguously worded congressional language that could abrogate treaties was also interpreted as not abrogating treaties (Getches 2011, 131). It would prove to be an interesting research exercise to figure how the Four Normative Assumptions played a role in the Canons of Construction interpretive method. Did the Fourth Normative Assumption of "helping Indians" dominate the debates?

It is fitting that we move into the 20th century with the emergence of William Rehnquist. It is quite mind-boggling, in some ways, how a 20th century mind can be so hostile toward Indians. Today, it seems fitting that we brand Rehnquist as the author of a new era (old) in Indigenous sovereignty: He can be the Founder of the Canons of Destruction. This Canon may be redefined as follows:

1. [A]mbiguous [treaty] expressions must be resolved in favor of ~~the Indian parties concerned~~ states' rights
2. Indian treaties must be interpreted as ~~the Indians themselves~~ states would have understood them
3. Indian treaties must be liberally construed in favor of ~~the Indians~~ states' rights (Getches 2011, 130)

There are two issues to raise with this above creep. First, it is clean and "race free" to say that debates over diminished Indigenous sovereignty have nothing to do with race and everything to do with states' rights. Secondly, both Canons of Construction and Canons of Destruction are deterministic decision-making models. This second issue deserves detailed attention.

To be fair, most legal scholars and jurists are carrying out some sort of decision-making model with a predetermined outcome in mind. This type of decision-making model may be better understood as "deterministic" or the idea that one condition is having tremendous impact on the outcomes while other potentially impacting conditions are diminished or ignored (Brady and Collier 2010, 146–147). The Canons of Construction is a deterministic model of decision-making. The Rehnquist model for decision-making, the Canons of Destruction, is also deterministic. In fact, I provide quantitative evidence of this fact in Chapter 6. Regardless, it was nice that some policy makers once believed in some form of special consideration with regard to Indigenous sovereignty but, sadly, that day is long gone. This chapter will outline how many legal minds on the Court have predetermined outcomes in mind and search only for premises that support their conclusion while ignoring premises that do not support their predetermined conclusions. Secondly, the chapter will provide evidence that the Four Normative Assumptions of the Marshall Court have been replaced with Rehnquist's Canons of Destruction. This replacement carefully negates Indigenous sovereignty by focusing on states' rights while ignoring racial hierarchies implied by Aboriginal Title. This chapter concludes with four mini-case studies on Supreme Court cases heard during the Rehnquist era from 1972 to 2005. The cases represent normative platforms for diminishing, expanding, and leaving Indigenous sovereignty as the Court found it. These ideal type cases set a foundation for Chapter 6, which is a quantitative test of the Rehnquist Court. At the end, there appears to be no room for co-existence between Indigenous nations and colonial actors in Rehnquist's Canons of Destruction.

What is a Deterministic Method?

Deterministic cases also rely on stereotypes in lieu of and/or in supplement of history or omit history entirely because the outcome is predetermined. With deterministic cases, the history must be carefully revised and stereotypes are meticulously invoked in order to arrive at the predetermined conclusion. The term "deterministic" is borrowed from social sciences. Within a social science discipline, the deterministic model is one in which the results of some quantitative test are manipulated to achieve the intended outcome. For example, an ordinary least squares regression can be manipulated by careful selection of cases based on some distinguishing characteristics being observed in order to obtain statistically significant results (King, Keohane, and Verba 1994). For the Supreme Court, they are essentially carefully selecting which history/stereotype (observations) they wish to include in their analysis to match the outcome (result) they already have in mind. The deterministic approach requires that one ignore history that conflicts with the predetermined outcome. In the absence of the "correct" history, some justices rely on stereotypes and pass it off as historically accurate. The majority of the cases that employ the deterministic approach tend to be direct assaults on Indigenous sovereignty. As a consequence, contemporary Supreme Court cases must talk about Aboriginal Title without mentioning the phrase. Although it is possible to use deterministic methods to improve the Indian condition, such as the Canons of Construction model, such methods can just as well cause tremendous harm as exemplified by the Oliphant case.

Ideal Type Cases and the 1972–2005 Court

This chapter is leading up to a systematic inquiry into Rehnquist's impact on the Court and the idea that scholars can test the Court's decisions for carrying out the Canons of Destruction. Many scholars have had a long debate in the journals and in books about the nature of Rehnquist, the Supreme Court, and their inept nature of impacting Indigenous sovereignty positively or negatively (Wilkins and Lomawaima 2001). This chapter is not merely offering a few case studies meant to deterministically prove that the Canons of Destruction are firmly in place. Instead, I'd like this chapter to lay down a foundation for comprehensive understanding of the Supreme Court between 1972 and 2005. This fairly ambitious approach requires the identification of some ideal cases that should work to further develop definitions of what future case types would look like. Ideal types allow us to form categories for all cases based on the case study of just a few ideal cases (Goertz 2006, 83). The Court might be the most powerful arbiter in terms of deciding the line between Indigenous sovereignty and domestic U.S.

mechanism. Indigenous sovereignty has become a moving target through no fault of Indigenous leaders trying to survive colonization in the face of federal Indian law and policy creep. Figure 5.1 showcases this in static form. If this book could animate Indigenous sovereignty in flux, it would animate a shift back and forth within and without Indigenous nations. This is not a "pendulum swing" but a constant pressure to eliminate remaining vestiges of Indigenous sovereignty (Deloria and Lytle 1984, 256–262). The Court is tied in to this creep toward elimination. It makes sense to identify some ideal type cases within the Court and use these case examples to further illuminate a method to identify all cases and plug them into a typology.

What will this typology look like? We know, or can imagine, that Court cases may Expand, Leave As Found, or Diminish Indigenous sovereignty. We may draw this idea along a continuum (Figure 5.1) with a 1 representing cases that happen to expand sovereignty, a 0 representing opinions that do not impact sovereignty as it has been found, and a -1 meaning the case has diminished sovereignty. Do not read too much into the negative number as I do not mean to imply that this is necessarily a negative. Our main concern should be that I have 1. Identified these ideal type categories, and 2. That it might be possible to arrange all cases along this continuum ranking them from Expand to Diminish. Of course, it would be very illustrative but also a methodological nightmare to try and map the changing trajectory of Indigenous sovereignty. We would probably need at least two continuums: one continuum based on the Canons of Construction and one based on the Canons of Destruction.

Figure 5.1: Indigenous Sovereignty, Ideal Types, and Their Relation to One Another

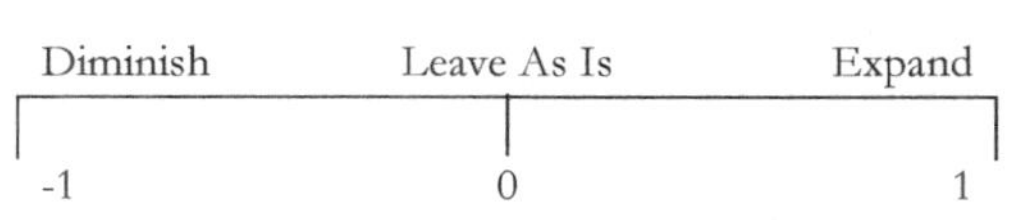

For our purposes, it is only necessary to draw one continuum based on the Court decisions from 1972 to 2005 testing for the presence of factors related to states' rights, also known as the Canons of Destruction. Again, it is instructive to take a lesson from case study legal scholars and explore some of the cases as miniature case studies. In this sense, we will now delve into four ideal type cases. Our most infamous case diminishes sovereignty. The Oliphant case held that Indigenous systems of justice are not adequate to incarcerate and prosecute non-Indian offenders (Oliphant v. Suquamish Indian Tribe et al. 1978). Oliphant is an ideal type case of diminished sovereignty. Mille Lacs is offered as an ideal type on when Indigenous sovereignty is expanded consistent with the Canons of Construction (Minnesota v. Mille Lacs Band of Chippewa Indians 1999). Mille Lacs found that an Indigenous nation that reserves use of land ceded to the U.S. can, in fact, use that land! Sometimes, as in the case of Ramah, Indigenous sovereignty is left as found (Ramah Navajo School Board v. Bureau of Revenue 1982). In Ramah, it was decided that the State of New Mexico CANNOT tax business operations in Indian Country . . . something that was supposedly settled long before. But it would be dishonest to state that all cases on federal Indian law have something to do with sovereignty. Hence, Klamath is offered as a case where it is not clear that sovereignty is at stake. Rather, it appears that sharing documents between the Bureau of Indian Affairs (BIA) and various Indigenous nations is required (Department of the Interior v. Klamath Water Users Association 2001). This appears to be a bit of bickering over U.S. policies that might contradict one another. As a consequence, this case is an ideal type of unclear impact on sovereignty.

Oliphant—Ideally Diminished Indigenous Sovereignty

Probably one of the most remarkable features of the Rehnquist Court involves the turn away from the Marshall Model and toward the Canons of Destruction. Such a development was necessary because, given the Four Normative Assumptions within the Marshall Model, at least two had the potential to aid Indians from the perspective of the U.S. Time, and political correctness probably did away with U.S. domination and exclusive acquisition assumptions. Yet, occupancy and civilizing the Indian could potentially benefit Indians in the eyes of the U.S., especially if the first two assumptions are no longer openly acceptable to the public. A couple of factors allow the deterministic method to work in the Supreme Court regarding federal Indian law. The first factor is that no one on the court seems to care one way or the other how federal Indian law impacts the Indian condition with the exception of Rehnquist. Rehnquist's attention is the second factor; given his track record, it is safe to assume Rehnquist was not a fan of recognizing anything to improve the Indian condition. These two factors created a situation in which the premise for federal Indian law could be supplemented with stereotypes and inaccuracies and the conclusions could largely be predetermined by Rehnquist without any butting in from the other justices. A closer look at Oliphant will support the above argument.

The Oliphant case will spell out the manner in which accurate history is replaced by stereotypes and selective source citation in order to arrive at the predetermined outcome (Oliphant v. Suquamish Indian Tribe et al. 1978). While technically not a Rehnquist Court case, the opinion was written by Rehnquist in 1978, eight years before he became chief justice. Concerning federal Indian law, Oliphant is the source of the Rehnquist Court Canons of Destruction. Oliphant considers whether tribal courts have criminal jurisdiction over non-Indians. Selective treaty citations signed by the Choctaw during the forced removal era indicate that the Choctaw "wish" to have criminal jurisdiction of non-Indians granted by Congress, thereby, indicating that the argument offered by the respondent is inaccurate. In other words, one treaty signed during forced removal indicates that criminal jurisdiction does not emanate from retained Indigenous sovereignty. The analysis further cites Ex parte Kenyon holding that Indians do not have criminal jurisdiction over non-Indians, (Ex parte Kenyon 1878). The case was overturned but no mention of this fact subsequently surfaces in the opinion. Without clear rules, the analysis instead relies on the opinion of the Executive branch of 1834 (President Jackson) and the federal courts of the time (namely Judge Parker) as history indicating a lack of tribal criminal jurisdiction over non-Indians. The analysis then cites termination era congressional hearings indicating the same as Jackson and Parker in the 1830s. Interestingly, the analysis moves on to the Four Normative Assumptions mostly out of convenience.

Note the invocation of "common assumptions of those who drafted" treaties and legislation (Oliphant v. Suquamish Indian Tribe et al. 1978). Given the reliance on the era of removal (1830s), the general assumptions are U.S. domination, exclusive right to acquire, Indian right to occupy, and Indian improvement via civilizing. Yet, it is difficult for Rehnquist in this time period to openly refer to the Four Normative Assumptions and must, instead, rely on silence by the tribe as an acquiescence to tribal criminal jurisdiction over non-Indians. The backdrop of the silence is the reliance on the Four Normative Assumptions to implicitly guide the opinion. Some citations, however, rely on the U.S. domination norms but are cited in a fashion that obscures the normative assumptions. For example, the analysis relies on United States v. Rogers (The United States, Plaintiffs, v. William S. Rogers 1846) to explicitly state the U.S. domination Normative Assumption that Indian laws may remain so long as they do not diminish the power of the United States.

A final quote at length is necessary to understand the massive reliance on selective histories. Rehnquist finds comfort in the ability to rely on the "nature and circumstances" of a case apparently meaning that a justice should utilize the "common assumptions" of the era. What follows is the rationale for the extension of U.S. law. The regular text indicates the original citation as included in Oliphant. The **bold** text will highlight the text omitted in Oliphant and replaced with ellipses.

> **It is a case where, against an express exception in the law itself, that** law, by argument and inference only, **is sought to be extended** over aliens and strangers; over the members of a community separated by race [and], **by** tradition, **by the instincts of a free though savage life,** from the authority and power which seeks to impose upon them the restraints of an external and unknown code, **and to subject them to the responsibilities of civil conduct, according to rules and penalties of which they could have no previous warning;** which judges them by a standard made by others and not for them, **which takes no account of the conditions which should except them from its exactions, and makes no allowance for their inability to understand it.** It tries them, not by their peers, nor by the customs of their people, nor the law of their land, but by **superiors of** a different race, according to the law of a social state of which they have an imperfect conception, **and which is opposed to the traditions of their history, to the habits of their lives, to the strongest prejudices of their savage nature; one which measures the red man's revenge by the maxims of the white man's morality.** (Oliphant v. Suquamish Indian Tribe et al. 1978; Getches 2011, 506; Williams 2005, 97–114).

Here the analysis has nicely weaved in the Four Normative Assumptions. To be clear, it seems that Rehnquist believes that the U.S. should dominate, the U.S. has a right to acquire, Indians can stay on the land at the pleasure of the U.S., and that civilizing Indians with criminal law will possibly improve the Indian condition. The conclusion of the case is that Indians do not have criminal jurisdiction over non-Indians.

It is risky to delve too far into the mind of Rehnquist only because it would be far too easy to lose a sense of objectivity, a concern Rehnquist himself apparently had no trouble abandoning. As such, all that can be said about Rehnquist's self-interest is best exemplified by the sources he cites as history that impact the conclusion. His reliance on forced removal era presidential and court wisdom coupled with his yearning to utilize the "assumptions" of the day speak volumes of the Rehnquist mind. How history is misused clearly outlines the Four Normative Assumptions of the Supreme Court as the Canons of Destruction. Although Rehnquist is willing to not call Indians savages and inferior, he still is able to conjure up the rationale that rests on the assumption of Indian savagery and inferiority. As such, there is a direct match between the interests of Rehnquist and the conclusion of the Oliphant case. Indians should not be able to incarcerate whites. As stated at the outset, because logic is nonexistent in the reasoning of this case, it is useless to consider how the case should have turned out had the outcome not been predetermined.

Mille Lacs—Ideally Expanded Indigenous Sovereignty

Consider Minnesota, et al., petitioners v. Mille Lacs Band of Chippewa Indians et al. as an example of a federal Indian law court case that expands Indigenous sovereignty (Minnesota v. Mille Lacs Band of Chippewa Indians 1999). The majority holding covered five points:

1. Usufructuary rights to land ceded to the U.S. in the 1837 treaty remains with the Mille Lacs Tribe
2. The 1837 treaty failed to address usufructuary rights leaving them open to interpretation
3. The Court held that usufructuary rights were not terminated in the 1850 executive order
4. The 1855 treaty failed to address usufructuary rights and only dealt with the purchase of land by the federal government from the Mille Lacs Band
5. The 1858 admission of Minnesota to the U.S. as a state did not address usufructuary rights.

As a result, the Mille Lacs band retained the right to enjoy land they sold to the U.S. even though they did not occupy the land anymore. While this case is a rare exception, it does make the point and demonstrate what a typical court case expanding Indigenous sovereignty might look like.

Consider Rehnquist's dissenting opinion in contrast to the majority ruling: First, Rehnquist was satisfied that the 1850 executive order was a valid revocation of usufructuray rights. Secondly, he argued that the 1855 treaty was broad enough to terminate usufructuray rights. Finally, the 1858 admission of Minnesota as a state eliminated such rights (Minnesota v. Mille Lacs Band of Chippewa Indians 1999). Clearly, had dissenting justices had their way, a diminishment of Indigenous sovereignty would have been at hand.

Ramah and Leaving Sovereignty as It Is Found

A second case to consider is Ramah (Ramah Navajo School Board v. Bureau of Revenue 1982). There are two major points to consider: 1. The Navajo School Board and a construction company were not required to pay taxes to the State of New Mexico for gross receipts involving construction of a school for Navajo children and 2. Federal law preempted state law thereby exempting the Navajo Nation from paying state taxes.

Rehnquist authored a dissent on this case stating, "[the] . . . court accorded a dependent Indian tribal organization greater tax immunity than the court accorded the sovereignty of the United States . . ." (Ramah Navajo School Board v. Bureau of Revenue 1982). Notice how Rehnquist discusses Navajo Nation as a "dependent Indian tribal organization." While disrespectful, the comment is also a denial of any Indigenous sovereignty whatsoever. I guess we should be happy he capitalized the word Indian. Federal Indian law at the time of the court ruling (1982) held that federal law does trump state law and that allows for Indigenous nations to be exempt from state taxation. Once again, had Rehnquist and company had their way, the tribal sovereignty of the era would have been diminished. As it stands, the case outcome preserved the sovereignty of tribes which already existed prior to the case decision. Given the above rationale, the Ramah case was designated as a "Leave As Is" outcome in relation to Indigenous sovereignty.

Domestic Bickering? When U.S. Institutions Fight Over Indian Individuals

Finally, the unclear ideal type example comes from Klamath (Department of the Interior v. Klamath Water Users Association 2001). This case was categorized as unclear because of the twists and turns it takes. First, Klamath sued to gain access to information about water allocation. The BIA did not want to disclose water allocation data supplied to them by various tribes. The holding was that the BIA must disclose documents because the transmission of data from tribe to agency was not intra- or inter-agency transmission. Is this decision a clear diminishment of Indigenous sovereignty, a preservation of that which already existed, or does it have nothing to do with sovereignty at all? The answer depends on one's perspective: Based on the assumption that economic interest trumps other interests, one might assume that the case left Indigenous sovereignty as found. On the other hand, evidence suggests, at the very least, that tribes do not always conform with the rules of "rational" economic thinking. As such, what if the documents outlined sacred knowledge or secret places? Given that these concerns are not satisfactorily addressed by the case outcome, the safest bet is to call this case "unclear" on Indigenous sovereignty.

Concluding Remarks

The Four Normative Assumptions underlying many Court cases are largely at work in deterministic cases. Although the outcome may be the same in many types of cases, it is still interesting to understand the manner in which enemies of the Indigenous sovereignty still exist in a supposedly contemporary and enlightened world. To the credit of the Marshall era court, as exemplified by M'Intosh, it was rather clear that the Four Normative Assumptions were at work driving the opinion. At least the presence of the assumptions was clearer than in future Supreme Court decisions. Separating the two highlights was the connection that deterministic cases have with the modern conservative Court. While more open-minded people may have long abandoned the need to dominate Indian peoples and to steal their land, there are still those in the world that harken back to a time when Indians were considered to be savage, inferior beasts, infidels who should thank Europeans for the privilege of holocaust, Christianity, democracy, slavery, capitalism, pollution, racism, assimilation, and all the other values underlying the American ethic. These are the Canons of Destruction and they are alive and well in the Court today. The most troubling notion is that those who hold the Four Normative Assumptions close to heart are the most powerful people in control of Indian policy. We can take comfort in our ability as scholars to point out their racist views as unacceptable then, now, and forevermore. Still, part of our responsibility is pointing out how this destruction process continues on in the late 20th century. We now turn to holding the Court responsible for its Canons of Destruction.

Chapter 6
The Rehnquist Legacy 1972–2005

It's one thing to take my word that Rehnquist has carried out his Canon of Destruction by way of unofficial, yet observable, judicial termination policy. It would be quite another thing to see the evidence for yourself. This chapter is a quantitative test of 45 cases heard during Rehnquist's tenure on the Court from 1976 to 2005. This chapter should serve as a model for carrying out small n research on Indigenous sovereignty in the 21st century. Small n research means that the number of cases is too high to be considered case study while too low to meet the assumptions of statistical analysis. Obviously, when you conduct research as in this chapter, some of the details are lost in the analysis. But that's okay. We need to start thinking about research as a Google map search. If we zoom out we can see a pattern. If we zoom in too close, all we see are the details. If we zoom halfway between "too far" and "too close" we see other details. All of these maps are "correct" representations of reality. I would never argue that case study research is any better than other types of research. I would much rather push for an inclusion and linking of case study and quantitative research focusing on tens of thousands of cases with research like small n research with only 45 cases. As the research unfolds in this chapter, I will point out how it can be tied to case study research.

Advocates of Indigenous sovereignty must be aware of the lies perpetrated on our tribal leaders with statistical analysis that washes us out of existence. We can't simply ignore the fact that, at times, junk science has been used to write about us with no benefit for our communities. Still, the nature of Indigenous studies research remains largely case study driven with little attention paid to small n and large n research. I often plead with students at Northern Arizona University to take courses on all ranges of research so that they can see the lies before they are carrying out damage in our Indigenous communities and beyond. We need to be as transparent as possible with our own assumptions as well as be trained to see the assumptions in other research. But that raises another question. Just what are MY assumptions? I've often teased elders and young Indigenous students that I make assumptions for a living. They all seem to giggle under their breath perhaps shocked that I would admit how idiotic I can be. But I think the lesson from this is that I make mistakes just as much as the next guy. While I have done my best to lay out all my assumptions, I'm sure I missed some. Again, this is another lesson for our Indigenous youth to learn now. Be clear and transparent with your research and if you make a mistake just own it and correct as necessary.

Federal Indian law and the U.S. Supreme Court are venues where the luxury of ignorance can be a source of fodder for undermining Indigenous sovereignty. This ignorance can often lead to a convenient diminishment of sovereignty. Chapters 4 and 5 offer several examples of the deep-seated level of willful ignorance in Supreme Court justices toward Indigenous nations.[7] When the Court diminishes sovereignty, citizens and leaders of Indigenous nations do not laugh. For scholars of Indigenous nation governance and Indigenous nation building, it is clear that a history of interaction with the United States presumes that Indigenous nations are sovereigns that pre-exist the U.S. constitution as well as the U.S. as a sovereign.[8] These details are outlined in Chapter 1. Regardless, states' rights advocates continue to assume away Indigenous sovereignty as a form of affirmative action. When the Court diminishes

7. Getches, David H. "Beyond Indian Law: The Rehnquist Court's Pursuit of States' Rights, Color-Blind Justice and Mainstream Values," *Minnesota Law Review* 86 (2001): 267–362. According to Getches, "The Court ignores precedent, construing statutes, treaties, and the Constitution liberally to reach results that comport with a majority of the Justices' attitudes about federalism, minority rights, and protection of mainstream values." This is a form of willful ignorance, a luxury that the Supreme Court may assume at will, that can only be afforded if the general public lacks interest in Indian Law case outcomes. See Williams Jr., Robert A. *Like a Loaded Weapon: The Rehnquist Court, Legal Rights, and the Legal History of Racism in America*, Minneapolis, University of Minnesota Press, 2005, for more information on the use of Native American stereotypes as sound premises for court opinions. Also see Williams Jr., Robert A. *Savage Anxieties: The Invention of Western Civilization,* New York, Palgrave Macmillan, 2012. for a lengthy discussion on "fear" of the other, in this case the Native American other, in the intellectual history of the West. My research here complements what many other critical race theorists have demonstrated in single case study descriptive research.

8. See Vine Deloria Jr, and David Wilkins. *Tribes, Treaties, and Constitutional Tribulations,* (Austin: University of Texas Press, 1999) for a lengthy discussion of the extra-constitutional nature of Indigenous nations. I argue that Indigenous nations belong within the literature on International Relations until around 1871 when treaty making, an instrument of international diplomacy, ceased to be carried out by the United States. See Getches, Wilkinson, Williams, and Fletcher, *Cases and Materials on Federal Indian Law 6th Edition* (St. Paul, MN: West, 2011).

sovereignty, Indigenous actors have few alternative options. This is a far from ideal scenario. Sadly, Indigenous actors lack a meaningful platform to object to the Court's judicial activism in a manner that encourages U.S. policy makers to address resulting problems. In this sense, the luxury of willful ignorance (the willingness to ignore facts as it suits individual needs), on the part of the Supreme Court, allows for an unchecked assault on sovereignty.

This chapter considers several questions related to the most recent and complete era of a single Supreme Court Justice, William Rehnquist. The scope should help guide conclusions about the power of a single justice in impacting Indigenous sovereignty. I will demonstrate how impactful Rehnquist was in diminishing Indigenous sovereignty from an institutional level. Legal scholars have offered valid case study evidence of judicial termination during the Rehnquist years; while their critics dismiss such claims as anecdotal (Johnson and Martinis 1995). The anaylsis in Chapter 6 bolsters arguments that, under Rehnquist, the Supreme Court did indeed carry out judicial termination under his Canons of Destruction approach to judicial activism. I present quantitative analyses demonstrating that deniers of judicial termination research are incorrect: Judicial termination is more than anecdotal evidence that a handful of cases were decided with unfortunate outcomes. The current consensus from the legal field is that the era of 1972 through 2005, during which 45 cases involving Indigenous sovereignty were decided, stands out because of blatant judicial attacks against sovereignty. My research design tests whether the Court ignored or was otherwise ignorant of precedent concerning Indigenous sovereignty to deliver opinions that would increase non-Indian control over Indigenous nations.

A Quantitative Test of the Supreme Court, 1972–2005—Beyond the Anecdotal Evidence

The U.S. Supreme Court exerts a powerful and inappropriate sway over federal Indian law (Getches 2011, 74–243; Williams 2005, 17–32). The cases decided by the U.S. Supreme Court during the Rehnquist years showcase an implicit hostility toward past decision norms and precedent. For example, states have taken advantage of vague treaty and federal statute language to deny Indian fishing rights (Johnson 1972). In Montana, an Indigenous nation that conveys land to non-Indians loses the right to use and occupy said land (Montana v. United States 1981). In all states, Indigenous nations are barred from bringing state officials accused of violating Indigenous rights into federal court (Idaho v. Coeur d'Alene Tribe of Idaho 1997). Legal scholars document, in great detail, a general pattern of diminishing Indigenous nation sovereignty (Getches 2011, 74–243; Williams 2005, 17–32). Still, skeptics may call previously published legal research into question.

U.S. policy makers have replaced missing or unknown premises in their decisions with stereotypes. The earliest Supreme Court decisions involved premises based on Indian savagery (Williams 2005, 33–45). Savagery served as a nice rationale for the U.S. to go to war with Indigenous nations (Getches 2011, 41–92), remove tribes (93–127), confine tribes to reservations (141–165), and allot what U.S. policy makers ultimately deemed "Indian Country" for the stated conclusion that these activities would improve the Indian by making them less savage (Williams 2005, 141–165). Evidence for European racial superiority is in early cases on federal Indian law and cited as contemporary international law of the era (Johnson and Graham's Lessee v. William M'Intosh 1823). Savagery as a premise within Supreme Court decisions continues to emerge involving plenary power of Indian nations (United States v. Kagama 1886). The legacy of savagery is evident in Crow Dog *United States v. Kagama 1886,* and the apparent need for U.S. interests to trump the Indian savagery for the good of the Indian (Williams 2005, 75–83). Language of savage Indians survives in the legal precedents of today in the form of *Tee-Hit-Ton v. United States, 1955,* and *Oliphant v. Suquamish, 1978.* The literature on the Supreme Court and federal Indian law appears to support the federal Indian law scholars. A systematic approach to Rehnquist era opinions may further convince the skeptic that there is evidence of judicial termination. This research will also reinforce what other critics on the Supreme Court opinions of federal Indian law and policy have argued for decades.

The best way to determine if a pattern of judicial termination exists is to comprehensively examine a plethora of Supreme Court decisions. Offered here is a systematic quantitative test of the impact (positive or negative) court opinions have on Indigenous nation sovereignty between 1972 and 2005. The analysis I present complements what legal scholars already believe to be true about the antagonism of the Court involving Indigenous nation sovereignty. Federal Indian law and policy scholars accuse the Court of doing what is best for the United States, while ignoring trust responsibility (Getches 2001). As a consequence, the term "judicial termination" has emerged as the current policy of the Supreme Court since many of the justices, either explicitly or implicitly, believe that Indians are better off being assimilated by force into the U.S. mainstream. This research lends support to those skeptical about the objectivity of the Supreme Court, to foster future institutional testing of the Supreme Court, and to spur a conversation about ways to resolve the Supreme Court's harmful impact on Indigenous nation sovereignty.

Research Design

In order to verify if a pattern of judicial termination exists, I collected Court opinions for 45 federal Indian law cases addressed by the Supreme Court between 1972 and 2005 into a data set.[9] There are two important aspects of the opinion under scrutiny: 1. Did a chief justice deliver or join an opinion? and 2. Did the case expand, leave as is, or diminish Indigenous nation sovereignty.[10] I used Qualitative Comparative Analysis (QCA) to examine the effects of the Court's decisions on Indigenous nation sovereignty. In QCA, qualitative data are examined for similarities and differences across observations (a unit of analysis) for the purpose of identifying conditions necessary for a given outcome to exist.[11] In this analysis, the conditions involve chief justice opinions as measured by Rehnquist opinions and the resulting relationship to the opinion's impact on Indigenous nation sovereignty (outcome). The 45 Court opinions were reviewed for evidence of their individual impact on Indigenous nation sovereignty. The Court's decision for each case was coded as having contributed to Indigenous nation sovereignty with the categories "expand," "leave as is," or "diminish." The characteristics of decisions falling in each category was established based on federal Indian law scholarship. Indigenous nation sovereignty can be impacted in one of four ways. Sovereignty is "expanded" when there is an increase in the relative level of sovereignty enjoyed by an Indigenous nation after the case has been decided rather than before. Sovereignty is "left neutral" if,

9. All cases can be located in Getches, Wilkinson, and Williams, *Cases and Materials on Federal Indian Law and Policy.*(St. Paul, MN, West, 2005). The original data set constructed by Michael Lerma is available at http://oak.ucc.nau.edu/ml572/publications.html. Feel free to build upon this data set if you believe it will serve a good purpose. The data set was built before Getches, Wilkinson, Williams, and Fletcher, *Cases and Materials* book was published. This nuance has no impact on this research because the time frame is 1972–2005.

10. Testing consistency and coverage across combined causal conditions is not possible. See (Bueno de Mesquita 2014, 482).

11. Charles C. Ragin and Claude Rubinson, "Comparative Methods," in *International Encyclopedia of Political Science*, ed Bertrand Badie, Dirk Berg-Schlosser, and Leonardo Morlino. (London: Sage, 2011), 331. See the following for a comprehensive discussion of various members of the comparative method family including QCA: Charles C. Ragin, *Redesigning Social Inquiry: Fuzzy Sets and Beyond* (Chicago: University of Chicago Press, 2008); Charles C. Ragin, "Set Relations in Social Research: Evaluating Their Consistency and Coverage," *Political Analysis* 14 (2006): 291–310; Charles C. Ragin, *Fuzzy-Set Social Science* (Chicago: University of Chicago Press, 2000); Charles C. Ragin, *The Comparative Method: Moving Beyond Qualitative and Quantitative Strategies* (Berkeley: University of California Press, 1987).

after the decision is rendered, there is no change in the level of Indigenous nation sovereignty. Sovereignty is "diminished" when it is decreased after an opinion is issued. And, finally, in some instances the impact is "unclear" when there is no clear-cut evidence of post-decision changes to Indigenous nation sovereignty.[12]

The history of federal Indian law is ripe with rulings and court opinions that inconsistently apply precedent impacting inherent Indigenous nation sovereignty (Getches 2011, 74–243). The act of judicial termination is best understood and analyzed in this study as instances of diminishing Indigenous nation sovereignty. A justice who consistently joins or delivers opinions that diminish Indigenous nation sovereignty is a justice carrying out judicial termination. The QCA analysis demonstrated the various (and often complex) relationships between the impact of a chief justice on sovereignty and judicial termination.[13] Several conditions were identified under which different patterns of judicial influence on Indigenous nation sovereignty occurred.

Indigenous Nation Sovereignty and the Supreme Court, 1972–2005

The original data presented here demonstrates how much impact a single institution, as measured through Rehnquist, can have on Indigenous nation sovereignty. I focus on this era because it is the most recent and diverse period in terms of data—45 cases pertaining to federal Indian law.[14]

12. It is certainly true that, in federal Indian law, cases may be simultaneously expansive and diminishing. In *U.S. v. Wheeler* (1978), for example, the court found that there were two sovereigns (United States and Navajo Nation) at work when criminal prosecution for a crime in Indian Country was being pursued. Hence, double jeopardy did not apply (435 U.S. 313 (1978)). While this case supported (left unchanged) Indigenous nation sovereignty, there were serious hints concerning the fragile nature of Indigenous nation sovereignty itself. There are two potential issues going on here. First, not allowing double jeopardy to have impact means that Indigenous nation sovereignty is intact yet this puts an individual in peril. On the other hand, many who wish to fight for individual rights will want to impede Indigenous nation sovereignty by having the Court prevent a second trial. For the purposes of this discussion, the impact in 1978 was is to leave sovereignty unchanged. It is beyond the scope of this research to reflect on future consequences of such decisions.

13. Fuzzy-Set/Qualitative Comparative Analysis 2.0. Department of Sociology, Tucson. Software can be downloaded here: http://www.u.arizona.edu/~cragin/fsQCA/software.shtml. Ragin, *Redesigning,* 13–20. Ragin. "Set Relations." Ragin, *Fuzzy,* Ragin, *Comparative.*

14. *Mescalero Apache Tribe v. Jones*, 411 U.S. 145 (1973), *Morton v. Mancari*, 417 U.S. 535 (1974), *United States v. Mazurie*, 419 U.S. 544 (1975), *Moe v. Salish & Kootenai Tribes*, 425 U.S. 463 (1976), *Bryan v. Itasca County*, 426 U.S. 373 (1976), *United States v. Antelope*, 430 U.S. 641 (1977), *Puyallup Tribe v. Washington Game Department*, 433 U.S. 165 (1977),

Further, legal scholars characterize the era as rampant with judicial activism in opposition to notions of Indigenous nation sovereignty (Getches 2001, xxxi–xiv; Getches 2011; Johnson and Martinis 1995; Williams 2005, 17–30). This research will analyze court opinion joining and authorship as "conditions" and investigate if the mere presence of joining or authorship can be tied to impact on Indigenous nation sovereignty. Case conditions involve a justice joining, delivering, or dissenting on an opinion. Ideally, these conditions should have nothing to do with a pattern of impact of Indigenous nation sovereignty.

The pattern of diminishing Indigenous nation sovereignty during this era is startling. Rehnquist was on the Supreme Court as an associate justice from 1972 to 1986, and later as chief justice until 2005. I used Getches, Wilkinson and Williams[15] as a source for federal Indian law

Oliphant v. Suquamish Indian Tribe, 435 U.S. 191 (1978), *United States v. Wheeler*, 435 U.S. 313 (1978), *Washington v. Confederated Tribes*, 447 U.S. 134 (1980), *White Mountain Apache Tribe v. Bracker*, 448 U.S. 136 (1980), *Central Machinery Company v. Arizona Tax Commission*, 448 U.S. 160 (1980), *Montana v. United States*, 450 U.S. 544 (1981), *Merrion v. Jicarilla Apache Tribe*, 455 U.S. 130 (1982), *Ramah Navajo School Board v. Bureau of Revenue*, 458 U.S. 832 (1982), *New Mexico v. Mescalero Apache Tribe*, 462 U.S. 324 (1983), *Rice v. Rehner*, 463 U.S. 713 (1983), *Three Affiliated Tribes v. Wold Engineering*, 467 U.S. 138 (1984), *National Farmers Union Insurance Companies v. Crow Tribe of Indians*, 468 U.S. 1315 (1984), *Kerr-McGee v. Navajo Tribe*, 471 U.S. 195 (1985), *Montana v. Blackfeet Tribe*, 471 U.S. 759 (1985), *California v. Cabazon Band of Mission Indians*, 480 U.S. 202 (1987), *Lyng v. Northwest Cemetery Protection Association*, 485 U.S. 439 (1988), *Cotton Petroleum Corporation v. New Mexico*, 490 U.S. 163 (1989), *Brendale v. Confederated Yakima Indian Nation*, 492 U.S. 408 (1989), *Employment Division, Oregon Department of Natural Resources v. Smith*, 494 U.S. 872 (1990), *Duro v. Reina*, 495 U.S. 676 (1990), *Oklahoma Tax Commission v. Citizen Band Potawatomi Tribe*, 498 U.S. 505 (1991), *Yakima v. Confederated Tribes*, 502 U.S. 251 (1992), *Oklahoma Tax Commission v. Sac & Fox Nation*, 508 U.S. 114 (1993), *South Dakota v. Bourland*, 508 U.S. 679 (1993), *Seminole Tribe of Florida v. Florida*, 517 U.S. 44 (1996), *Babbitt v. Youpee*, 519 U.S. 234 (1997), *Strate v. A-1 Contractors*, 520 U.S. 438 (1997), *Idaho v. Coeur d'Alene Tribe of Idaho*, 521 U.S. 261 (1997), *South Dakota v. Yankton Sioux Tribe*, 522 U.S. 329 (1998), *Alaska v. Native Village of Venetie*, 522 U.S. 520 (1998), *Montana v. Crow Tribe of Indians*, 523 U.S. 696 (1998), *Kiowa Tribe of Oklahoma v. Manufacturing Technologies, Inc.*, 523 U.S. 751 (1998), *Arizona Dept. of Revenue v. Blaze*, 526 U.S. 32 (1999), *Minnesota v. Mille Lacs Band of Chippewa Indians*, 526 U.S. 172 (1999), *El Paso Natural Gas Company v. Neztsosie*, 526 U.S. 473 (1999), *Amoco Production Co. v. Southern Ute Indian Tribe*, 526 U.S. 865 (1999), *Rice v. Cayetano*, 528 U.S. 495 (2000), *Department of the Interior v. Klamath Water Users Association*, No. 99–1871 (2001).

15. Getches, Wilkinson, and Williams, *Cases and Materials,* xxxi-xlv. The joined in part [which means a justice may have agreed with part of the opinion and may have written a separate dissent] and dissented in part [which means a justice may have disagreed with the opinion but also did not agree with a dissent] cases are categorized as "mixed" and are excluded from the overall analysis (*Washington v. Confederated Tribes* 1980; *Idaho v. Coeur d'Alene Tribe of Idaho* 1997). These cases represent 4.4 percent of all federal Indian law cases, which means that their arbitrary categorization into any of the four outcomes will have an almost unnoticeable effect on the quantitative outcomes. Since these cases are not included in the analysis, they have no effect on the interpretations and conclusions offered.

cases to analyze. Table 6.1 is a comprehensive list of the conditions and outcomes being tested in this research. Rehnquist authored 10 of the 45 opinions, and he joined in an additional 32 opinions. He dissented on four majority opinions, and he joined in part and dissented in part on two additional cases. (Table A provides all of the technical details about categories of conditions and outcomes.) Ideally, a justice merely joining or authoring a majority opinion in a case should not be linked to a specific outcome. In the case of Rehnquist, however, there is a pattern of negative impact when he joins or authors cases on federal Indian law.

Table 6.1. Condition and Outcome Codes Used in Qualitative Comparative Analysis of U.S. Supreme Court impact on Indigenous Nation Sovereignty, 1972–2005

Condition Variables	*Definitions of Condition Variables*
Delivered	A justice authors an opinion and other justices may join if they agree with the opinion. This article codes delivery of any dissent or majority opinion as delivered.
Join	A justice signs on to an opinion as it is written by another justice. Although a justice may join a majority opinion or a dissent, this article codes join as a justice who joins a majority opinion.
Dissent	A justice disagrees with a majority opinion and joins a dissenting opinion authored by another justice. Although a justice may join a majority opinion or a dissent, this article codes dissent as a justice who joins a dissenting opinion.
Join in Part or Dissent in Part	A justice may join in part meaning they agree with an opinion with the exception of some sections. This could lead to a justice responding in writing to an overall decision where a comprehensive and accompanying opinion is authored explaining the position of a single judge. Other justices may join.
Outcome Variables	*Definitions of Outcome Variables*
Expand	An opinion that enlarges the sovereign reach of an Indigenous nation.
Leave as is	An opinion that leaves Indigenous nation sovereignty as it was found. (There is no expansion or diminishment of Indigenous nation sovereignty).
Diminish	An opinion that decreases the level of sovereignty to be exercised by an Indigenous nation.
Unclear	An opinion that is not clear about its impact on Indigenous nation sovereignty. Are the opinions expanding, leaving as is, or diminishing sovereignty?

*The Supreme Court will not see their actions as linked to these outcomes. However, these are the definitions used throughout this chapter.

Figure 6.1 highlights the general layout of federal Indian law cases Rehnquist took part in deciding between 1972 and 2005. The outermost circle represents the 45 cases in question. The conditions tested by the analysis, whether or not Rehnquist joined or authored an opinion, are represented by the largest subset of 41 cases. Also, within the body of the 45 total cases, are 10 case opinions authored by Rehnquist. Rehnquist wrote 9 majority opinions and 1 dissenting opinion.[16] We may further examine details of case relationships to the role Rehnquist took in the decision as pertaining to Indigenous nation sovereignty (Figure 6.2).

16. Note: There are two cases that remain unclear to me. Collaboration with other scholars would illuminate if either of these cases diminished, expanded, or left neutral Indigenous nation sovereignty as it was found.

Figure 6.1: All Cases Heard with Rehnquist on the Bench 1972-2005

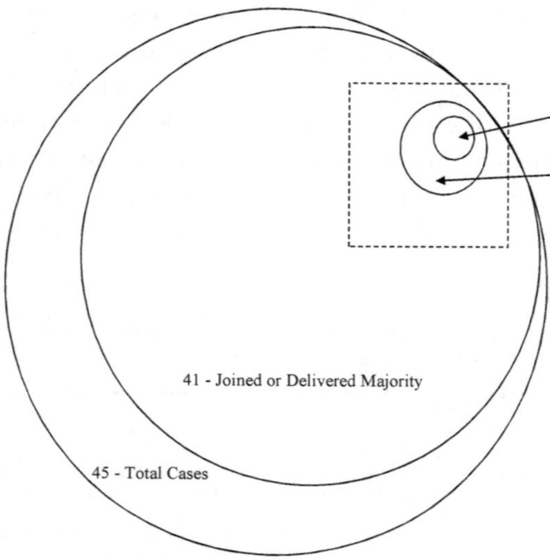

Figure 6.2: Exploded View of Figure 6.1

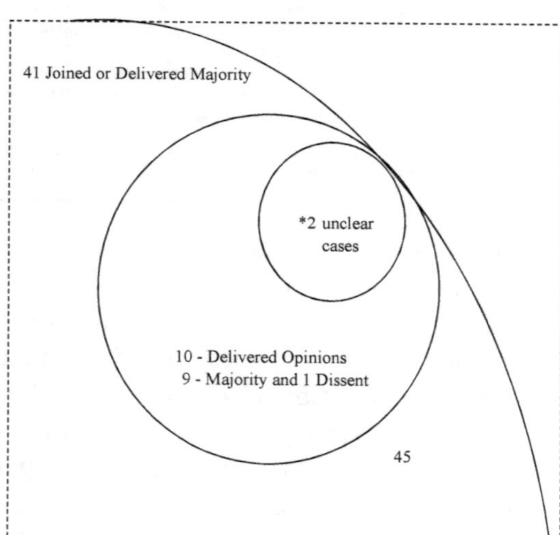

45 total = 10 delivered + 31 joined + 4 dissented
41 delivered or joined majority = 9 delivered majority + 32 joined only
10 delivered = 9 delivered and joined + 1 delivered and dissented
5 dissented = 1 delivered dissent + 4 joined dissent
* 2 mixed = joined in part and dissented in part on both - excluded from total count

Figure 6.2 focuses on the court case relationships in more detail. In other words, we can see the detailed relationship of cases authored, joined, and dissented by Rehnquist that involve Indigenous nation sovereignty. The overlapping circles indicate Rehnquist's pattern of action in authoring and/or joining an opinion on remaining aspects of Indigenous nation sovereignty at the time the case is decided.[17] It highlights Rehnquist writing nine majority opinions and joining 31 others over his tenure on the Court. In the single case where Rehnquist wrote a dissent, the Court expanded Indigenous nation sovereignty. It is also worth noting that there were four additional cases where Rehnquist joined a dissenting opinion. All relationships can also be expressed as follows:

$$45 \text{ total cases} = 10 \text{ delivered} + 31 \text{ joined} + 4 \text{ dissented}$$

The above equation details the makeup of the case outcomes and provides a wealth of information on the 1972–2005 period. Of the 45 cases in the data set, 10 were delivered by Rehnquist, 31 were joined by Rehnquist and 4 were dissented by Rehnquist. Other equations can be referenced in Figure 6.2. This information can now be linked as conditions that can change Indigenous nation sovereignty and outcomes in positive or negative ways.

Cause and Effect in Plain Sight

The pattern of judicial termination can be seen when we explore Supreme Court behavior as linked to the pattern of impact on Indigenous nation sovereignty. Scholars have long argued that justices intentionally disregard or are willfully ignorant of federal Indian law (Getches 2001; Wilkins 2008).[18] If justices are objective, then there should be no relationship between a mere authorship or joining of an opinion and an impact on remaining vestiges of

17. Note that the two mixed cases are not included in the overall analysis. One case is in the majority group, and one case is in the dissent group population. Perhaps a discussion of Youpee would illuminate this confusion: In this case the Department of the Interior Secretary challenged the finding of the United States Court of Appeals granting an Indian individual a judgment. This finding was based on the premise that an amended Indian Land Consolidation Act violated another act called the Just Compensation Clause of the 5th amendment. Hence, I cannot be sure if this actually expanded, left as was, or diminished Indigenous nation sovereignty. This decision could leave as was based on a court case falling outside the time frame for this study. Alternatively, this case could leave Indigenous nation sovereignty as it was found. But, again, this could fall into a time frame beyond the scope of this research. Hence, the safest thing to do is code this case as unclear and transparently declare that these types of cases are NOT included in the overall analysis.

18. Getches, "Beyond Indian Law," 267 discusses willful ignorance while Wilkins, "Disrespect" discusses privileged ignorance of federal Indian law.

Indigenous nation sovereignty. Testing this relationship requires us re-examining authorship and joining of majority opinions as conditions which might impact sovereignty. There are four conditions tested in this analysis to examine the impact that a chief justice has on the Court's decisions:

1. Did the chief justice author the opinion of the Court?
2. Did the chief justice join the opinion of the Court?
3. Did the chief justice dissent on the majority opinion?
4. Was Rehnquist chief justice at the time the court case outcome was decided?

If conditions one through four consistently appear with a particular Indigenous nation sovereignty outcome (expand, leave as is, or diminish), we have observable evidence of influence based on authorship or joining.[19] The act of a chief justice authoring or joining is not what should be influencing Indigenous nation sovereignty positively or negatively. Rather, these decisions should be grounded in some reason beyond the action of a judge (Deloria and Wilkins 1999, 33). For now, I focus on analyzing the existing patterns of delivering or joining an opinion on Indigenous nation sovereignty.[20]

Indigenous Nation Sovereignty in the Supreme Court (1972–2005) and Qualitative Comparative Analysis [21]

QCA was used to investigate any pattern of expansion or diminishment of Indigenous nation sovereignty through the U.S. Supreme Court opinions. Should this research highlight a systematic pattern of Indigenous nations losing sovereignty, this evidence would corroborate accusations of judicial termination. Recall, 45 cases were coded to represent one of four categories of outcomes: Cases that 1. Expanded, 2. Left as is, 3. Diminished, or 4. Mixed remaining Indigenous nation sovereignty (Ragin 2000, 2008).[22] This means that all of the

19. This pattern of impact (positive or negative) can be much more complex if multiple condition and outcome scenarios emerge. This area could be further explored in the "mixed" and "unclear" cases. They are prime candidates for in depth case study research due to the parsimonious explanation required to fully understand their impact on Indigenous nation sovereignty.

20. A more technically oriented way of stating the test focus is as follows: Considered here is whether the delivery or joining, delivery and dissent, delivered majority only, or delivered dissent only of an opinion has an impact on Indigenous nation sovereignty.

21. Tables A through H in the appendix detail the steps of the analysis leading up to the quantitative test of Rehnquist's impact on Indigenous nation sovereignty.

22. Ragin, *Redesigning*, 4–5; Ragin, *Fuzzy*, 113. A slippery slope of sort is often at work when an analyst has a vested interest in the outcome of the research product. In a methodological sleight of hand, it is easy to slip some of the order into the category of chance, thereby changing the outcome to one's desire. As such, one cannot really argue

past case study research on federal Indian law can be analyzed in the same manner, providing clear ties between past chief justices and patterns of Indigenous nation sovereign fluctuations (Ragin 2000, 20–25). Again, case study research that ties Rehnquist to judicial termination will be supported by this research because it looks at all cases and points to a pattern of judicial termination. This research will further bolster claims made by case study research and dismissed by skeptics as anecdotal (Ragin 2000, 23–25). QCA provides a mechanism for linking causation (who wrote or joined the opinion) with outcome (impact on Indigenous nation sovereignty) (45–63) in a manner not discussed in the extant literature (Ragin 2000, 20).

Two QCA operations are relevant to U.S. Supreme Court impact on Indigenous nation sovereignty—consistency and coverage. Consistency is a percentage related to the frequency of a given causal condition observed with a given outcome (Ragin 2000, 45–54). In other words, how consistently does a justice writing an opinion link with a particular Indigenous nation sovereignty outcome (Table A). We might better understand the broader pattern if we explore the relationship between opportunities to write or join and the resultant impact on Indigenous nation sovereignty. If there is a clear tie between a justice delivering, joining or dissenting and an impact on sovereignty, we have demonstrated that an objective review of the facts may not be at work when drawing conclusions. This problem highlights a larger issue in federal Indian law and policy. It appears very little thought has been given to the consequences of policy outcomes. How many opportunities did Rehnquist have to impact sovereignty?

---

that foul play is at work if the argument is not of a sophisticated enough caliber to call the research design into question. The gap between order and chance, then, is filled with whatever the analyst feels like choosing. Such a charge is often lobbed at the Supreme Court for reasons covered by legal scholars but stated in different words. And even when the *Oliphant* v. *Suquamish* case discussed earlier, is objectively presented, analysts cry foul because *Oliphant* represents a shifting of order and chance in favor of concluding that the opinion is less than objective. Put differently, no one has quantitatively tested more than one federal Indian law case in search of bias until now. See King et al, *Designing Social Inquiry,* 59. See Ragin, *Redesigning,* 4–6.

Veristic models of quantitative research deal only with a relatively low number of cases when compared to statistical research. Given that federal Indian law is a subset of federal law, the population of cases has been severely limited meaning that statistical analysis is inappropriate. A versitic model will allow for analysis of fewer cases, and affords the researcher an opportunity to map every case in the data set. There is ample room to become well versed in cases under study allowing for a more qualitative approach to quantitative research. Some might call such an approach deterministic because the deep knowledge of the cases is often misconstrued as shifting the cases in a direction more in line with a predetermined outcome. Yet, with clear definitions of categories, publicly available data, and the utilization of standard mathematical calculations, the research is largely replicable by anyone who desires to do so. See Ragin 2008 pg. 23–26.

Rehnquist used 32 opportunities to join opinions and he used 19 of the 32 opportunities to diminish Indigenous nation sovereignty. Table 6.2 shows how consistently the causal conditions (delivered, joined, dissented, chief, and associate) are related to the Indigenous nation sovereignty impact outcomes (expand, leave as is, diminish, and unclear). These associations are measured for consistency and opinion coverage. In the example above, we know that Rehnquist had 32 opportunities to deliver, join, or dissent on an opinion. How consistently did he dissent leading to an outcome such as expand? The consistency score is based on a dichotomous breakdown of case categorization. Complementary to consistency is a coverage score which is the true measure of causal impact between condition and outcome. Again, in our example, we know that Rehnquist had 32 opportunities to impact sovereignty. After we discover a consistent pattern of, say, dissent and expand, we can then ask how many opinions reflect this pattern. This pattern is known as coverage. Coverage scores indicate how many cases exhibit a particular outcome. For example, a combination of conditions and outcomes that only covers 1 case is less useful than a combination that covers 26 cases. Coverage scores above 50% are considered reliable data to support conclusions that a causal relationship exists between a condition and an outcome.

Table 6.2: Analysis of Mutually Exclusive Necessary Conditions

		Expand		Leave As Is		Diminish		Unclear	
		consistency	coverage	consistency	coverage	consistency	coverage	consistency	coverage
	delivered	1.00	0.11	0.41	0.78	0.32	0.84	0.67	0.30
	joined	0.67	0.02	*0.84*	*0.45*	**0.94**	**0.68**	0.92	0.11
conditions	dissented	0.33	0.08	0.24	1.00	0.12	0.67	0.42	0.42
	chief	1.00	0.04	0.57	0.40	**0.73**	**0.71**	0.83	0.14
	associate	0.33	0.04	**0.76**	**0.62**	0.57	0.62	0.50	0.10
	total cases	1		17		23		4	

Assumptions

expand = (delivered) or (joined) or (dissented) or (chief) or (associate)
neutral = (delivered) or (joined) or (dissented) or (chief) or (associate)
diminish = (delivered) or (joined) or (dissented) or (chief) or (associate)
unclear = (delivered) or (joined) or (dissented) or (chief) or (associate)

Table 6.2 shows the results of QCA testing for all the possible relationships between conditions and outcomes outlined for the analysis. QCA protocol states that we cannot base our conclusions on relationships if the coverage score is below 50 percent (Ragin 2000, 45–63). A coverage score is a measure of how many cases fit the combination of conditions and outcomes. So if a condition (e.g. joined) is linked to an outcome (e.g. expand) but the number of cases that reflect this configuration are below 50 percent, the links are not viable to draw a conclusion. For example, where Rehnquist delivered the majority opinion (which means the justice joined by default), the expansion of Indigenous nation sovereignty occurred in less than 1% of Court decisions (Table 6.2).[23] Based on the results, we cannot conclude that Rehnquist was a fair and just mediator of federal Indian law over a broad spectrum of topics. To be technical, this relationship would be characterized as follows:

ASSOCIATE JUSTICE + CHIEF JUSTICE + JOIN = LEAVE AS IS

We now can point to some evidence that Rehnquist may have been a fair jurist. During his entire career on the bench, this analysis demonstrates that when he joined any opinion on federal Indian law, he would likely leave sovereignty as he found it. The coverage level is 45%, falling slightly below a minimum 50% level of significance. Note, however, that the consistency rate is at 84%. One might carefully conclude that there is something to the relationship beyond a coincidence but such a finding is tenuous at best. In plain language, there are not enough cases that cover this combination of conditions to draw strong conclusions. We cannot conclude that Rehnquist was at all neutral regarding remaining vestiges of Indigenous nation sovereignty.

Three conditional relationships of note (bolded on Table 6.2) are:

1. Justice Rehnquist Generally Agrees: Justice Rehnquist (Chief and Associate eras) Joins or Delivers AND diminished Indigenous nation sovereignty (In Table 6.2, this is the intersection of column "Diminish" and row "Joined").
2. Young Rehnquist Agrees: Rehnquist joins or delivers as an associate justice (1972–1986) AND leaves Indigenous nation sovereignty as is. (In Table 6.2, this is the intersection of column "Neutral" and row "Associate Justice").
3. Chief Rehnquist Agrees: Chief Justice Rehnquist Joins or Delivers AND diminished Indigenous nation sovereignty. (In Table 6.2, this is the intersection of column "Diminish" and row "Chief Justice").

The most powerful and startling conclusion to be drawn from this research is also no surprise to case study federal Indian law scholars. As U.S. Supreme Court Justice, where I combine his associate and chief years, Rehnquist took numerous opportunities afforded him to diminish Indigenous nation sovereignty. In equation form:

---

23. This event is a single case where tribal citizen hunting and fishing rights over land that was no longer a part of the Indigenous nation were acknowledged and respected. *Minnesota v. Mille Lacs Band of Chippewa Indians*, 526 U.S. 172 (1999).

ASSOCIATE + CHIEF + JOIN = DIMINISH

In technical terms, the joined/diminished Indigenous nation sovereignty relationship covers 68% of the cases in the data set. In other words, this is very strong evidence that Rehnquist, by putting pen to paper, ended up diminishing sovereignty during his career on the Court. The consistency of the relationship envelops a substantial 94% of the Supreme Court case outcomes. Almost all cases Rehnquist had a hand in diminished sovereignty and scholars can now look up each of these cases. This is one of the clearest examples of a U.S. Supreme Court Chief Justice (in this case Rehnquist) having tremendous termination-based and systematic causal impact on Court opinions above and beyond single case examples.[24] As such, this research supports the finding that there is simply too much unchecked institutional power in the hands of individuals completely separate from Indigenous nations. Supporting what previous research has argued, this result is the most compelling evidence available that the U.S. Supreme Court, as an institution of the federal government, has substantial authority to arbitrarily diminish the sovereignty of Indigenous nations and with few opportunities for remedial action.

Rehnquist's rank is related to his willingness to leave Indigenous nation sovereignty as he found it. As an associate justice, Indigenous nation sovereignty was left as found more than three-fourths of the time. The equation would be as follows:

ASSOCIATE JUSTICE + JOIN = LEAVE AS IS

Technically speaking, this relationship covered 62% of the cases in the data set. The combination of Rehnquist joining an opinion as a junior jurist should result in him leaving sovereignty as he found it. The rate of consistency is 77%. The coverage of cases is satisfactory to call this more than a coincidence. This means that there is an influence associated with the power of Chief Justice Burger that impacted Indigenous nation sovereignty outcomes while Rehnquist was an associate justice. Hence, this configuration deserves further attention as future research. For now, we can be confident that Rehnquist waited until he was the chief justice before venturing away from federal Indian law precedent. Again, this is powerful systematic evidence for what case study scholars have long argued: The era of judicial termination did not take place until after 1986.

24. It can also be inferred that Chief Justice Burger had a tremendous impact on federal Indian law and policy. Future research on the Burger Court would determine if any discernible pattern of impact exists on Indigenous nation sovereignty.

The third significant finding involves the relationship between Rehnquist's position as the chief justice and the outcome of diminished Indigenous nation sovereignty. Again, in formal terms:

CHIEF + JOIN = DIMINISH

As Chief Justice of the U.S. Supreme Court, Rehnquist had a hand in diminishing Indigenous nation sovereignty in 70% of cases. This is an alarming rate. His rank could have bolstered his confidence to haphazardly diminish sovereignty at every opportunity. This relationship represents the largest percentage of court cases in the current data set (23 out of 32 cases). Now scholars may look up these 23 cases as evidence of his judicial termination agenda. The relationship is observable in 73% of the cases.

When this result is interpreted in conjunction with Rehnquist leaving Indigenous nation sovereignty as found when he was an associate justice on the U.S. Supreme Court, it may suggest the influence of Chief Justice Burger on the Court during his term of office, although a study examining Burger's tenure would be required to substantiate this hypothesis. This lends even more support to the thesis that U.S. Supreme Court chief justices have tremendous unchecked sway over Indigenous nation sovereignty. Again, additional analysis of the total time other justices served on the bench would need to be carried out to confirm judicial impact on Indigenous nation sovereignty. These relationships deserve further investigation. Advocates for the maintenance and expansion of Indigenous nation sovereignty cannot prevent all cases from coming before the Supreme Court (Barnes 2013). Still, I offer this future strategy: Where possible, it may be prudent to prevent cases involving Indigenous nation sovereignty from coming before the Supreme Court. Since this is not always possible, exploring fiscally conservative approaches to sway the Court toward maintenance and expansion of Indigenous nation sovereignty could be key when these cases appear on the Supreme Court docket. In a climate where it is expedient to cut budgets, Indigenous nations may gain traction by agreeing to incur the costs associated with maintaining and expanding their sovereign reach.

Concluding Remarks

The results of this analysis supports what legal scholars have anecdotally argued for decades—that judicial termination, a serious threat to Indigenous sovereignty, has been carried out between 1972 and 2005.[25] The

25. Johnson and Martinis, "Chief Justice Rehnquist," 1. Rehnquist will only uphold Indigenous nation sovereignty to the extent that his rulings will not impact U.S. sovereignty.

analysis presented here has highlighted an astonishing pattern of diminishing Indigenous sovereignty from 1972 to 2005. The more nuanced analysis holds that Rehnquist, as an associate justice, left sovereignty as he found it. Later, as chief justice, Rehnquist diminished Indigenous sovereignty. His chief justice activity, however, made up for his associate justice activity. This analysis confirms what many scholars have attempted to demonstrate with case study research: After 1986, Rehnquist was nearly unstoppable as he pursued the extinguishing of any remaining vestiges of sovereignty.

Critics of federal Indian law may also find this research useful since the tests demonstrate that the U.S. Supreme Court's impact rises above levels of mere coincidence. The research also suggests that the influence of any chief justice on the outcome of Indian law cases is massive and unchecked. Future research could also look back to all cases starting with the Marshall Trilogy, the first federal Indian law cases to come before the Supreme Court. Perhaps more importantly, the research should be used to forecast the current Roberts Court outcomes and consider how to prevent further erosion of Indigenous sovereignty. Predetermined outcomes (outcomes that justices *feel* are okay for everyone including Indigenous actors) are consistent with what other scholars argue: Justices ignore precedent not consistent with their values (Getches 2001, 267). We can now definitely state that Rehnquist was prejudging federal Indian law cases so that "outcomes" diminished sovereignty. The research must be used to create forecast models on post-2005 outcomes so that future legal strategies may account for and mitigate predetermined outcomes if possible. If cases continue to be decided based on how a justice *feels* they ought to be decided, there is little hope that any future decisions could ever fully respect Indigenous nation sovereignty.

Whether it is willful ignorance or blatant disregard, our challenges as advocates for the maintenance and expansion of Indigenous sovereignty are immense (Getches 2001, 267). As Wilkins notes: "Roberts and Justice Antonin Scalia, in particular, display both a profound ignorance of Indigenous status and, more depressing, indicate a degree of rank disrespect and rudeness toward Indigenous nation businesses and governments that rival anything in American jurisprudential history." He goes on to write:

> The sarcastic tone . . . from the justices and the laughter they elicited on the bench and in the courtroom—though we do not know specifically who laughed—powerfully affirm that Native-owned corporations, the tribal nations these corporations

> operate on, and the federal rules and regulations governing such operations, are being accorded far less respect than [other non-Native individuals] displayed towards tribes more than a century and a half ago (Wilkins 2008).

Our challenges remain immense and the magnitude overwhelming. Our one virtue might be that we refuse to keep quiet about continued genocide. Yet, one of our biggest challenges is convincing a powerful minority elite that paths toward economic development rarely produce a quality of life improvement for citizens within Indian Country. There is a long overdue discussion about contemporary colonization that takes the form of "jobs, resource development, and efficiency."

Section III
Indigenous Resources, Colonial Wealth, Indian Dependency

The methods used to marginalize Indigenous nations are hiding in plain sight. So far we have revisited a narrative forgotten or buried in the confusion of the American myth. Next, we revisited the Courts and their codification of myth followed by the ethnic cleansing of the record where race is edited out of the narrative. Today, the greatest challenges to Indigenous sovereignty involve resources located in Indian Country. The wealth of the U.S. and all colonial actors in the Americas, was extracted from peoples with an inherent obligation to guard those resources or Indigenous peoples. Contemporary colonization rages on without mention of Aboriginal Title or states' rights. Our own Indigenous leaders may be culpable in "self-colonization."

The chapters in Section III involve the notion of economic liberalism in Indian Country. This phrase has probably never been written in conjunction with Indian Country economic development. Many activists and scholars, however, are talking about the lack of understanding that grossly misrepresents existing attempts to bring economic development to Indian Country with no discussion of economic liberalism. Chapter 7 begins this discussion by making an analogy between post-World War II Europe and Indian Country of the 1930s. The Marshall Plan was successfully carried out in Europe in the aftermath of World War II. Some would say that the war itself was convenient. War destroyed infrastructure during World War II. After peace was declared, the eviscerated European infrastructure was rebuilt. Many U.S. companies were paid to rebuild Europe after the war. This was the short-term benefit to the U.S. economy. But the architects of the Marshall Plan also understood that rebuilding European economies in a way that embeds those economies with the U.S. would make the rebuilding enhance the U.S. political economy for generations, or perhaps centuries. This same logic is applied to Indian Country in Chapter 7.

The ties between war, destruction, and rebuilding are explored in Chapter 7. It is quite convenient that the U.S. destroyed Indigenous ways of feeding themselves in the course of war with Indians. Traders also decimated animal populations and this also compromised the ability for Indigenous nations to feed themselves. This dependency was created by design. Had it not been for this dependency, how could Indigenous nations be expected to sign treaties under duress? With their economies decimated, the U.S. was forced to provide rations and other supplements to Indigenous nations. These provisions are observable in treaty articles contained in the massive treaty record. Any economic development that did take place in Indian Country can largely be tied to individual white men in border towns making their first million. As a consequence, any real economic development in Indian Country that could lift Indigenous citizens out of poverty is quickly quashed. These types of economic development are perceived as threats to the status quo border town local economic hegemons or the regional hegemons. Until these variables are directly addressed, there can never be economic development on the reservation. But Indigenous leaders themselves deserve some credit for this stasis.

Indigenous leaders deserve some blame for the lack of economic development in Indian Country. More importantly, however, institutional barriers present even greater hurdles to true economic development. Chapter 8 explores the variables that inhibit economic development in Indian Country. Namely, the main culprit in economic stasis in Indian Country is federal aid to Indigenous nations. There are simply too many strings attached to funding procedures. While this idea is not new, the application of selectorate theory to this process is very illuminating. The U.S. will never fund projects that do not, first and foremost, ensure that U.S. leaders and constituents benefit. Secondly, Indigenous leaders will never accept aid from the U.S. unless the Indigenous leaders also benefit. This means that Indigenous leaders are in a difficult position. They can either enrich themselves and their loyal supporters with aid or turn down the aid and not be returned to office. For the U.S., the situation is win-win. Hence, U.S. aid is actually purchasing a policy concession from Indian Country. When U.S. constituents like the purchase, they reelect the leaders that obtained the concession. When Indigenous leaders accept aid, they enrich themselves and their cronies by distributing contracts to preferred loyal followers. Everyone wins but the citizens of Indigenous nations.

The future of Indigenous nations is bright given these barriers. There are too many Indigenous nations to lose sight of this optimism. The key is coming together based on shared interests in renewable energy. The key to understanding the barriers to renewable energy are laid out in Section III. These barriers are immense but they are surmountable. The way to save the planet from environmental catastrophe has always been in the philosophies of Indigenous ties to homeland.

Chapter 7
Economic Liberalism and Sustainable Colonization[26]

One of the relatively neglected areas of Indigenous sovereignty involves questions of economic development. Most of the research on Indigenous nation building tends to focus on institutions such as writing or modifying constitutions (Lemont 2006). One of the areas recently coming into view is the economic development of gaming nations (Corntassel and Witmer 2008). There have also been some minimal discussions, but more so in communities, about green economic development. Many seem frustrated, and correctly so, by the level of bureaucracy that stymies many attempts at economic development in Indian Country.

Some have questioned this red tape stagnation as more than a mere coincidence (Holm 2005, 155–180). This chapter introduces the idea of economic liberalism as it applies to Indian Country. This idea was first introduced in Chapter 2 but is more heavily analyzed here. Similar to post-World War II rebuilding of Europe, we must begin thinking about Indigenous nations as the testing ground for the Marshall Plan that was carried out a century later (Bueno de Mesquita 2014, 386). Today we must confront the reality that the U.S. does not want any economic development to take place in Indian Country unless it feeds well within the regional and global economic hegemons. This chapter will introduce economic liberalism as it applies to Indian Country, examine recent research on Indigenous nation building that ignores economic liberalism problems, discuss cultural, political, and economic institutions in Indian Country as tools for contemporary economic development for the future, and showcase how gaming accidently benefited some communities in spite of U.S. efforts to curtail its impact through regulation. This chapter is meant to showcase how these institutional barriers are as tough as brick walls but they can be torn down if we strategize toward that goal. Only after current institutions are rebuilt to serve Indian Country can true economic development flourish.

26. Thanks to Sean Parson for saying this title out loud and allowing me to steal it.

Economic Liberalism in the 21st Century—Neo Colonialism?

Former Soviet bloc countries are currently going through the process of developing their own institutions for governance. Former colonies are dismantling the remnants of their past crowns and they are making mistakes in the process. Meanwhile, a relationship of unequal trade continues to be maintained by more powerful and established nation states. Emerging polities in recognition of "free trade" protocols are quite aware of the unequal trade practices and, hence, are building their domestic and international mechanisms for interaction to offset the unequal trading practices to the best of their ability. And while the majority of attention has gone to emerging third world nations, Indigenous nations will necessarily need to grapple with their own individual orientations towards one another, states (especially colonial actors), and towards the international political economy. Complicating matters will necessarily be the role that Indigenous institutions can play in international interaction. Yet, to ignore the future of global interaction is guaranteeing failure to have some control over one's Indigenous nation in the international community. If an Indigenous actor is deemed not relevant, there is no way that they can have much of an impact on the future interaction it has with other international actors.

Recall our discussion of economical liberalism assumptions from Chapter 3. States are rational unitary actors. International politics are hierarchical as opposed to anarchic. Hierarchy implies the presence of an actor that can enforce norms of conduct between states. Cooperation, not war, is the natural state of affairs between states. International affairs include issues of political economy (trade, organizations), not just security. Distribution of power is not as important as distribution of shared interests. These are the main normative assumptions of neoliberalism today (Richardson 2001). One consequence of these assumptions is that today Indigenous nations are under the thumb of neoliberalism. Colonial actors remain the dominant hegemonic power in proximity to Indigenous nations today. In the U.S., policy toward Indigenous nations may be confused (Holm 2005) but the rational outcome has been as outlined in Chapters 1 and 2. This rational approach has always been about imposing hierarchy upon Indigenous nations. Economic development is typically reserved for the benefit of colonial actor elites and perhaps colonial actor constituents (Mahoney 2010). Hence, the main objective, as outlined in Chapter 2, has always been to impose norms for assimilation in Indian Country. A glaring omission by most researchers has been the footnote mentality of the various trade and intercourse acts which, today, should be thought of as clear declarations that colonial actors and the U.S. wished to wrap up Indigenous nations within the U.S. political economy. This is the liberal definition of coerced cooperation. When Indigenous nations do not behave, they can easily be locked out of economic interaction until they do behave. Hence, the shared interests have less to do with cooperation than with the most powerful actor's interests. These assumptions have impacted all attempts for 20th century Indigenous nation building.

Indigenous Nation Building in the United States

Generalizing about contemporary reservation conditions is obviously difficult. There is so much diversity that generalizations must be carefully undertaken. One potential hurdle is that Indigenous nations continue to struggle with their perception by outsiders as trapped in history and this perception can obscure the assessment of current-day problems and solutions (*The State of the Native Nations Conditions under U.S. Policies of Self-Determination* 2007, xix). Colonial legacies that have set the stage for contemporary Indigenous nation building can be reviewed elsewhere if necessary (Jorgensen 2007, 55–77). Hence, with the assumption that an Indigenous nation is attempting to rebuild itself in the aftermath of colonial activity, many potential solutions have been visited and revisited by policy makers and theorists. Research on North American Indigenous nations (mostly focused on Indigenous nations within the United States) can be organized along at least three central themes: Indigenous philosophical institutions, political institutions, and economic institutions. The themes themselves are not strict categories. They will be used here to better organize the current research on Indigenous nation building.

Nation Building In Terms of Indigenous Philosophical Institutions

The most general (non-specific) research attempts to focus on Indigenous philosophy-based literature. The research primarily deals with traditional characteristics, political entanglements, and economic consequences of the political entanglements collectively. Perhaps as a consequence of the focus, such research is more broad and abstract relative to institutional or economic research. Examples for Indigenous philosophy-based research focus on reconciliation with pre-contact philosophy and contemporary issues (Champagne 2007, 9–24, 25–44, 66–106). A general theme involves pointing out the contradictions inherent in a given Indigenous philosophy as compared to a European political philosophy. Philosophical themes are supplemented with case study examples which may only fit in specific areas. Cases or examples will have less of a fit when trying to generalize the specific pattern to other Indigenous nation experiences. As recent research gets into more specific details, it has focused more on institutional and economic issues.

Indigenous Institutions and Nation Building

Political research involving Indigenous nation building has focused primarily on the United States followed by Canadian experiences. Once again, it is difficult to generalize about the level of attention given to traditional institutions of governance. In many ways, the focus has justifiably been a response to a given federal Indian policy. It should go without saying that Indigenous nation-building experiences have been impacted by federal policies directed at interaction between colonial actors and Indigenous nations. This area has been previously discussed in Chapter 2.

Since at least 1934, the proposed interaction process between the U.S. and Indigenous nations has revolved around some form of constitutional development. Experiments with written constitution (presidential/legislature) style governments for Indigenous nations have had very diverse impacts as evidenced by the history and aftermath of the Indian Reorganization Act (IRA) of 1934 (Lemont 2006, 49–106; Getches 2011). As a result, some argue that Indigenous nation building should continue with constitutional reform to resolve the issues left in the wake of colonial impact, as long as the match between culture and government is at least not contradictory and, at best, complementary to one another (Jorgensen 2007, 78–114; Cornell and Kalt 2000; Lemont 2006, 184–219).

Other advocates for constitutional reform focus on merging Indigenous tradition with contemporary challenges such as globalization (Lemont 2006, 11–34). Notwithstanding, constitutional discussions have also relied upon pre-contact Indigenous constitutions, which students of European philosophical thought may neglect or refuse to recognize as a legitimate constitutional government (Lemont 2006, 144–183). All research on Indigenous governance gets even more complicated when considering that no one definition of "constitution" currently exists. Indigenous nation policy-maker definitions and cross-cultural definitions make the term "constitution" subject to conceptual stretching (Sartori 1970). As a consequence, the challenges for constitutional reform within Indigenous nations remain an enormous undertaking (Lemont 2006, 252–332). One caveat is that constitutional reform should be addressed in pursuit of the best interests of a given constituency by Indigenous nation policy makers. Regardless of individual Indigenous nation policy makers and their inherent and explicit self-interest, all Indigenous nations must necessarily address their interaction with other Indigenous nations, with the U.S., and with other colonial actors.

The impact of varying institutions and their tug of war over current and future policy language must acknowledge the current situation between the United States and Indigenous nations. At the very least, Indigenous nations must interact with four governing institutions. As self-governing bodies,

Indigenous nations are domestic polities unto themselves and must begin to reconsider their international policy preferences and platforms. Secondly, Indigenous nations are constantly interacting with the U.S. federal government. Third, Indigenous nations are constantly interacting with neighboring U.S. states. And, finally, local or regional municipalities and counties become a factor (Wilkins 2007; Corntassel and Witmer 2008). Complicating matters are varying polities with co-existing policies which directly contradict one another. In other words, what may be technically legal in Indian Country may violate state or federal law and vice versa (Biolsi 2007, 100–204). To be certain, American Indians are today still subject to tribal, state, and national citizenship, which makes their benefits and obligations all the more tenuous to briefly and clearly explain (Wilkins 2007, 52–59). With these large issues in the background, one can envision that a diversity of foci and proposed solutions currently exist.

The journey of policy switches by the federal government is a subset of the colonial legacy Indigenous nations must face and surmount to be successful on their own terms. From war to self-determination, the overly simplistic view has almost exclusively been that Indigenous nations are forced to interact with other polities (colonial actors) that refuse to see Native peoples as nothing more than "obstacles" or as a collective "problem" (Porter 2005, 185–186). A more simplistic way of putting it is that Indigenous nations have not been allowed to experience change on their own terms (Holm 2005, xi). For our purposes, it is necessary to revisit the most recent era of federal policy toward Indigenous nations. The details are covered in Chapter 2.[27] Briefly, the Era of Self-Determination has been characterized as the culmination of a pan-Indigenous revolt against termination policies (Getches 2011, 216–243). The results were the Indian Self-Determination and Education Assistance Act of 1975, the Indian Child Welfare Act of 1978, and the American Indian Religious Freedom Act of 1978, to just name a few (Wilkins 2007, 122). These U.S. Congressional acts, more or less, held the spirit of Indigenous nation building and rebuilding on terms set forth by Indigenous nations independent of non-Indigenous influence. In practice, the policies have proven less than ideal but are still an improvement over past federal policies geared as a fix to the "Indian problem" (Holm 2005, 14; Porter 2005, 186–187). The congressional activity of the 1970s opened the door for Indigenous nation policy makers and scholars to begin focusing on nation building and not merely nation preservation in political terms.

Many Indigenous nations today are attempting to reconcile their philosophies and world views to co-exist alongside the U.S. polity. Challenges

27. Some argue that forced federalism is the current Indian policy era.

remain daunting from various polities including state and municipal governments (Corntassel and Witmer 2008). Challenges aside, efforts have yielded links between traditional knowledge and contemporary Indigenous nation government. For example, the San Carlos Apache currently utilize an Elders Cultural Advisory Council so that traditional knowledge has a place in contemporary San Carlos Apache policy (*The State of the Native Nations Conditions under U.S. Policies of Self-Determination* 2007, 24). Also, Navajo Nation has made overt efforts to incorporate the Fundamental Laws of the *Diné* into their own branches of government (Council 2002). Diné Policy Institute, or DPI, was recently commissioned to address Navajo Nation government reform (Yazzie et al. 2008; Begay 2008). Unrelated to the reform question, the Navajo Nation voted to reduce its legislature from 88 to 24 (Begay 2009). The Navajo Nation Council further requested information on implementing Navajo philosophy into their current legislature (Yazzie et al. 2011). Some recommendations were later incorporated into the Council by the delegates (Smith 2011). The story continues on with various DPI research projects meant to incorporate Navajo philosophy into contemporary Navajo institutions of governance (DPI 2012).

Other issues of interest include restarting and expanding tribe to tribe interaction both politically and economically (*The State of the Native Nations Conditions under U.S. Policies of Self-Determination* 2007, 29). The challenges of incorporating Indigenous philosophy with contemporary tribal government have most overtly been addressed in terms of tribal constitutional revisions and amendments (Lemont 2006, 11–34). This makes sense because many Indigenous nations currently work with a modified version of the Indian Reorganization Act (IRA) constitution they first adopted during the mid-1930s to 1940s. As laid out in the Act, tribes were given the option to vote for accepting or rejecting IRA provisions (Getches 2011, 187–199). New questions surrounding IRA constitutions and 21st century tribal governments are further explored in Chapter 8. For now, political restructuring cannot occur without addressing economic concerns.

The Economics of Indigenous Nation Building

Research on economics and Indigenous nations grants the least attention to the intersection of Indigenous philosophy and contemporary issues. A report by Diné Policy Institute on food sovereignty is currently exploring a centuries-long relationship between war, removal, assimilative practices, and contemporary bureaucratic red tape as it contributes to contemporary food desert conditions on Navajo Nation (Eldridge et al. 2014). This process is nothing new, yet, it may not be connected to contemporary U.S. war practices. Basically, a strategy of U.S. war making carried out today was perfected with Indigenous nations over the last two centuries. The U.S., and all colonial actors, carried out wars of genocide. Part of this genocidal process involves the destruction of Indigenous political economies. Hence, if an Indigenous nation cannot feed themselves, they cannot carry on a war with the U.S. and they are forced to surrender and be confined to a reservation. The U.S., recognizing this lack of ability to feed oneself and coupled with the fact that the U.S. wished to convert Indians into white farmers, supplemented the loss of the Indigenous political economy with rations (Holm 2005, 5). This was the first step in transforming the Indigenous political economy into an economy that feeds the border towns surrounding reservations today.

Next, the U.S. would typically assist with infrastructure in a way that, again, fostered an extraction process with Indigenous nations only. There is compelling research about the integration of Indigenous arts and crafts into the U.S. political economy (Lomawaima and McCarty 2006). In essence, the U.S. is tasked with valorizing wage-based economic activities because the U.S. can then extract tribute from the wage labor. Secondly, valorizing wage labor ensures that Indigenous individuals enter the wage labor market on terms most beneficial to employers and this means depressed wages. Third, this process is accompanied by boarding school education that de-valorizes sharing, enterprising, and otherwise creates an illegal or illicit economy within Indian Country (Peterson 2003). For Indigenous peoples, this means devalorizing clan-based relationships and responsibilities. With minds shaped appropriately by U.S.-style thinking as taught in mainstream schools, many Indigenous individuals see no chance for individual prosperity on reservations and self-relocate to urban centers for employment. These are the barriers that many at home in Indigenous nations face: no jobs, no healthy food, and plenty of red tape to undermine even the most ardent rebuilders of Indigenous political economies. This is why, in many ways, rebuilding Indigenous political economies is basically illegal for at least two reasons: 1. Rebuilding is already monopolized by a corporation or 2. The red tape is so immense that it cannot be surmounted (Regan 2014). This is the preferred outcome of economic liberalism.

Contemporary advocates for economic development on Indigenous nations fail to address economic liberalism and the assumptions inherent in having a subservient role to colonial actors. This misstep is a by-product of focusing too heavily on cases of red tape. When we do this, we miss the pattern across all Indigenous nations. The trends in Indian Country economies have been organized around the typical indices one might see in non-Indigenous community research. Comparative research indicates that unemployment rates continue to be higher among Indigenous communities than non-Indigenous communities in the U.S. (Wilkins 2007, 165–168). These comparatively lower employment rates are consistent with economic liberalism because U.S. border towns (towns in proximity to an Indigenous nation border) have greater priority in promoting economic development on the U.S. side. Typically, the only levels of economic development that are not squashed outright involve the extraction of resources in manners that 1. Potentially place laborers' health at risk, 2. Potentially create environmental disasters in terms of pollution or envi ronmental degradation, and 3. Bring raw materials to the U.S. political economy at rates below fair market value. This pattern goes back to the first days of contact with non-Indians.

The original extraction process involved gold but 20th century concerns revolved around oil. In the 1920s a massive oil deposit was discovered in Oklahoma on Indian reservations (Fixico 2013, 153). It is difficult to ignore the coincidence involving the discovery of natural resources in Indian Country and the strategy to create Indian Reorganization Act constitutions within a decade. This process of discovery and constitution writing would culminate in the 1970s when the U.S. was hungry for cheap finite resources. In 1975, tribal leaders came together in order to capitalize on this demand forming CERT or the Council of Energy Resource Tribes. CERT appears to have obtained the blessing of the U.S. government by virtue of funding. In 1980, CERT built up a 3.9 million-dollar budget. About 74% of the budget came from the U.S. The U.S., essentially, obtained cheap natural resources, including oil, for their contribution. For example, the largest strip mining operation in the late 1980s was managing to extract resources in the four corners region or Indian Country. Typically, the coal in Indian Country was purchased for far below fair market value. In 1989, resource extraction corporations were able to purchase coal for 20 cents per ton while the going rate was 6 dollars per ton (Fixcio 2013, 157–158). This brief analysis should give pause to those who claim CERT members were benefiting from their relationship with resource extraction companies. Was the U.S. paying CERT members to sell coal for dirt cheap? Still, this type of relationship is only possible if an Indigenous nation happens to have natural resources on their lands and will sell at a cheap price which implies environmental destruction.

Supposedly positive aspects of reservation economies involve better utilization of land, land consolidation, and land recovery in the face of allotment, termination, and self-determination policies (Wilkins 2007, 169–171; *The State of the Native Nations Conditions under U.S. Policies of Self-Determination* 2007, 93–110). Natural and agricultural resources (such as energy and timber) have also been a focus for some reservation leaders depending on their particular assets (Wilkins 2007, 180–188; *The State of the Native*

Nations Conditions under U.S. Policies of Self-Determination 2007, 159–176). Environmental issues also remain a concern, generally, as Indigenous nations continue to grapple with their experiences with the global political economy (*The State of the Native Nations Conditions under U.S. Policies of Self-Determination* 2007, 177–196). Additionally, tourism remains a vital pipeline for economic development for some reservation communities (Wilkins 2007, 188–190). One of the most ambitious treatments of contemporary Native North American governance looks at many examples of positive occurrences today (*The State of the Native Nations Conditions under U.S. Policies of Self-Determination* 2007). The text begins with many qualifications over the necessity with which readers accept the breadth of the subject matter at hand and its inherent diversity.

> "If there is a "message" to [Native nation building research] . . . , it is that Native nations, communities, and peoples are living real lives on the contemporary stage of our increasingly globalized world" (*The State of the Native Nations Conditions under U.S. Policies of Self-Determination* 2007, xix).

The diversity of topics covered includes social development (197–274), culture, arts, and media (275–318), and less commonly studied topics on Alaska Natives, Native Hawaiians, and Urban Indians (*The State of the Native Nations Conditions under U.S. Policies of Self-Determination* 2007, 319–376). Again, it is telling that there are no current economic development trajectories carried out in Indian Country that could be considered competitive with non-Indigenous enterprises, perhaps with the exception of gaming. Again, resource extraction on Indigenous nations can only happen when those resources are not as cheaply extracted or obtained elsewhere. As mentioned in Chapter 3, Indigenous leaders are completely enveloped within the U.S. economy forcing them to either sell their finite resources to the U.S. and corporate interests or allow economic stagnation to become depression. Tourism tends to offer "an experience" that the U.S. cannot provide. Additionally, cultural objects for sale to non-Indigenous collectors also do little to compete with non-Indigenous producers for now. Even gaming remains well embedded within the U.S. political economy.

The Impact of Gaming on Indigenous Nation Building

Economic research receiving the most recent treatment has primarily focused on issues surrounding the contemporary phenomena of gaming (*The State of the Native Nations Conditions under U.S. Policies of*

Self-Determination 2007, 145–158). In the late 1970s and early 1980s, some tribes (Seminole and Cabazon) began running gaming operations (Wilkins 2007, 173). State officials moved in to ban the practice but tribes cited the lack of jurisdiction most states have in Indian Country (Getches 2011, 709–715). In 1987, the U.S. Supreme Court upheld the legality of gaming in *California v. Cabazon.* Cabazon opined that states which authorized some form of gambling must also allow tribes to run gaming operations (Wilkins 2007, 173). It is telling that the case had two competing issues that could not co-exist. Cabazon successfully argued that they had an economic development interest in carrying out gaming. California argued that they wished to stop gaming because they did not want to have organized crime fester within their state. Ultimately, the Court declared that the interest Cabazon expressed was consistent with many congressional attempts to foster economic development in Indian Country. This economic development interest should trump state concerns about organized crime (California et al. v. Cabazon Band of Mission Indians et al. 1987, 1092). I believe both the U.S. and Indigenous nations sorely underestimated the magnitude of the coming economic shock and influx into Indigenous political economies with successful gaming enterprises.[28] However, both Indigenous nations and the U.S. recognized that gaming would create new funding. To their credit, the U.S. moved swiftly to quash the coming windfall about to befall Indian Country.

In 1988, the U.S. Congress passed the Indian Gaming Regulatory Act or IGRA (Wilkins 2007, 173). Note that this was a very fast 1 year turnaround. Identifying three classes of gaming, IGRA required Indigenous nations to negotiate a compact between themselves and the U.S. state that currently surrounds them (*Indian Gaming Regulatory Act* 1988). Congress, then, is openly ordering states to play a dangerous game of negotiating with subunits of the U.S. and this is an erosion of Indigenous sovereignty. "In compact negotiations since 1988, states have largely ignored historic, treaty-based relationships that Indigenous nations have had with the federal government" (Corntassel and Witmer 2008, 16). Congress did attempt to "regulate" the nature of gaming so that it 1. Allowed Indigenous nations to prosper economically, 2. Prevented organized crime, and 3. Ensured that Indigenous nations were the primary beneficiary from gaming operations (*Indian Gaming Regulatory Act* 1988, section 2702). One of the most controversial instruments of IGRA is the Tribal-State Compact. IGRA legislation provides, from my point of view, limited direction regarding the goals of compacts.

28. The term "shock" refers to Indigenous nations impacted by punctuated equilibrium, critical junctures and path dependency (Lerma 2014).

> (C) Any Tribal-State compact negotiated under subparagraph (A) may include provisions relating to—(i) the application of the criminal and civil laws and regulations of the Indian tribe or the State that are directly related to, and necessary for, the licensing and regulation of such activity; (ii) the allocation of criminal and civil jurisdiction between the State and the Indian tribe necessary for the enforcement of such laws and regulations; (iii) the assessment by the State of such activities in such amounts as are necessary to defray the costs of regulating such activity; (iv) taxation by the Indian tribe of such activity in amounts comparable to amounts assessed by the State for comparable activities; (v) remedies for breach of contract; (vi) standards for the operation of such activity and maintenance of the gaming facility, including licensing; and (vii) any other subjects that are directly related to the operation of gaming activities (*Indian Gaming Regulatory Act* 1988, section 2710 C)

Many scholars have suggested that states are taking advantage of the issues raised as important by Congress in IGRA to further erode Indigenous sovereignty.

IGRA letter((C)(iii)) on the amounts required to defray the costs of regulating gaming is key to potential abuses by state governments. It remains rather unclear whether the amount of revenue directed back to state governments is solely a function of the costs of regulating gaming. Two key issues should be on our minds. 1. To what extent does this regulation inhibit economic development in Indian Country and 2. How does stagnant economic development in Indian Country prevent competition for off-reservation economic enterprises such as border town economies? These questions do not get asked unless we are focused on the assumptions of economic liberalism. Indigenous leaders are wise to understand how the U.S. is now enforcing new norms of economic interaction by forcing Indigenous nations to negotiate compacts with states. As a more powerful actor among the hierarchy of nations, the U.S. would prefer a coerced method of cooperation among Indigenous actors and states. Again, readers should explore the multiple challenges to gaming elsewhere (Getches 2011, 715–726). When individual Indigenous actors fail to negotiate a compact, they are frozen out of the gaming business and, hence, do not get to "cooperate" in the political economy at all. When gaming does occur, it probably does not compete with other economic activities deemed important by the state. When gaming might compete with another municipal or state-based economy, we should expect any number of red tape-based attacks to prevent gaming as evidenced by the burgeoning state legislature activity to limit gaming (Corntassel and Witmer 2008, 46–55). Still, the gaming phenomena has never been as much of a windfall in reality as it is in the imaginations of many onlookers.

One of the most comprehensive studies of the gaming impact on reservation economies is the comparative research on the U.S. economy, reservation economies with gaming operations, and reservation economies with no gaming operations between 1990 and 2000. The findings suggest that all reservation income rose by 20 percent while the U.S. income rose by 11 percent (Taylor and Kalt 2005, i). Poverty rates among non-gaming areas dropped by seven percentage points, gaming areas dropped by ten percentage points and U.S. rates dropped by eight-tenths of a percentage point (Taylor and Kalt 2005, 6–19). Non gaming unemployment dropped by two and a half percentage points, gaming unemployment dropped by more than five percentage points and U.S. unemployment dropped by half a percent during the same 10-year period (Taylor and Kalt 2005, 20–27). As a result, the gaming phenomenon has had immense impact on Indigenous nations with gaming operations. However, gaming is just one aspect of economic development.

Independent of the gaming impact on Indigenous nation political economies is the general treatment of economic development in Indian Country. Some instances of economic development have been framed as a consequence of self-determination. Although a great deal of Indigenous nations continue to live under conditions of poverty, various examples of successes have been documented (Taylor and Kalt 2005, 28–39). After continued monitoring of conditions in Indian Country, the findings indicate some interesting patterns. After acknowledging the very serious constraints on development, it seems that at least three necessary conditions are present within successful Indian Country economic development: external opportunity, internal assets, and development strategy (Cornell and Kalt 1992, 3). The lens of economic liberalism might do a better job of contextualizing these necessary conditions.

External opportunity really means that the U.S. market, off the reservation, exists and is willing to pay for some resource or service. This could be a finite resource or perhaps a tourist opportunity. Again, it seems more attractive opportunities for the non-reservation populations co-exist with pricing the resources below fair market value. Internal assets have to do with infrastructure. If a community in Indian Country can extract the resource or house and tour the visitors, then there is a higher probability that the resource will be utilized. Finally, the development strategy is, again, a process where the resource can be accessed cheaply and sold to non-Indian communities. Now, typically, the assumption is that a given tribe won't know how to manage their resources consistent with the demands of economic liberalism. This means tribes will be advised to employ an expensive consultant, and the consultant will advise the tribe to hire a management company. The management company will come in and advise the tribe on how to extract the resource as cheaply as possible so that there is enough profit left for the managers, the companies that build the infrastructure, and for the non-Indian world to buy at a bargain. Whatever is left is divided up by the tribe and there probably won't be much left. The research cited does not say all of this but, again, the lens of economic liberalism does a better job of making these connections. As a consequence, Indigenous nations with institutions that look like neighboring county and state institutions just so happen to be the Indigenous nations in the best position to carry out self-colonization-style economic development.

Specifically regarding the notion of capable institutions, the research findings indicate that in the face of poor conditions on reservation lands (such as a lack of natural resources), the fact that governing institutions are similar to off-reservation institutions seems to promote sustained economic development (Cornell and Kalt 1992, 53–54). In other words, Cornell and Kalt argue that a "cultural match" between a contemporary culture of "good governance" and contemporary institutions of governance matter. This line of thinking is regurgitated several times in subsequent Indigenous nation-building research (Cornell and Kalt 1996, 18). Cultural match arguments are based on other Cornell and Kalt research, in which findings are incorrectly supported by statistical regression and qualitative comparative analysis methods (Cornell and Kalt 1995). This is a very subtle argument that if you have a "culture" within your tribal government for, basically, feeding the demands of the U.S. political economy "efficiently," then you will have economic development. As I understand it, this means if your tribe has 1. "Any" resource (that does not happen to compete with non-Indian resources), 2. You are willing to sell for dirt cheap, and 3. Manage the resource extraction in a way that keeps the costs down, you can have economic development too. Yet, the research on "capable institutions" is not as bulletproof as it is made out to be.

There are many problems with the misuse of methodology in the source research, which should have us call all of the findings on cultural match into question. The cases in support of the findings seem cherry-picked to reinforce the conclusions (Cornell and Kalt 2000). It is unclear why "strong executive" is used as the baseline for running statistical regression analysis.

Using "strong executive" as a baseline for regression implies that a strong executive government is necessarily a point of governmental mediocrity and can only be improved upon. Such a leap of faith requires a built-in normative assumption that has not been made explicit by the researchers (Ragin 2008, 20–23). Furthermore, the levels of significance must be extrapolated from the data in a way that seems to obscure the research premises. Regardless, the data is not showing any levels of significance traditionally accepted by statisticians (Cornell and Kalt 2000, 461). In other words, the data is not statistically related to cultural match and institutions, hence, we should reject the null hypothesis that institutions matter. At the very least, we can conclude that the economic research is still up for debate. Nevertheless, the policies that Indigenous nations choose to restructure go a long way toward explaining what is working and not working in Indian Country. So maybe institutions do not matter? Regardless, there is a better explanatory model that can properly situate why Tribal leaders may have little choice in the matter of taking new trajectories toward economic development.

Chapter 8
Misplaced Blame? Institutionally Captured Indigenous Leaders

For all of the discussion behind economic liberalism, many still believe that Indigenous leaders should just simply stop playing games with non-Indigenous governments. Hopefully, readers have a greater appreciation for why this "halt" strategy is not going to work. The U.S. may unilaterally plunge any Indigenous nation into depression but it won't so long as the resources stay flowing cheaply. So we can't really blame Indigenous leaders for this. Still, we can blame Indigenous leaders for having their taste of the spoils in continuing to embed themselves and Indigenous citizens within the U.S. political economy. This chapter will not single out a particular Indigenous leader. Certainly there are a multitude of great leaders in Indian Country and just as everywhere else in the world there are bad leaders. Rather, this chapter was written to inform readers about the inherent losing bet we place when we endeavor to seek office and change the world in our home communities. It's not that easy and here is why.

This idea of captured Indigenous leaders will be explained as a function of selectorate theory holding that a set of variables in Indian Country can be fine-tuned to further exploit Indigenous nations. This process works by considering leaders and constituents in the U.S. and in Indigenous nations. This chapter assumes that all leaders wish to remain in office. Hence, leaders, and their winning coalitions, work together to reward themselves and maintain their status quo, namely, economic stagnation. This chapter will explain why Indigenous leaders are unwilling to fully engage economic development on terms that actually serve Indigenous constituencies.

Relationships and Foreign Aid Analysis

The first step toward understanding co-opted leadership is to rethink how federal funding for Indigenous nations is labeled. We should re-examine the impact federal funding as FOREIGN AID has on most nations, including

Indigenous nations. There is no reason to call federal funding to Indigenous nations anything other than foreign aid. Bueno de Mesquita defines foreign aid as "[a]ssistance given by one country or organization to another country, ostensibly to improve conditions in the recipient state" (Bueno de Mesquita 2014, 528). My point of view is that U.S. federal funding to Indigenous nations based on treaties and the federal Trust Doctrine is not any different than foreign aid. Readers may explore this debate on their own (Wilkins and Stark 2011, 104–111).

We must next understand some simple variables for the nations involved.

Indigenous Nations:

- Leaders of Indigenous Nations (LIN)
- Constituents of Indigenous Nations (CIN)

Colonial Actor Nations:

- Colonial Actor Leaders (CAL)
- Colonial Actor Constituents (CAC)

One strategic approach for international interaction is called the selectorate theory (Bueno de Mesquita 2014, 64–95). Selectorate theory identifies the manner in which developing nations interact with more powerful nations. This theory showcases some striking explanatory power when applied to Indigenous nations. All nations have some form of selectorate. The selectorate are the population that has some sway over leadership selection. Any group of individuals qualified to select a leader are members of the selectorate. For Indigenous nations, any person eligible to vote for Indigenous leaders is a member of the selectorate population. In the U.S., if you can vote, you are also a member of the U.S. selectorate. Put simply, the selectorate are non-essential and replaceable members of the population. If one member of the selectorate defects from a leader, that member can be replaced with another voter.

Within the population of the selectorate are members of the winning coalition. The winning coalition is a subset of the selectorate. The winning coalition members are the individuals who select the next leader of a nation. For example, if you voted for Barack Obama in the 2012 U.S. election, you are a member of the U.S. winning coalition. (If you voted for John McCain, you are a member of the selectorate but not a member of the winning coalition.) Loyalty from the winning coalition is essential during an election period. The size of the winning coalition determines the strategy by which loyalty is maintained. Size also informs the level of democracy or dictatorship a particular nation experiences. Figure 8.1 is a two-dimensional model of selectorate theory.

Figure 8.1: Selectorate Theory: Large Selectorate and Winning Coalitions Denotes a More Democratic Regime. Smaller Selectorate and Winning Coalitions Indicate Dictatorship. (Based on Bueno De Mesquita 2014, 64-95).

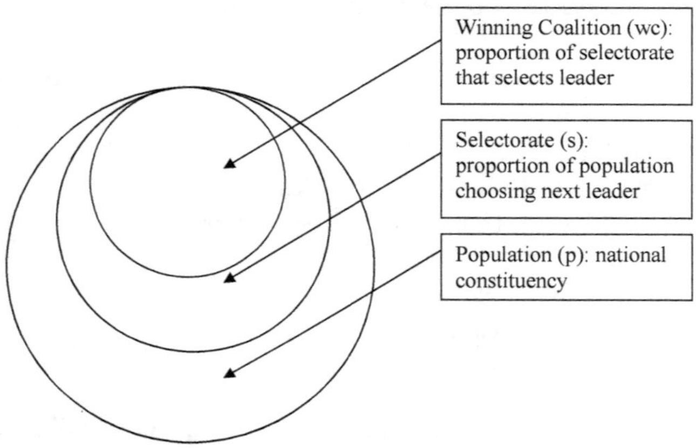

When a nation has a large winning coalition, the loyalty of the winning coalition can most effectively be maintained by providing public goods (Bueno de Mesquita 2014, 393). A public good is a good that is not exclusively distributed across citizens of a nation. Clean air, good roads, and clean water are examples of public goods. No matter if you voted for one party or another, your vote does not give you more or less access to air quality, road quality, and water quality. In other words, your vote for a particular candidate cannot be tied to access to a public good. Figure 8.1 is a visual representation of a nation with a large winning coalition. Some nations have small winning coalitions. Loyalty in a small winning coalition nation is a much different matter than loyalty in a large winning coalition nation.

A nation with a very small winning coalition may be a military junta or dictatorship. A leader can provide private goods to a handful of selectorate members if he or she only needs a handful to remain in power (Bueno de Mesquita 2014, 397). In a military junta, a leader may only need the consent of the military generals to remain in power. Some Indigenous nations appear to operate in this manner today. A leader with a small winning coalition maintains loyalty using private goods. Private goods are excludable resources delivered to members of the winning coalition exclusively. Examples of private goods may be contracts to build pollution-control devices to maintain clean air, contracts to build and maintain roads, and contracts to build water-delivery infrastructure and pollution-control devices to maintain clean water. Private goods can also be delivered via exclusive access to natural resources privileging members of the winning coalition. Private goods might involve price-setting for such natural resources. Private goods are excludable. Members of the selectorate in a small winning coalition nation could involve as few as 12 individuals (corporations included). Members loyal to the leadership are typically handsomely rewarded for their loyalty via private good delivery. Figure 8.2 depicts how a small winning coalition nation works. Hence, it is critical to accurately estimate the size of an Indigenous nation selectorate and winning coalition. The smaller the size of the winning coalition nation, the more likely the nation is susceptible to varying outside (international) influence in the form of foreign aid. Foreign aid compromises a small winning coalition nation's ability for recipient nations to economically develop in ways that actually serve the nations constituency. We should expect a small winning coalition nation with heavy foreign aid funding to serve the interests of the donor nations economic interests.

Figure 8.2: Selectorate Theory Showcasing a Small Selectorate and Winning Coalition. Loyalty of the Selectorate Must Be Maintained Using Private Goods, (Based on Bueno De Mesquita 2014).

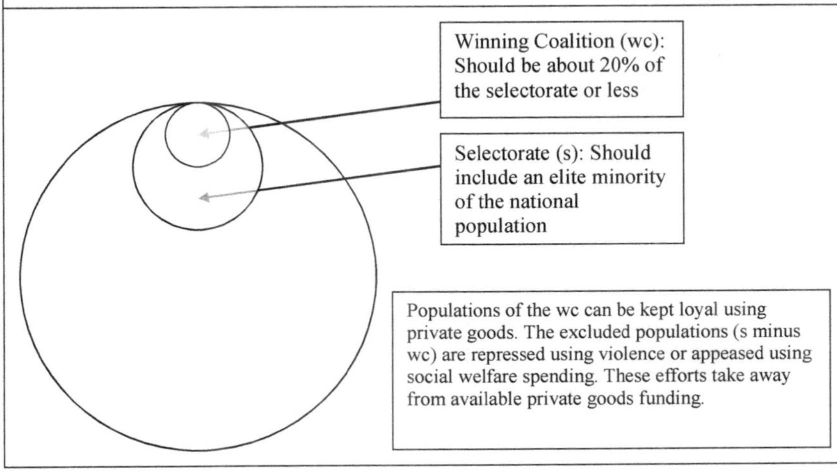

It is often said that "foreign aid comes with strings attached." But what does that really mean? How does the impact of foreign aid change the likelihood that a nation can carry out economic development on its own terms? More succinctly, does receipt of foreign aid compromise Indigenous nation leaders' ability to faithfully serve their constituents? Many leaders in Indian Country have complained that money from the U.S.

comes with so many regulations about spending that the money is not useful when it makes it to the local level. A recent report cited various problems inhibiting the "unlocking [of] wealth" in Indian Country citing the usual concerns: Energy resources are undeveloped, the federal government bureaucracy makes development difficult, and tribes lack enough controls over their own resources to develop properly (Regan 2014). Some have called these regulations just an unfortunate consequence of unstable federal policy towards Indians since 1871. Other scholars have argued that the indefinite trajectory has forced Indigenous nations to be subject to whims of the most recent liberal policy makers in Washington.

Others see a potentially sinister attempt to stymie economic development on Indigenous nations by putting some Indigenous civil liberties on "time out" status so the inept Indians will not harm themselves with too much individual freedom (Holm 2005, 171). There are more economic-based reasons to ensure Indigenous nations remain under or undeveloped. The contemporary interaction between the U.S. and Indigenous nations is one of international trade. Yet, when trade policy is too heavily influenced by the outside, the chances of building toward economic development on terms that serve Indigenous nation citizens are minimized. The U.S. government is contributing (per the Trust Doctrine) foreign aid to many, conceivably all, 566 Indigenous nations. Perhaps not coincidentally, many Indigenous nations have historically sold resources to U.S. corporations for under fair market value (Fixico 2013, 158). Many of the episodes noted in Chapter 2 revolve around natural resources. After treaty making ended in 1871, the original natural resource sought was the land. As is outlined in detail in Chapter 2, the original domestic U.S. policy for divesting Indigenous peoples of their lands was allotment.

Fixico (2012) offers a rich historical narrative complete with the stories of individual victims and victors of the allotment era (1871–1934). For our purposes, knowing the patterns is sufficient. Indigenous lands held in common by a collective (tribe) where thrown further into chaos as individuals received 160 acres of land, or less, and the so-called surplus was sold to non-Indians and corporate interests.[29] Many times, non-Indians would use various methods to cheat Indian individuals out of oil and gas extraction royalties tied to allotments. Other times, Indian individuals would cheat other Indians out of royalties and entitlements (Fixico 2012, 3–26). Perhaps the divisions created within Indigenous communities during the allotment era survive today in the form of contemporary divided communities. Note, however, that not all Indigenous nations underwent allotment. Still,

29. Osage ended up deviating from this norm but the same principle applies.

allotment might be the fuzzy era in which selectorate theory does not quite establish the shift from attachment to homeland, as expressed in Chapter 3, to contemporary (and often divisive) tribal government. For selectorate theory to work in explaining the allotment era, we must find concrete evidence that the U.S. 1. Contributed foreign aid to Indigenous leaders and 2. Obtained a policy concession from those leaders, such as their support for allotment. The U.S. leaders could benefit from this relationship if their opening up of Indigenous lands for non-Indian settlement could be translated into sustaining their leadership tenure. For U.S. constituents, the benefit was free or cheap Indian land or the resources on that land. An example of this operation may showcase how this operation might work. While it is only one case, it could point to a pattern or be an anomaly. Interestingly, the example will follow what selectorate theory predicts should occur.

Osage Nation: A Case for the Explanatory Power of Selectorate Theory

This case study will, hopefully, highlight the explanatory power of selectorate theory in Indian Country and the Osage Nation. Osage experiences with the U.S. do not ideally represent all aspects of selectorate theory and that is okay. It would be disingenuous to claim that selectorate theory explains all interaction. It does represent a great deal of the issues we often ignore in Indigenous relations with colonial actors and the U.S. Researchers are encouraged to apply selectorate theory to their Indigenous nations of interest as it may re-focus future policy strategies meant to maintain or bolster Indigenous sovereignty.

First, it is important to me that readers understand the dangers of carrying out research from afar. I will make no claim to know Osage people and I have never visited Osage country. The following research is primarily based on primary and secondary documents researched by Fixico (2012) and Burns (2004). The purpose of this section is to highlight the multitude of vulnerabilities inherent in contemporary Indigenous institutions of governance. Secondly, this section will highlight a typical pattern on how these vulnerabilities emerged. The focus of this entire book, and this chapter, involves institutions first and foremost. There are few mentions of individuals. When individual names appear, they are a part of the public record. I have no desire to learn new names of individuals not already in the public record. I have no desire to "blame" any individuals for the consequences of policy-based decisions long ago. I, most importantly, acknowledge that the following section may not be the only version of this story. There is always going to be dispute in these sensitive issues. Citizens of Osage Nation may not like what they read, however, I am only sharing what exists and is available to an outsider. This section is intended to showcase the explanatory power selectorate theory has for understanding Indigenous nations and nothing more. Hopefully, this section will serve as an example on how others might apply selectorate theory to any Indigenous nation.

The history of Osage colonization is complex. Having undergone occupation by various colonial actors, the U.S. ultimately envisioned Osage traditional homeland as a destination for many other removed Indigenous nations from the Southeast. There is a clear case to be made regarding U.S. policy-maker ignorance, arrogance or both. Contemporary Osage (and Indigenous) historians remind us of the U.S. assumptions inherent in their stance on how to resolve the appropriation of Osage homelands. The U.S. wanted to solve its "Indian problem" or the "Indian question." The most arrogant (and likely impossible) solution was to annihilate all Indians or commit genocide. Another solution was to confine Osage, and all other Indians, to reservations. As explained in previous chapters, these reservations could be located on undesirable lands completely removed from an Indigenous nation's traditional homeland. Alternatively (and as is the case with Osage) the reservation could be a diminished iteration of a nation's traditional homeland. This solution may combine both ignorance and arrogance. Some also talked of creating an "Indian state" in current-day Oklahoma (Burns 2004, 172–185). While there is little clarity on what such an Indian state might look like institutionally, it probably did not mean an equal state in the Union with equal representation in Congress. The fourth solution was to incorporate all Indians into U.S. society but, ignorantly, this solution sorely underestimated the very existence of Indigenous nationhood itself (Burns 2004; Holm, Pearson, and Chavis 2003; Lerma 2014; Lerma 2012; Lerma 2008). This section will briefly look at the intersecting and evolving interests of Osage citizens as they navigated conditions that provoked many policy changes from assembling a tribal government to addressing allotment. These conditions are the typical stresses experienced by many other Indigenous nations including war, land cessions, removal, and allotment questions.

In order to successfully use selectorate theory to explain the evolution of the Osage Tribal Government, we must brush over some seriously critical events between 1800 and 1920. Readers may refer to Burns on the *History of the Osage People* (2004). This section will only identify members of the selectorate within the Osage Nation. While Bueno De Mesquita, the author of selectorate theory, would typically highlight strategies to remaining in office, I will alternatively tie the theory to obtaining a specific policy, such as allotment and resource extraction, to the pursuit of factional policy preferences that transcend tribal government. The origin of the Osage chaos began when colonial actors carried out war and trade policies. The U.S. entered into seven treaties with the Osage between 1808 and 1839. These seven treaties mainly involved peace, commerce, non-Indian squatters, and land cessions (Burns 2004, 152–171).

After treaty making was no longer required, due to the destruction of the Osage political economy, the U.S. was able to forcibly remove Osage to even smaller portions of their traditional homeland between about 1864 and 1871 (Burns 2004, 314–334). At the risk of redundancy, all of these eras (treaty making, land cessions, removal) created the legal fiction of extinguishing Osage title to their traditional homeland as it was discovered by colonial actors. Interestingly, the Osage also signed a treaty with the Confederacy during the U.S. Civil War in 1861. One article of note mentions how Osage land will not be incorporated into a U.S. state or a Confederated States of America (Burns 2004, 261–263). The Civil War not only impacted many in battleground states, it also impacted Indigenous nations within those states including the Osage prompting a need for "Indian Reconstruction" (Burns 2004, 267–268). The reconstruction prompted the U.S. to reestablish an alliance but also took the opportunity to extinguish more Osage (Aboriginal) title.[30] The post-removal era prompted the Osage to, again, re-form a tribal government. As is always difficult, the re-formation of any tribal governments had to balance many interests, remain somewhat philosophically consistent with the particular Indigenous values, and also properly negotiate co-existence with the U.S., emerging state governments, and businessmen. In the case of the Osage, this task was nearly impossible (Burns 2004, 431).

Between about 1870 and 1875, the Osage were in a period of transition and, perhaps on the cusp of no longer existing as a people or a nation (Burns 2004, 335). Faced with removal and the push to convert the Osage from their cultural foundation to settled farmers and individuals, this transition period is likely the origin of contemporary factions in their government today. Demographically, the Osage population was estimated to be about 3,150 citizens (Burns 2004, 336–337). This demography brings in an uncomfortable label tossed around at the time as "matter

30. Even this notion of Aboriginal Title may not fit the Osage situation. Evidence suggests that the Osage reservation may have once been held in fee simple by the Osage. This was likely a result of the complexity of removing other tribes to Osage traditional homelands and then removing Osage from one location within their traditional homelands to another section within their traditional homelands first promised to other removed tribes. Even so, the deed to the Osage reserve is currently held in trust by the U.S. government despite requests and demands that the deed be handed over to Osage leaders of the era. See Burns 2004 345–346.

of fact" but, ultimately, founded in the racist attitudes of the West (Williams 2012). Census records of the time were intently interested in so called "full blood" and "mixed blood" Osage. Sadly, these racial categories would later develop into factions within nearly all tribal governments. I would prefer to use the term "traditional" meaning that an individual Osage adhered to an Osage philosophy of leadership. The full blood category likely (epiphenomenally) reflected this traditional perspective due to an immersion from birth into a home with Osage language, Osage sacred history, Osage ceremony, and Osage place (Holm 2003). While not all Osage "full bloods" were traditional, and not all traditional Osage were "full blood," I carefully offer this modification. I fully acknowledge that terms like "traditional" remain problematic. Western influences tended to impact the children of Osage and non-Osage interracial marriages (or mixed bloods). During this time period, then, the majority of the Osage population was traditional (or full blood) (Burns 2004, 337).

Efforts to start life anew after the removal process involved the creation (or more accurately the re-formation) of an Osage government. The traditional and non-traditional citizens were incorporated together into a 14-member council (Burns 2004, 337). This council is credited with arranging for the current-day Osage reserve, perhaps, to avoid the farming expected of them and to limit interaction with non-Osage. Non-interaction would be less disruptive of hunting practices that were, more or less, consistent with Osage traditional knowledge. We should expect, then, that non-traditional (mixed bloods) citizens were more inclined to be farmers consistent with the expectations set forth for them by the U.S. government. From the Western point of view, this idea that the non-traditional individuals (mixed bloods) were the bright future of the individual people was contrasted with the notion that the traditional folks were uncivilized barbarians and better off gone as soon as possible. During a time when the traditional Osage still had greater influence than the non-traditional leaders, the Osage were invited to join the so-called Five Civilized Tribes but declined as they did not wish to surrender any more autonomy to an international organization made up of other Indigenous nations with heavily compromised governing bodies (Burns 2004, 338). The balance between following traditional policies and appeasing U.S. interests would erode as more non-Osage influence crept into the Osage governing body.

While it is not possible to conclusively estimate the size of the traditional Osage selectorate, we could venture an educated guess that decentralized and consensus-based decision-making ruled the day. This would mean that of the more than 3,000 Osage citizens, probably every adult needed to agree to a policy in order for the nation to follow said policy. Nearly every resource (or good) the Osage worked to keep control over was essentially a public good. The introduction of private good access, through the non-traditional sect, likely trumped the collective public good perspective of the traditional leadership. Only a handful of non-traditional leaders could halt obtaining consensus among the adults to incapacitate the traditional approach to managing the reservation. Some of the earliest pressures to abandon the traditional ways involved the consequences of removing a people to a diminished portion of their traditional homeland while adding more people from other tribes to neighboring portions of the same homeland.

The war and treaty process essentially harmed the traditional Osage political economy and put more pressure on the natural resources (public goods). Non-Indian businessmen extracted resources and other removed tribes attempted to also survive in proximity to Osage people. It should be no surprise that economic stagnation led to more supposed Osage lawlessness when they attempted to feed themselves during harsh times (Burns 2004, 344–366). Like with many other Indigenous nations, these factors likely led to a crisis of traditional Osage leadership. Perhaps Osage selectorate questioned the traditional way of doing things and assumed they no longer worked. Perhaps the Osage creator had abandoned them and it was time for the non-traditional selectorate to take over. The non-traditional leaders would find great allies off the reservation.

Many Osage would begin to find their fortune with ranching. It would be overly simplistic to call this move a "non-traditional" approach. We can be certain that the ranching process was attractive to any Osage wishing to feed themselves and their families. In other words, ranching might be a transition from a public good to a private good. This transition is a slippery slope process. How much should each Osage extract from the land? How consistent would the extraction be with their traditional teachings about the Osage homeland? When non-Osage interests intersected with the need to eat, it became more and more difficult for individual Osage citizens to turn away from the attractive offers to ranch themselves or to lease their reservation lands to non-Osage ranching interests. Collective land rights were giving way to private good exclusive access to resources on the land. All of these factors conspired to further erode the Osage traditional teachings especially the notion of land as a public good for all members of the selectorate. Non-traditional-leaning Osage citizens could easily see their path toward prosperity in concert with non-Osage ranching interests, U.S. federal ambitions to civilize the Osage people. Their clear obstacle was the traditional Osage leaders (Burns 2004, 368–375). Figure 8.3 is a Venn diagram of the intersecting Osage interests emerging in the late 19th century.

Figure 8.3: Emerging Interest Groups on Osage Reservation

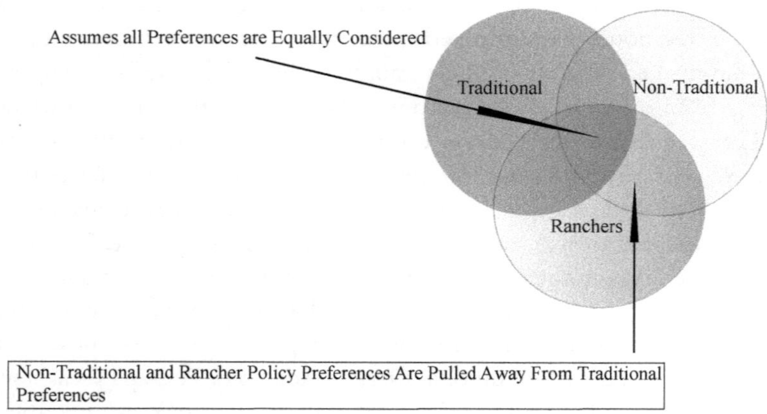

The traditional Osage continued to push for their policy preferences. Non-Osage ranchers and the Osage interested in pursuing ranching and leasing of land for non-Osage ranching collaborated to drag the actual ranching policy away from the preferences of the traditional citizens. Again, all this did for the domestic Osage leadership is pit citizens against one another.

There remains debate about the impact of writing a constitution on tribal government itself. There are several assumptions that should be mentioned here. I refuse to assume that Indigenous nations and the Osage, in particular, lacked a government prior to contact with colonial actors. Rather, I would argue that their ceremony cycle, language, sacred history, and land constituted a government at the very least while simultaneously constituting a comprehensive set of norms for living a good and long life. Other scholars are encouraged to re-examine evidence of Indigenous philosophy pertaining to specific Indigenous nations. I expect they may find much the same is true for those nations as it is for the Osage Nation.

Few scholars have, thus far, explored the impact of Indigenous nations writing a constitution in English. Although I call discussions about the impact of writing a constitution a "debate," I believe I am being generous. Rather, discussions continue to take place among interested parties and they correctly point out that much is lost in translation. While the majority of Indigenous English language constitutions came about in the 1930s and 1940s, Osage deviates from this trend by attempting to write constitutions in the 1860s. As I would surmise, other scholars correctly point out that there would be no need for a constitution during a time when a particular Indigenous nation had a functioning leadership protocol in place made up of traditional knowledge holders (Burns 2004, 390). From an Indigenous point of view, nearly every push for an Indigenous nation to write a constitution in English had a two-fold impact: It concentrated the Indigenous nations' power in the hands of fewer (perhaps even one) leaders and it coincided with the U.S. interest to have more impact on future domestic Indigenous policy making. In selectorate theory terms, constitution writing shrank the selectorate and the winning coalition creating a dictatorship that could be more easily controlled by the U.S by creating or expanding the reach of private goods control over natural resources.[31]

In 1881, the Osage Nation attempted to write a constitution for a second time. Some scholars appear content to call it an exercise of the Osage people. Closer inspection of the motives trace to traditional versus non-traditional factions in concert with the non-traditional shared interest with non-Osage for individual land rights, and thus leasing profits, related to grazing. This is a shifting of the land from a public good to a private good. By the early 1880s, the traditional mechanisms for dealing with crimes against an individual remained intact. However, the advent of individually held property rights complicated matters. Since individual property ownership (a private good) had not existed prior to the 1880s, there was a gap in the traditional methods for dealing with disagreements (Burns 2004, 391–392). If we could interview traditional Osage from the 1880s today, they would likely lament this move toward private property rights due to this problem of creating conflict about who has exclusive access to specific portions of land. This process confused the notion of land as either a public or a private good. We are wise to look back into the factions. As the non-traditional Osage gained vested interest in privately held land rights they yearned to create a government that could protect that privileged access.

Recall earlier my claim that traditional Osage norms may have demanded all land access should be held as a public good and based on some method of determining the needs of extended families. From the Western point of view the problem was simple. The traditional Osage "savages" were clinging to the past and the civilized Osage wished to move forward

31. Burns makes this same point by writing, "A dictatorship is not only cheaper than a democracy but it is more efficient." (2004, 393)

into the 20th century. Regardless, for a whole host of reasons that the U.S. government could not satisfy today, the Osage Constitution was set aside and Indian agents were tasked with appointing a Principal Chief and an Assistant Principal Chief citing a more efficient method for decision-making (Burns 2004, 393–394). This is as small a selectorate (an Indian agent) and a winning coalition (an Indian agent) that can possibly be constructed. That single Indian agent, then, would have massive authority over the distribution of land as a private good.

Soon, the question of allotment appeared on the horizon. Allotment is a selectorate theory scheme to assign private good access to land and export the access to non-Indians. U.S. interests were clearly impacting the creation of a government consisting of a Chief, Assistant Chief, and a Council. Elections were held and carefully supervised by the Bureau of Indian Affairs to ensure candidates who supported allotment would fill the newly created Osage government openings. The U.S. carefully promoted a winning coalition that would promote private goods access to land. This Osage government wrote the Osage Allotment Act of 1906. The language of the Act created a third government tasked with the distribution of mineral rights (private goods) from the allotment process (Burns 2004, 394). This same government of 1906 remains in place today (Burns 2004, 395). Then there is the question of citizens or the selectorate.

One of the tried-and-true methods of impacting the selectorate is declaring some individuals invalid and disenfranchising them. The horrific story of calling some people "full blood" and "mixed blood" has all sorts of implied racial connotations that need not be addressed here. In short, the factions in Osage government sought to protect their policy preferences (private goods access). While it was once the motives of the traditional folks to enfranchise the non-traditional individuals, it was the strategy of many non-traditional individuals to protect their self-interest by contesting the citizenship of many other Osage. All the while the traditional Osage deplored the fact that future financial windfalls were capitalized upon by a minority Osage elite (Fixico 2012, 32–35). As fate would have things, the financial windfalls were about to get lucrative.

In 1895 an oil boom was about to take place. This boom would, essentially, replace the need for the U.S. to provide foreign aid to Osage. In other words, while many Indigenous nations today are heavily embedded within the U.S. political economy based on foreign aid, the Osage would prove to be quite rewarding to the U.S. political economy without such aid. All that needed to be built were clear mechanisms that tied exclusive access to mineral rights for Osage citizens to resource extraction companies. Henry

Foster applied to the Secretary of the Interior for a lease over the entire Osage Reservation. The Principal Osage Chief signed off on the lease. This, essentially, would set up the population of Osage Nation for royalties should oil be profitably extracted. In 1895, there was no guarantee that any usable oil could be extracted. Edwin Foster inherited Henry's obligations upon his passing (Fixico 2012, 29–30). By 1900, several wells struck oil prompting more oil drills on and in the vicinity of the Osage reservation. By 1902, the wells were producing a great deal of oil, creating demand for more wells, producing more oil, etc. This also increased demand for the land itself to be owned by non-Indians and not leased from Osage citizens through the Secretary of the Interior. Prior to this, Oklahoma was still "Indian Territory" or a location designated as a potential concentration of tribes removed from other areas, especially the southeast U.S. However, the oil boom coupled with interest in the Oklahoma land for cattle grazing and farming, prompted local non-Indian politicians and businessmen to seek statehood for Oklahoma. Meanwhile, unscrupulous white men married Osage women, perhaps, to inherit the oil wealth (Fixico 2012 30–32).

Collectively, Osage people with non-Indian parents (mixed bloods) cooperated with businessmen to push for allotment in Oklahoma. Allotment, as readers will recall from Chapter 2, meant that all Indians would receive, at most, 160 acres as an individual land holding. This would then "free up" the surplus land that could be sold to non-Indians for resource extraction and farming. Again, these allotment schemes are shifting land from a public good to a private good. Traditional Osage citizens had deep concerns about allotment and believed the membership accounting, or "tribal rolls," containing a list of Osage was filled with the names of non-Indians while leaving out many traditional (full blood) Osage. Secondly, the "full blood" sect was apparently also interested in purging some "mixed blood" names in order to maintain majority control (Fixico 2012, 32–33). Some Osage leaders wanted to become a state as well. However, their ambitions involved a joining of forces with the other so-called "Five Civilized Tribes" (Cherokee, Chickasaw, Choctaw, Creek, and Seminole). Hence, they wished to prevent allotment and make Oklahoma an "Indian State" governed and controlled by the six nations collectively (Fixico 2012, 33). We might call the traditional Osage strategy a move to have exclusive control over the land and keep it a public good for all including, perhaps, the civilized tribes. Obviously, this Indian State could not be allowed to happen or the businessmen and farmers could not profit directly from Oklahoma resources. All the while, squatters (prospectors) simply moved onto land on the Osage Reservation for living or for extracting resources.

This narrative can further highlight the various emergent factions: 1. Resource extraction businessmen, 2. Farming businessmen, 3. Non-Traditional Osage, and 4. Traditional Osage. These factions are represented in Figure 8.4, which is an updated illustration of the varying factions linked to policy preferences.

Figure 8.4: Converging Interests Involving Allotment on the Osage Reservation

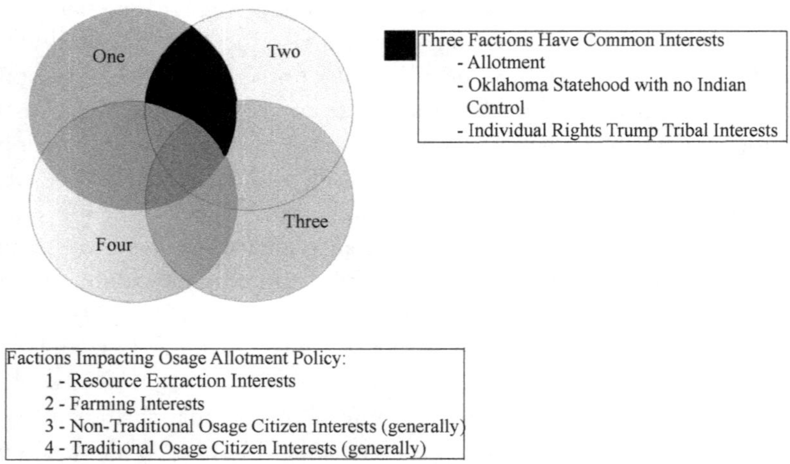

Factions 1 through 3 have the most interest in a. allotment and b. Oklahoma statehood, but only after allotment and surplus land is sold to non-Indians. Resource extraction royalties can be paid directly to individuals with land holdings if the allotment is carried out (Fixico 2012, 34). The simpler allotment royalty payments can be made, the cheaper the extraction process. On November 28, 1904, the Osage tribal government agreed to send a delegation to Washington to pursue allotment on their reservation. Selectorate theory suggests that the delegation should have been made up, perhaps exclusively, of non-traditional Osage representatives. The Osage Allotment Act was approved by U.S. Congress on June 28, 1906 (Fixico 2012, 34–36). The Act was unclear, in some instances, regarding royalties.

Ordinarily, royalties would go to a property owner. However, who owns the allotments? The post allotment Osage reservation was a can of worms. Many non-Osage (non-Indigenous) individuals could be considered property owners of record. Secondly, not all Osage individuals held an equal interest in the post allotment land distribution (Burns 2004, 425). This confusing mess allowed for resource extraction companies, allottees with the most valuable rights, and non-traditional members of the Osage Tribal Council to work toward their common goals. As forecast by selectorate theory, the traditional Osage were left out and their policy preferences were no longer viable.

As Figures 8.3 and 8.4 highlight, there were more factions interested in maximizing the efficiency and rates of royalty payments for fewer individuals than there were factions interested in more egalitarian distributions. It is much simpler, and less expensive, for resource extraction companies to pay royalties to fewer individuals (Burns 2004, 425). This interest coupled with the emerging elite within Osage leadership who wished to ensure fewer Osage citizens would benefit from royalty payments. The fewer the beneficiaries the higher the royalty payments. Finally, the U.S. markets also benefited from lower extraction costs which led to lower retail prices. At the time there were 2,229 Osage citizens. Allotment impacted 1,465,380.56 acres. The distribution was handled by lottery. The lottery distribution went so far as to assign a blindfolded "full blood" boy and another blindfolded "mixed blood" boy to draw the lottery numbers presumably to avoid any controversy over the drawing assignments (Fixico 2012, 34–35). Each citizen received about 657.41 acres. The Osage did better than most considering federal policy spelled out, at most, 160 acres. These allotments came with sources for revenue such as grazing permits, oil revenue, and gas extractions royalties. From July 1, 1904 to May 13, 1905, the royalties amounted to $108,567. Individual Osage royalty incomes were high, ranging from about $40,000 in 1920 to $65,000 in 1925. In 1905, other oil companies called Foster out for violating U.S. anti-trust laws when his Osage wide lease came up for renewal. His lease renewal was only approved so long as it covered the eastern side of the Osage reservation. The lease included 680,000 acres (Fixico 2012, 34–36).

Between 1905 and 1912 the western portion of the Osage reservation remained unleased. Oil companies began harassing allottees, cutting fences, and illegally hauling wood (to build oil drills) across allottee lands. Non-Indian extraction companies continued pressuring the Osage tribal government to allow more leasing in the western area. Allottees, apparently, had concerns about leasing. They formed the Osage Protective Association (OPA) in 1911 to see that their interests were met. Originally, the royalties due to allottees were only for surface rights, not sub-surface mineral rights. Sub-surface rights were held in common by all Osage citizens and not by individual allotees. The OPA pushed for, and received, legislation allocating rights to individual allottees if they were less than 1/2 Indian (Fixico 2012, 36–37). There is a serious implication in this policy. It could be that a 1/2 Osage or less was "more civilized" and thus more apt to properly manage his royalty payments.

In May of 1912, the Osage Principal Chief was instructed to sign four new leases that would cover the majority of the western reservation. The Secretary of the Interior disallowed this and wanted to try other methods to ensure the royalties made it to more Osage citizens (Fixico 2012, 37). A blanket lease policy was replaced by instead leasing in smaller parcels between 300 and 5,120 acres. Secondly, no one entity could lease more than 25,000 acres (Fixico 2012, 37). While this scheme seems to have no impact on allottee royalty payments, it appears to prevent monopolization of the leases from the outside.[32] There is no reason to think the situation has changed today. U.S. corporations end up selling Indigenous natural resources for a profit to citizens of the United States. This is no accident. The systematic interaction between Indigenous leaders, U.S. leaders, and U.S. constituents is heavily at work here. This process can be easily described. Selectorate theory details the explanation for why this process started back in the treaty making era and continues to this day.

To recap this section, nearly all of the post-removal strategies for ensuring good governance with Osage citizens are really attempts to shift the size of the Osage selectorate. The selectorate was not only shrinking, but also ensuring that the policy preferences involved changing the land and natural resources from public to private good status. Typically, the foreign aid incentive to make these shifts occur would involve direct payment of money to the recipient nation in exchange for a policy concession (land shifted to private good). However, this case study may be better explained by looking at "aid" in terms of advice from non-Indians on allotment. The results are essentially the same. A near dictatorship emerges that can more efficiently provide private and exclusive access to resources on the land. These resources are then divided up among the non-Osage and the elite Osage citizens supporting exclusive resource access. Not all Indigenous nations will have the "benefit" of natural resources. Regardless, the same principles apply.

Selectorate Theory, Indigenous Nations, and Treaty Obligations—Foreign Aid?

Selectorate theory more generally explains the interaction between Indigenous nations and the U.S. The application will also pinpoint a compromise for Indigenous economic development. There are four key groups to identify. Two groups tie into each nation. Indigenous nations have 1. Leaders (LIN) and 2. Constituents (CIN). The U.S. also has 3. Leaders (CAL), and 4. Constituents (CAC). Each of these groups ties into the other nation as members of the selectorate, winning coalition, and leadership.

32. There are no indications that anyone is considering the market value versus the rate of pay for Osage allottees. This would provide some interesting future research.

Each nation must distribute public and private goods. One assumption is that each set of leaders wishes to remain in power for as long as possible. (Power retention can be personally held or held via a party or associates.) Essentially, each of the leaders must distribute public and private goods to his or her respective winning coalitions. Foreign aid plays a critical role in the process (Bueno de Mesquita 2014, 79–94).

Foreign aid, as a function of policy concessions, works hand-in-hand with international trade. The more foreign aid impacts trade policy for a recipient nation, the less likely the recipient nation can retain the ability to sustain economic development that serves its citizens. The U.S. is a large winning coalition nation needing public goods to keep voters loyal to a particular leader. U.S. leaders retain loyalty during election cycles based, for example, on securing resources. These resources are distributed as public goods to the U.S. constituents. Resources cannot be privately distributed to only those who voted for the winning leader. This would amount to pennies per vote so individual voters must be served using public goods. Yet, the U.S. relies on a distribution scheme allowing U.S. corporations to also serve the selectorate. In this way, corporations also have access to private goods. Private goods, with respect to Indigenous nations, involve resource extraction. U.S. corporations serve their leaders and the U.S. selectorate by providing jobs, cheap energy, water, and the like to non-Indigenous American citizens first and foremost. If we assume this extraction process is zero sum, then someone must lose in the scheme.

The second part of the equation is the particular Indigenous nation relationship to the interaction. Indigenous leaders are essentially being bought by foreign aid in the form of federal aid with strings attached. This is a clear threat to Indigenous economic development that challenges the economic hegemon or the U.S. This challenge is neutralized with "strings attached" or foreign aid. It is in the best interest of the U.S. to retain small winning coalition nations in place. In other words, U.S. interests "abroad" are better represented if the foreign aid is distributed only to puppet democracies or moderate to small winning coalition nations as represented in Figure 8.2. When Indigenous nations have a small winning coalition, the U.S. can more easily purchase policy concessions from Indigenous leaders using private goods or federal aid. Again, I am calling this funding foreign aid. If Indigenous leaders only need a handful of loyal members in order to retain their leadership roles, the policy concessions can remain in place. Indigenous leaders, then, do not need Indigenous constituent loyalty to retain leadership. So long as Indigenous leaders have a small winning coalition, they may buy the loyalty of winning coalition members with private goods. This is, potentially, how best to explain the Indigenous economic interactions with the U.S. today.

How Does the U.S. Benefit From the Foreign Aid Relationship?

U.S. leaders win when they obtain cheap natural resources from the Indigenous nations, such as natural gas and water. The U.S. constituents win because they obtain cheap natural resource distribution as a public good. The U.S. constituents, happy with their representatives due to cheap water and natural gas, reelect U.S. leaders. Indigenous leaders, then, continue to retain foreign aid revenue in order to pay off their winning coalition, and stay in office. Indigenous leaders distribute the revenue as private goods via contracts for future resource extraction, such as new leases for fracking. Indigenous citizens, finally, must bear the cost of Indigenous leaders giving a policy concession to the U.S. Foreign aid, then, purchases a policy that should otherwise serve the Indigenous citizens. Whether or not this scheme accurately reflects the current situation is not the main point. The important point is that, should this model be in place or continue, it is certainly NOT an example of conditions conducive to economic development serving Indigenous citizens. The foreign aid with strings attached model here is a snapshot of what could be going on between the U.S. and all Indigenous nations. But this only works if we can determine that Indigenous nations have small winning coalition governments.

Do Indigenous Nations Reflect Small Winning Coalition Nations?

None of this selectorate theory explanation works unless we can determine that Indigenous nations have small winning coalition governments. Again, review Figure 8.2 for some reference about what constitutes a small winning coalition government. We are wise to review some scant descriptive statistics on the consequences of the Indian Reorganization Act (IRA) era constitutions. IRA explains how contemporary Indigenous nations are set up today. The evidence on the impact of IRA on tribal government is varied. Interestingly, the maneuver is difficult to view absent a federal strategy to further solidify an envelopment of Indigenous governance, once dominated by Indigenous philosophies, within a frame that was more similar to a U.S. model. In other words, IRA was potentially designed to trump and replace tribal governance (Porter 2005, 187–188). Obviously, another part of the debate involves whether IRA policy did more good or more traditional damage to specific Indigenous nations (Getches 2011, 188).[33]

---

33. Still, the unrelated debate also surrounds whether IRA created a boilerplate constitution or if it was fine-tuned for specific Indigenous nations. Some contend that IRA was nothing but a boilerplate model (Champagne 2007, 67). Others contend that this boilerplate argument is inaccurate and seriously flawed (Lemont 2006, 49).

IRA was the first time, since prior to treaty making, that Indigenous nations had a "choice" in the matter of self-determination if one considers voting a method of self-determination. Indigenous nations could vote to accept or reject IRA. The scant data suggests there were 258 elections, 181 nations accepted, 77 rejected, and 14 did not hold elections. By 1946, 12 years after IRA was passed, there were 161 Indigenous constitutions and 131 corporate charters in place (Getches 2011, 193). Still, I have often wondered if this federal movement to organize Indians in the 1930s was somehow related to new technology that would allow the detection or extraction of natural resources on Indigenous nations. (Much more research similar to the Osage analysis would verify if this process occurred broadly.) It would be rather convenient if corporations could obtain tribal council approval if IRA-type constitutions were in place to approve land leases. Many IRA constitutions started out with a proviso that the U.S. Secretary of the Interior approve of tribal government acts. Hence, for all the fervor around how IRA would garner self-determination, it is striking how the Secretary of the Interior had more control of Indian affairs after IRA due to unilateral veto power over any tribal legislative action. In any case, we currently could have as many as 292 IRA-related constitutions and corporate charters, some nations have both, with questionable and under-researched traits. I'd like us to focus on one pattern.

The literature on tribal constitutions has yet to be fully engaged and a full engagement is beyond the scope of this research. One key component of contemporary IRA constitutions involves a concentration of power in the hands of a relatively small council that legislates based on principles that are very similar to those exercised by the U.S. Congress. It's odd that no other researcher has ever conducted a survey of tribal legislature size. Cornell and Kalt state that they have collected data on approximately 70 tribes and consider whether a legislature made up of between 7 to 15 members has an impact on economic development (2000, 458). I would argue that a legislature made up of 50 legislators is a small winning coalition government. This means that these types of governments are susceptible to foreign aid influence through private goods purchase of policy concessions for the donor's aid. Cornell and Kalt hypothesize that these types of small councils should out-perform nations with a general council.

General councils are made up of a large legislative body composed of all citizens of a nation. Citizens choose individual levels of involvement with policy making (2000, 458). Again, there is no count given on the number of Indigenous nations with a general council. Perhaps these types of nations are large winning coalition legislatures and, thus, less susceptible to foreign aid impact. The logic here is simple: An Indigenous nation with a legislative body of about 88 members would require about 45 to 59 legislators to agree to policy concessions for a donor nation. It's simply more expensive to buy off this many legislators with private goods. If a legislature is only 7 to 15 members, then a donor can more cheaply purchase a policy concession by obtaining the consent of between 4 to 7 members with private goods.

The anecdotal evidence points to a great number of Indigenous nations with small winning coalition governments. Table 8.1 is a list of some Indigenous nations and their number of legislators. This table is NOT meant to be comprehensive.

Table 8.1: Limited Data on Indigenous Nations and Legislature Size – Based on Original IRA Constitution that May Have Been Modified.

Indigenous Nation	Number of Legislators in Council
Cayuga Oklahoma	7
Colorado River Indian Tribes	9
Fort McDowell Apache	5
Gila River Indian Community	17
Hopi	18 to 36
Hualapai	7
Navajo	24
Pascua Yaqui	11
San Carlos Apache	7
Southern Ute	General Council – All Citizens Over 18
White Mountain Apache	11
Yavapai Apache	9

Table 8.1 represents Indigenous nations in alphabetical order but this could easily be re-arranged to show the largest to the smallest councils. It should be noted that most of the data is based on original IRA constitutions which could have been modified. The largest council might be Southern Ute and the smallest known number would be Ft. McDowell Apache. It is telling that the second largest Indigenous Nation, Hopi, would only require between about 10 to 12 votes to furnish a policy concession to the U.S. Hence it seems clear that this small sample of Indigenous legislatures is very susceptible to foreign aid influence.

Out of frustration, I have attempted to collect some data on Indigenous nations recognized by the U.S. government. According to the "Federal Register" there are currently 566 Indigenous nations recognized by the U.S. (Federal Register 2014). I endeavored to create a table with as many Indigenous nations as possible. While it would be most transparent to list all Indigenous nations here, space limits our attention to minimal descriptive statistics. Table 8.2 is a list of 336 Indigenous nations. This list does not include the 230 Native Entities within Alaska.

Table 8.2: Descriptive Statistics on Contemporary Indigenous Nations (48 States Only)

Council Size	Nations	Name if less than 2
no data	89	
3	7	
4	6	
5	59	
6	23	
7	65	
8	7	
9	25	
10	11	
11	12	
12	9	
13	3	
14	5	
15	4	
16	0	
17	3	
18	1	Crow Tribe of Montana
19	1	Seneca Nation
20	1	Muscogee Creek
21-23	0	
24	2	
26	1	Tohono O'odham
27	1	Te-Moak
28-29	0	
30	1	Seminole Oklahoma
Total Nations	336	

* Data Collected by Stefanie Kunze

Again, the story has not changed much since 1934 when many of these nations accepted and drafted IRA era constitutions. Creating Table 8.2 was challenging. Of the 336 nations that exist, excluding Indigenous entities in Alaska, only 247 disclosed information about the size of their governing body. All of the data was collected by visiting official Indigenous nation websites or some pan-Indigenous organization websites such as that of the National Council of the American Indian. There are 77 nations with fewer than 5 members of a legislative body. Many of these bodies have varying names such as "tribal council" or "business council." I have assumed they operate as a legislature. The largest legislature is the Seminole Nation of Oklahoma at 30 members. In theory, this means that anyone with enough money to buy off the votes of 16 council members could do so with the largest Indigenous legislature in the U.S. In other words, a business person could calculate the maximum dollar amount for each of the 16 members and if the endeavor would net a surplus after the payouts to council members, this would be a good deal. It is worth reminding readers that I am not accusing any legislators of accepting bribes. I am questioning the ability for small size legislatures to fully represent their constituents needs while turning away foreign aid from the outside.

It seems clear that nearly all Indigenous legislatures are susceptible to foreign aid influence. There are many other missing portions of information that would be key in answering a great deal of other questions. Does legislature size correspond with IRA acceptance? Does a non-IRA nation tend to have a larger legislature? As other research has pointed out, the more concentrated the decision-making process of a nation, the more likely they will see economic development (Cornell and Kalt 2000). This sounds like a great outcome, however, what economic development, as discussed in Chapter 7, has more to do with supporting the U.S. political economy than growth that can be enjoyed by citizens of an Indigenous nation. If we cross-listed the nations discussed by Cornell and Kalt with Table 8.2, we might discover that nearly all of these nations have small winning coalitions. We should expect to find heavily concentrated leadership, insulated from public constituent criticism, and heavily embedded within the U.S. political economy. Success on terms dictated by the colonial actor is no success at all.

Concluding Remarks

Indigenous leaders may believe they are carrying out economic development when they allow resource extraction on their homelands that destroy the environment and places workers at risk. These leaders will be the first to lament the bureaucratic nightmare inherent in any economic development on Indigenous nations. We are wise to remind ourselves of two important issues: 1. Our pre-contact philosophies have preserved finite resources that have contributed to colonial actor development today and 2. This process of Indigenous economic co-optation began long ago when colonial actors elevated an Indigenous elite to self-colonize while paying tribute to colonial actors (Mahoney 2010). Previous chapters have explained the process and this chapter outlines how it continues today. Our one remaining strategy may be that we refuse to fall victim to the amnesia of the American myth, Aboriginal Title, and the most invasive racial and ethnic entitlement policy ever carried out on the planet. The tie between Aboriginal Title and 21st century colonial actor wealth is a well-known secret. When colonial actors discovered Indigenous nations, they extinguished Indian rights to occupy homelands, and appropriated the resources stored in our homelands to enrich themselves and an elite Indigenous leadership caste. I still remember traditional homelands, sacred histories, ceremonies, and languages. These reminders should nag us all as we fall asleep late at night. These memories should frighten us as they begin to dim. Social science fiction abounds and our only reality may be the one left to us by our ancestors. Do not forget their lessons. Remember what Aboriginal Title means.

Epilogue
Aboriginal Title: The Originial Ethnic and Racial Entitlement

On February 25, 2014, Time Magazine's website posted a story about a study of Los Angeles immigrants being "the most successful" (Lee 2014). This brings up, yet again, the issue about who are the immigrants and who are the natives. This is not meant to disrespect any other racial group. Rather, this book was written as a reminder to all that the most successful immigrants on the planet are people from Spain, Portugal, and England. These are the immigrants who have had a lasting impression on the Western and Southern Hemispheres. Yet, few consider these groups immigrants because they have been so successful at resetting the agenda. How successful have immigrants from Spain and Portugal been? Research on post-colonial economic development in Latin America may be one of the few quantitative treatments of this discussion. The findings indicate that colonial actors in Latin American have been relatively more successful than their neighbors if they can accomplish one of two things: 1. Eliminate the previously existing network of economic ties or 2. Eliminate the heads of these previously existing economic ties and install themselves as the heads (Lee 2014). What do these findings actually mean.

Colonial actors in Latin America—immigrants—took it upon themselves to carry out the most egregious genocide in the history of the world. They had at least two methods of carrying out this genocide. They could completely annihilate the Indigenous political economic networks. Alternatively, these colonial actors could remove Indigenous leaders and replace the leaders with themselves. Mahoney's research suggests that there are three levels of relative economic development: high, medium, and low (Mahoney 2010, 5). This research becomes more interesting as we explore the "pre-colonial societies" and their level of "complexity." The exploration of institutions is key to understanding genocide and post-genocide development. So long as institutions can be either taken over or eliminated entirely, the levels of development after the genocide can take on differing characteristics. These institutions can be economic, political, or social (Mahoney 2010, 24). The research goes on about the type of colonization: mercantilist or liberal. Mercantilist colonial actors tended to prefer complex pre-colonial societies because they could, again, seize control of these complex institutional networks that, quite frankly, were similar to European states. Both mercantilist colonial actors and Indigenous nations with complex economic networks coerced labor and utilized powerful institutions for extracting taxes from the populations. Hence, we find that mercantilist colonial actors developed by co-opting Indigenous economic networks (Mahoney 2010, 26). For liberals, the path to colonization involved "less complex" pre-colonial institutions. Liberal colonial actors took a path toward societies in which the entire network of institutions could be wiped out and replaced with their own rebuilt institutions (Mahoney 2010, 26). There are several interesting consequences to the outcomes of the research for Indigenous peoples in Latin America now.

We should be reminded of Peoplehood as a method of recognizing Indigenous sovereignty prior to contact with colonial actors (Mahoney 2010, 29). This process, in its infancy, was explored in Chapter 3. I've demonstrated elsewhere that Indigenous peoples today are willing to fight and give up their lives for their traditional homelands using independently collected data (Holm, Pearson, and Chavis 2003; Lerma 2012). Still, it should be noted that there is evidence that some Indigenous societies have made mistakes even prior to contact. As Mahoney suggests, there are certainly Indigenous empires that took hold prior to contact with colonial actors but he calls them "complex" (Lerma 2012). Although there is no judgment explicitly stated in Mahoney's work, I have to wonder if lower complexity really means Peoplehood. Tom Holm, Professor Emeritus of American Indian Studies at the University of Arizona, and myself disagreed about why Western scholarship tended to put Aztec, Inca, and Mayan civilizations upon a pedestal. Holm would say that Western civilization wished to discuss how advanced these civilizations were and, still, colonial actors were able to conquer them. I believe otherwise. These "complex" or "advanced" Indigenous civilizations looked in the Westphalia sense like Western ideas of the state. They looked like infidel societies that had no Christianity. And, much like Islamic nations, it was quite proper to destroy these Indigenous empires upon arrival because they are an affront to Western notions of god. For this conclusion, I'll assume I'm right.

So, what is a supposedly complex society? Well it probably has drifted away from Peoplehood and notions of 1. sacred history, 2. ceremony cycle, 3. language, and 4. place (Holm, Pearson, and Chavis 2003). These "simple" societies were more in tune with their sacred duty to lead their people, take care of their traditional homelands, and otherwise promote a long and wisdom-filled life for themselves and their future children. "Complex" Indigenous empires lost touch with these obligations to their surroundings. They decided to build permanent institutions to extract tribute from neighboring Indigenous peoples, use their sacred knowledge of the stars (Indigenous astronomy) for less than sacred purposes, and otherwise monopolize resources. It's odd that there are no longer any Indigenous empires in the Americas. Why did they go away? The simple answer is that they were conquered but I have to bring up the possibility that the creator removed them for their bad deeds. We are left with many Indigenous societies today that have survived by only taking from mother earth what they need and no more or less. They have sustained themselves with "superstitions" related to their ceremonies, their histories, their languages, and their traditional homelands. Again, this would be consistent with Figure 3.1 on the concept of pre-contact Indigenous sovereignty. This Indigenous knowledge transcends all notions of federal recognition, treaties, and books. As my teacher, Avery Denny, would say, "It's already there." This Indigenous sovereignty was never fully appreciated by colonial actors then or now.

One of the biggest stumbling points for many is the tie between Indigenous sovereignty, spirituality, and natural resources. Some have said that Indians worshipped everything! Maybe you heard that guy say this simple idea. Or maybe you heard that Indians worshipped the wind and prayed to the sun. Atheists must be laughing and falling out of chairs as they read this line. But, pretend for a minute, that science and religion can co-exist and actually complement one another. This is a huge idea to grasp for some but quite easy for others. I would argue that Indigenous peoples did this all the time and some still do this today. They see their spirituality intrinsically linked to their management of their environments! Spirituality is religion and environment is natural resources. Our Indigenous sciences are about ensuring that all individuals maintained a good and proper relationship with everything around them. If you take too much from the earth now it won't be there for the taking tomorrow. So leave a little bit for tomorrow, for your neighbors, and so on. Indigenous nations left a great deal sitting there waiting to be consumed.

There is no need to go into great detail about how we Indians wasted the land and never developed it correctly! I obviously find this idea idiotic. It would be great if someone would extend Mahoney's research to the U.S., New Zealand, Australia, and Canada. Each of these colonial actors "found" either complex or simple societies. Based on their discovery they each made a choice. They either wiped out the entire Indigenous political economy or they co-opted it. Those who did a good job at their genocide became massively powerful global actors today regardless of the method they chose to take. I would anecdotally argue that the G4, that stands for genocidal four, also known as the U.S., New Zealand, Australia, and Canada, all encountered "simple" Indigenous societies and destroyed the Indigenous political economies. My anecdotal evidence for this claim is that we now have Indigenous nations with decimated political economies surrounded by G4 borders. There is also less evidence of Indigenous societies in the G4 countries that built pre-contact empires. This means the "simple" Indigenous peoples did not start treating mother earth like an ATM machine. So how does this tie to economic development today?

The G4 countries are four of the most economically developed and powerful nations on the planet. Why? I say it is because of Peoplehood. Our ceremonies, our sacred histories, and our languages required us to protect and preserve our homelands. And what exactly did we save using our religions? We saved natural resources! Then, along came a "horde of refugees from another continent" (Alfred 2009, 79) who took what we saved since time immemorial (natural resources) and used it to become the wealthiest nations on earth. The activities of the G4 have proven my point too. If we do not care for our mother earth through the ceremonies, use of languages, taught to us and carried in our sacred histories, our world will come to an end. Here we are in 2014 about to see this reality take place. Our climate has changed and our future is seemingly bleak. Still, the tie between spirituality and environment is a constant relationship. Indigenous peoples were in the way of economic development. And as the G4 countries destroyed Indigenous political economies and extracted the natural resources persevered because of Peoplehood, they became the most powerful nations because they were able to develop so fast. The research offered by Mahoney seems very applicable to the G4. This dysfunctional relationship between spirit and environment appear to be the most salient to our coming Indigenous spring and it remains intrinsically tied to our sovereignty.

Even the very root of what counts as a tribal government is so embedded in colonial actor terms that I cannot write this book in any other language than English. Not being satisfied to simply write, I have attempted to provide several two-dimensional figures of contemporary Indigenous sovereignty. The most important notion of Indigenous sovereignty must wrestle with the young minds who could be reading this now. We have to reconcile sovereignty based on Peoplehood and reconsider our original binary in the form of Aboriginal Title. Recall that colonial actors decided amongst themselves that they had superior rights to the Western and Southern Hemispheres based on the Doctrine of Discovery. The doctrine stated that any Christian nation could claim an exclusive right to discover lands held by Indians. They claimed discovery, and then had to do the genocidal work of extinguishing Aboriginal Title by purchase, conquest, or abandonment (Getches 2011). No Indian tribe could ever live up to Aboriginal Title standards . . . not even the Indigenous empires could qualify. They all had to go.

Many scholars call out the race-based metric of colonization. Still, there is a cleaner way of discussing these matters. I won't deny that racism plays a major role in colonization then and now. I will, instead, remind readers to fully engage this idea of Aboriginal Title or the right to occupy one's traditional homeland at the pleasure of the European Christian sovereign crown. Remind yourself and others about how this is a weakest link argument. Ethnic groups from another continent decided that they would adopt an ethnic-based affirmative action program that made their claims superior to notions of organic attachment to homeland based on Peoplehood (Getches 2011, 45). Indigenous activists cannot simply adopt a Western notion in response, lest, we risk repeating the mistakes of our relatives on this continent when they experimented with Indigenous empire building and paid a heavy price. Our children, grandchildren, and all future generations of Indigenous individuals deserve a much better example than that.

Going forward, we have much to gain by reminding policy makers today that we should all dismiss racial and ethnic-based entitlements. We should all be in favor of abandoning hierarchies and non-level playing fields. Many scholars have carved out a very narrow view of these discussions in terms of affirmative action, wealth disparities, health care disparities, educational concerns, and environmental racism. Reversing the Doctrine of Discovery, then, is not a racial or ethnic-based entitlement. We are talking about the recognition that many Indigenous political economies were destroyed for the purpose of building so much wealth in the hands of so few immigrants. Mahoney's research hints at this reality. Where did all of the wealth of the U.S. and Canada come from? Where did the wealth of colonial actors come from? These are the consequences of race-based affirmative action policies for the appropriation of lands in the Americas.

I have been teaching tribal government classes and Native American politics classes for the last five years. We always discuss the Doctrine of Discovery. In the first couple of years of teaching these classes, I would go into the class on the day or week that we discussed the Doctrine of Discovery ready to explain this reality. After I was done with the lecture, I often felt dissatisfied. I felt like I had failed to truly convey the magnitude of this equally beneficial and destructive policy. Beneficial for the most successful immigrants in the history of the world and downright genocidal for the focal point of this race-based policy. By the third year of teaching these courses, I started telling students about my concern. I don't want to "over sell" the idea and be hyperbolic about the whole thing. Being honest about this concern seemed to help. I could, perhaps, go overboard and yet leave them with a public service announcement that maybe I was about to go off the rails for a few minutes. Still, I left these classes unsatisfied. Nowadays, when we discuss the Doctrine of Discovery and Aboriginal Title, I still feel dissatisfied. I see many Indigenous students with a slight grin on their faces and sitting on the edges of their seats. After five years, I may be making end roads toward fully disseminating the magnitude of this ethnic entitlement policy. It's so massive that it is difficult to truly over sell it even now. But, again, these are not excuses to be bitter.

The coming Indigenous spring needs to be carried out by very patient teachers. We need to re-explore how we can reconnect with peoples from diverse cultures over these issues of ethnic entitlement policies. We should not be interested in rebuilding Indigenous empires. We must acknowledge this fact here and now. We are not trying to do anything other than return to some notion of Peoplehood. This means we must cooperate with one another, perhaps in ways that were once attempted ceremonially, in order to survive the coming environmental catastrophe. Recall the advice of one First Nations elder when he said that if we all come together and think the same thing for about two or three seconds, a miracle will occur (Holm, Pearson, and Chavis 2003; Wilson 2008, 69). Our Indigenous experiments with coercive states failed prior to contact, in the 19th century, and continue to fail today in contemporary tribal governments. We have learned to be very obedient and fearful of the U.S. institutional apparatus that has been used against us in war, in education, in policies directed toward exterminating us, and in terms of funding. We have seen a generation of tribal leaders play it safe. We have personally, at times, adopted roles in the dominant society in order to feed our families and, thus, may have compromised our morals to play a role in our own suppression. I too can claim credit for playing a role in buying into the false dichotomies of Aboriginal Title because I have fee simple title, along with a bank, to my current home.

If there is only one voice saying that Aboriginal Title is an ethnic entitlement, this Indigenous spring is doomed to fail. Our "victories" will continue to involve some notion of "settling Indigenous rights" which, today, means erasing those rights and allowing subunits of the U.S. government to set the agenda again. We need not join an Indigenous elite that is incapable of exercising some notion of sovereignty, perhaps based on Peoplehood, because if we ever threaten the political economy of the local hegemon, such as the U.S., your funding will dry up. Our foreign aid requires a policy concession to the non-Indian world (Bueno de Mesquita 2014, 383–414). Our collective efforts must also include all of the reminders mentioned throughout this text or we are doomed to repeat the same mistakes our recent ancestors have made.

Indigenous peoples of the world have been tricked into believing some of the hype about ourselves. We tried to deal with colonial actors as humans but the military men of Europe may have been the lowest form of humans. As Deloria has stated, these may have been the weeds of mankind (Deloria 1974, 80). Obviously, the early immigrants are not representative of the people inhabiting the Western and Southern Hemispheres today. As I say in my classes, there is virtually no one individual left, besides the 1%, who can claim some massive victory today for the colonial ambitions of their ancestors. Most of the wealth monopolized during the post-Aboriginal Title period has not magically redistributed itself in any equal way to current populations. Instead, all individuals regardless of their ethnic background share in a very serious issue related to wealth mal-distribution, the further erosion of the environment, and the continued legacies of colonization itself. All the while, we are often recruited to contribute to a "sustainable colonialism." There are only a handful of individuals, be they VERY powerful, willing to continue extracting resources, poisoning the environment, and continuously telling the world that these practices are inevitable. Our coming together is very likely required based on our shared interests.

The young people of the world seem hungry for some kind of spiritual grounding. This is both a profound yearning and a very scary idea. Many Indigenous youth (maybe those under 30 years of age) have very limited access to their elders and knowledge holders. Sadly, the notion that Indigenous knowledge is rapidly disappearing is largely correct. A world of 140 character attention spans has created a serious strain on those elders who remain tolerant enough to put up with our inability to shut up and listen to them. This has placed some strain in the minds of the contemporary Indigenous youth. Encouraged to seek higher education, they learn how to be adversarial at the exact wrong time, just when an elder is about to say something important.

I leave you with this final note of optimism. I have learned that our Indigenous knowledges (and yes, there are multiple knowledges) were acquired by individuals like us long ago. They were not any more special than we are now. I certainly take these creation stories seriously even if they are, at times, contradictory toward one another. Why would I place such faith in these systems of knowledge? For one, these systems discouraged

Indigenous empire building. Perhaps the Mayan people walked away from their elites just before Spaniards showed up to finish the job we started on ourselves. Perhaps had Aztecs and Incas been given some more time, they too would have abandoned empires as unsustainable. So if we leave these types of societies out for a minute, there is a very long history of sustainable communities built upon a foundation of oral accounts of creation. Individuals, probably like us, had a much more open-minded perspective about what their senses were telling them. They listened to their thoughts and were not limited to five senses. Readers are encouraged to rediscover these tales in one of the few places they are recorded (Deloria 2006). The creator(s) ordained Indigenous peoples with responsibilities to one another, to bird people, to hooved people, to people who crawled on the ground, to insect people, etc. We respected one another. Sometimes we gave our lives for the other. We learned this from a higher being.

Some Indigenous philosophies maintain that our knowledges take care of themselves. (Yes, not itselves but themselves!) If we are not in the correct "way" this knowledge will avoid us. We have to come at these tidbits of knowledge in the correct way. And we may only get one chance to pay attention. Many of the Indigenous creation stories involve a single individual being taught a song. A holy being will come to them and say, "Learn this song." And the track record for how these "stories" remains hidden in plain sight is clear as mud. Hopi may lay claim to the longest continuously inhabited settlement in all of the Western Hemisphere. Indigenous peoples didn't survive this long by accident. Our sacred histories, our ceremonies, our languages, sustained us in our traditional homelands from time immemorial until about 1492 at the earliest. Some still sustain themselves to this day! No one takes these empirical observations seriously and it is time to reconsider that decision. The Indigenous youth seem willing to ask these questions even if they may not understand how to do this. The elders seem willing to share this knowledge yet may be turned off by some of the habits the youth learned in our modern day higher education boarding schools. And even if there are no elders around anymore, there is always the possibility that you, the reader, could be that one with the special ability to hear what others dismiss as "the wind" or "just an intuition." Next time you are asked, because you won't be ordered, to learn a song, I suggest you learn it. You could be the one who teaches the rest of us how to save the world!

Appendix to Chapter 6

In the interest of transparency, various tables are offered to ensure that quantitative operations are carried out correctly. QCA uses both a qualitative and quantitative approach to research analyses. It is specifically designed to deal with subset relationships (such as Supreme Court opinions and Indian law opinions) and a small number of cases (as in the 45 cases within federal Indian law and policy). They can be followed as a step-by-step strategy to carry out your own analysis of other eras in the Supreme Court. My first task was to identify all possible conditions and outcomes. Table A is this list and an internal check on the data collection process. Note that the total column and row equal the same amount verifying that the cases are arranged in a logical manner. This table also gives us the clearest view of the cases in matrix form.

Table A: Matrix of Cases by Condition and Outcome

		Outcome				
		expand	neutral	diminish	unclear	totals
Conditions	delivered	1	3	4	1	9
	joined	0	10	19	3	32
	dissented	0	4	0	0	4
	de or j	1	13	23	4	41
	de or di	1	4	0	0	5
	de maj	0	3	5	1	9
	de di	1	0	0	0	1
	chief	1	6	14	3	24
	associate	0	11	9	1	21
		5	54	74	13	146

Step 2 would be to narrow in on some of the typical conditions. They are listed as "joined," "delivered," and "dissented." Table B is a basic table of causal conditions cross tabulated with corresponding outcomes. Note that the distribution of court cases centers on the categories of diminishment and leaves as is labeled as "neutral" in the table. The percent of neutral cases is 38% while the percentage of diminished cases is at 51%. These two statistics combine into a whopping 89%. As a result, we can conclude that between 1972 and 2005, the potential for expanding Indigenous nation sovereignty was very low. In fact, only one case during this time period expanded Indigenous nation sovereignty. The low likelihood of expanding Indigenous nation sovereignty is one finding while another is that sovereignty was diminished approximately half of the time.

Table B: Matrix of Cases by Mutually Exclusive Conditions and Outcomes

		Outcome				
		expand	neutral	diminish	unclear	totals
Conditions	delivered	1	3	4	1	9
	joined	0	10	19	3	32
	dissented	0	4	0	0	4
	total	1	17	23	4	45
	percent	2.22%	37.78%	51.11%	8.89%	100.00%

Step 3 is more fact checking. One way to ensure that operations are working well is to negate conditions to examine if the outcome also is impacted. Hence, I negate dissent with "not dissent." "Not dissent" means that the justice either delivered or joined a majority opinion. It is an inversion of Table B in that the main logic here is seen in the behavior of a Chief Justice (Rehnquist) concerning his failure to dissent. Note that Rehnquist never dissented when Indigenous nation sovereignty was being diminished by the court outcome. Also note the few dissenting opinions that hover in the neutral category (9%). Note that Table C represents a total of 4 cases.

Table C: Distribution of Cases Dissented Only

		Outcome				
		expand	neutral	diminish	unclear	total
Conditions	dissented	0	4	0	0	4
	not dissented	1	13	23	4	41
	percent	0.00%	8.89%	0.00%	0.00%	8.89%

Step 4 is more thorough fact checking but applied to delivered and joined as well as its logical negation not delivered and not joined. Table D is the first time causal conditions are combined and their impact on outcomes investigated. Here the condition of Chief Justice (Rehnquist) delivering an opinion (majority or dissenting) is combined with the condition of chief justice joining a majority opinion. Notice, again, how the cases center around the neutral and diminish outcome. While I do not interpret "neutral" as a bad outcome, I do interpret diminish as negative. The majority of cases, accounting for 51%, have an outcome of diminishing Indigenous nation sovereignty. To be clear, this information is based on a single case.

Table D: Distribution of Cases Delivered or Joined (de + j)

		Outcome				
		expand	neutral	diminish	unclear	total
Conditions	de or j	1	13	23	4	41
	not de or j	0	4	0	0	4
	percent	2.22%	28.89%	51.11%	8.89%	45

Step 5 examines delivered dissent or joined dissent as well as the logical negation. Table E is a concentration of expanded and neutral cases in which a chief justice delivered or joined a dissenting opinion. One can infer that when the chief justice dissented, he disagreed with the outcome of the case. This action can be interpreted as follows: When dissenting to Indigenous nation sovereign expansion, this only means that the chief justice was in favor of either leaving Indigenous nation sovereignty neutral, diminishing Indigenous nation sovereignty, or (although logically not likely) being unclear on Indigenous nation sovereignty. Leaving Indigenous nation sovereignty neutral is consistent with the same logic applied to dissent. We can only infer that a chief justice either wanted to expand, diminish, or leave the question of Indigenous nation sovereignty unclear. Once again, note the behavioral trait of Rehnquist's non-action in terms of not dissenting. The majority of cases involve diminished sovereignty followed by leaving sovereignty neutral.

Table E: Distribution of Cases Delivered Dissent or Joined Dissent (de + di)

		Outcome				
		expand	neutral	diminish	unclear	total
Conditions	de or di	1	4	0	0	5
	not de or di	0	13	23	4	40
	percent	2.22%	8.89%	0.00%	0.00%	45

Step 6 investigates delivered majority and the logical negation not delivered majority. Table F looks at the nature of cases in which a chief justice delivered the majority opinion. The number of cases is low (9) making quantitative research all the more tenuous. More than half of the cases delivered by Rehnquist involved a diminishment of Indigenous nation sovereignty followed by leaving the level of sovereignty neutral. These 9 cases would make excellent case study candidates.

Table F: Distribution of Cases Delivered Majority						
		Outcome				
		expand	neutral	diminish	unclear	total
Conditions	de maj	0	3	5	1	9
	not de maj	1	14	18	3	36
	percent	0.00%	6.67%	11.11%	2.22%	45

Step 7 examines delivered dissent only and the logical negation not delivered dissent. Table G looks at the single case in which a chief justice (in this case Rehnquist) delivered the dissenting opinion. The conclusions based on Table F are the most difficult to support in isolation of the other outcomes. On one occasion, Rehnquist dissented to the expansion of Indigenous nation sovereignty.

Table G: Distribution of Cases Delivered Dissent Only						
		Outcome				
		expand	neutral	diminish	unclear	total
Conditions	de di	1	0	0	0	1
	not de di	0	17	23	4	44
	percent	2.22%	0.00%	0.00%	0.00%	45

Step 8 involves examining case impact as a result of status: chief justice or not chief justice. Table H deals with the impact Rehnquist's rank (associate or chief) had on federal Indian law case outcomes. Rehnquist was more likely to diminish sovereignty as a chief justice than as an associate justice. This may be true of all chief justices but further research is needed to be conclusive.

Table H: Distribution of Cases based on Associate or Chief Status						
		Outcome				
		expand	neutral	diminish	unclear	total
Conditions	chief	1	6	14	3	24
	not chief	0	11	9	1	21
	total	1	17	23	4	45
	percent	4.17%	25.00%	58.33%	12.50%	

References

Alfred, Gerald R. *Peace, Power, Righteousness: An Indigenous Manifesto.* 2nd ed. Don Mills, Ont.; New York: Oxford University Press. 2009.

Aronilth Jr, Wilson. *Foundation of Navajo Culture.* Tsaile. 1991.

Austin, Raymond Darrel. *Navajo Courts and Navajo Common Law: A Tradition of Tribal Self-Governance, Indigenous Americas.* Minneapolis: University of Minnesota Press. 2009.

Bailey, Garrick Alan, and Roberta Glenn Bailey. *A History of the Navajos: The Reservation Years.* Santa Fe, N.M.: School of American Research Press. 1999.

Barnes, Robert. Supreme Court to Examine Indian Child Welfare Act requirements in adoption dispute. *Washington Post,* January 4, 2013.

Begay, Jason. Reform study aims at discussion, sharing of ideas. *Navajo Times*, November 6, 2008.

———. Voters: Yes! Majority of Diné Vote for 24-member council, line-item veto for president. *Navajo Times*, December 17, 2009.

Bell, Derrick A. *And We Are Not Saved: The Elusive Quest For Racial Justice.* New York: Basic Books. 1987.

Benally, AnCita. "Diné Binahat'a', Navajo Government." Dissertation, Arizona State University, Phoenix. 2006.

Bighorse, Tiana, Gus Bighorse, and Noël Bennett. *Bighorse the Warrior.* Tucson: University of Arizona Press. 1990.

Biolsi, Thomas. *Deadliest Enemies: Law and Race Relations on and Off Rosebud Reservation.* Minneapolis University of Minnesota. 2007.

Blackhawk, Ned. *Violence over the Land: Indians and Empires in the Early American West.* Cambridge, Mass.: Harvard University Press. 2006.

Bobroff, Kenneth. "Diné Bi Beenahaz'aanii: Codifying Indigenous Consuetudinary Law in the 21st Century." *Tribal Law Journal* 5, no. 4 (2004-2005).

Brady, Henry E., and David Collier. *Rethinking Social Inquiry: Diverse Tools, Shared Standards.* 2nd ed. Lanham, Md.: Rowman & Littlefield Publishers. 2010.

Brinkley, Alan. *The Unfinished Nation: A Concise History of the American People.* 6th ed. 1 vols. New York: McGraw-Hill. 2010.

Bruyneel, Kevin. *The Third Space of Sovereignty: The Postcolonial Politics of U.S.-Indigenous Relations, Indigenous Americas.* Minneapolis: University of Minnesota Press. 2007.

Bueno de Mesquita, Bruce. *Principles of International Politics.* 5th ed. Los Angeles: Sage/CQ Press. 2014.

Burns, Louis F. *A History of the Osage People*. New ed. Tuscaloosa: University of Alabama Press. 2004.

Carey, Harold. "Navajo creation story - Nihalgai - The Glittering or White World." 2011.

Champagne, Duane. *Social Change and Cultural Continuity Among Native Nations, Contemporary Native American Communities*. Lanham: Altamira Press. 2007.

———. *Notes from the Center of Turtle Island, Contemporary Native American Communities*. Lanham: AltaMira Press. 2010.

Cornell, and Kalt, eds. *Reloading the Dice: Improving Chances for Economic Development on American Indian Reservations*. Edited by S. Cornell and J. P. Kalt, *What Can Tribes Do? Strategies and Institutions in American Indian Economic Development*. Los Angeles: American Indian Studies Center, UCLA. 1992.

Cornell, Stephen, and Joseph P. Kalt. Where Does Economic Development Really Come From? Constitutional Rule Among the Contemporary Sioux and Apache. *Economic Inquiry* July:402–426. 1995.

———. Where's the Glue? Institutional and cultural foundations of American Indian economic development. *Journal of Socio-Economics* 29:443–470. 2000.

Cornell, Stephen, and Joseph P. Kalt, eds. *Successful Economic Development and Heterogeneity of Governmental Form on American Indian Reservations*. Edited by M. Grindle, *Getting Good Government: Capacity Building in the Public Sectors of Developing Countries*. Cambridge: Harvard Institute of International Development. 1996.

Corntassel, Jeff, and Richard C. Witmer. *Forced Federalism: Contemporary Challenges to Indigenous Nationhood, American Indian Law and Policy Series; v. 3*. Norman: University of Oklahoma Press. 2008.

Council, Navajo Nation. "Amending Title 1 of the NNC to Recognize the Fundamental Laws of the Diné." Navajo Nation Council. 2002.

Crawford, Neta C. A Security Regime Among Democracies: cooperation among Iroquois nations. *International Organizations* 48 (3):345–385. 1994.

De Laguna, Frederica. *Under Mount Saint Elias: The History and Culture of the Yakutat Tlingit*. 3 vols, Smithsonian Contributions to Anthropology,. Washington,: Smithsonian Institution Press; for sale by the Supt. of Docs., 1972.

Deloria, Vine. *Behind the Trail of Broken Treaties; an Indian Declaration of Independence*. New York,: Delacorte Press. 1974.

———. *The world We Used to Live In: Remembering the Powers of the Medicine Men*. Golden, Colo.: Fulcrum Pub. 2006.

Deloria, Vine, and Raymond J. DeMallie. *Documents of American Indian Diplomacy: Treaties, Agreements, and Conventions, 1775–1979*. 2 vols, *Legal History of North America*. Norman: University of Oklahoma Press. 1999.

Deloria, Vine, and Clifford Lytle. *The Nations Within: The Past and Future of American Indian Sovereignty:* Univeristy of Texas Press. 1984.

Deloria, Vine, Steve Pavlik, and Daniel R. Wildcat. *Destroying Dogma: Vine Deloria, Jr. and His Influence on American Society*. Golden, Colo.: Fulcrum Pub. 2006.

Deloria, Vine, and David E. Wilkins. *Tribes, Treaties, and Constitutional Tribulations*. 1st ed. Austin: University of Texas Press. 1999.

Denetdale, Jennifer. *Reclaiming Diné History: The Legacies of Navajo Chief Manuelito and Juanita*. Tucson: University of Arizona Press. 2007.

———. *The Long Walk: The Forced Navajo Exile, Landmark Events in Native American History*. New York: Chelsea House Publishers. 2008.

———. *The Navajo, History & Culture of Native Americans*. New York: Chelsea House. 2011.

Department of Interior. Available from http://www.bia.gov/WhoWeAre/BIA/OIS/TribalGovernmentServices/TribalDirectory/. [cited May 31, 2014]

DPI. Diné Policy Institute Policy Domains. Diné College. 2012.

Echo-Hawk, Walter R. *In the Courts of the Conqueror: The Ten Worst Indian Law Cases Ever Decided.* Golden, Colo.: Fulcrum Pub. 2010.

Eldridge, Dana, James McKenzie, Robyn Jackson, Avery Denny, Robert Yazzie, Amber K. Crotty, and Crystalyne Curley. Diné Food Sovereignty: A Report on the Navajo Nation Food System and the Case to Rebuild a Self-Sufficient Food System for the Diné People. Tsaile: Diné Policy Institute. 2014.

Fearon, James D. Rationalist Explanations for War. *International Organizations* 49 (3):379–444. 1995.

Fixico, Donald Lee. *The Invasion of Indian Country in the Twentieth Century: American Capitalism and Tribal Natural Resources*. Niwot, Colo.: University Press of Colorado. 1998.

———. *The American Indian Mind in a Linear World: American Indian Studies and Traditional Knowledge*. New York: Routledge. 2003.

———. *The Invasion of Indian Country in the Twentieth Century: American Capitalism and Tribal Natural Resources*. 2nd ed. Boulder: University Press of Colorado. 2012.

———. *Indian Resilience and Rebuilding: Indigenous Nations in the Modern American West, Modern American West American indian tribal law, Aspen elective series*. Austin: Wolters Kluwer Law & Business. 2013.

Fletcher, Matthew L. M. *American Indian Tribal Law*, Aspen Elective series. Austin: Wolters Kluwer Law & Business. 2011.

Forbes, Jack D. *Native Americans and Nixon: Presidential Politics and Minority Self-Determination, 1969–1972*. Los Angeles: American Indian Studies Center, UCLA. 1981.

General federation of women's clubs. Public welfare Department [from old catalog], and Corinna Haven Putnam Smith. *A bulletin on the Meriam report.* Washington, D.C. 1928.

Getches, David. Beyond Indian Law: The Rehnquist Court's Pursuit of States' Rights, Color-Blind Justice and Mainstream Values. *Minnesota Law Review* 86:267–362. 2001.

Getches, David H. *Cases and Materials on Federal Indian Law*. 6th ed, *American casebook series*. St. Paul, MN: Thomson/West. 2011.

Getches, David H., Charles F. Wilkinson, and Robert A. Williams. *Cases and Materials on Federal Indian Law*. 5th ed, American Casebook Series. St. Paul, MN: Thomson/West. 2005.

Goertz, Gary. *International Norms and Decision Making: A Punctuated Equilibrium Model.* Lanham, Md.: Rowman & Littlefield. 2003.

———. *Social Science Concepts: A User's Guide*. Princeton: Princeton University Press. 2006.

Hämäläinen, Pekka, and William P. Clements Center for Southwest Studies. *The Comanche Empire*, *The Lamar Series in Western History*. New Haven: Yale University Press. 2008.

Henson, Eric C. The *State of the Native Nations: Conditions under U.S. Policies of Self-Determination: The Harvard Project on American Indian Economic Development.* New York: Oxford University Press, 2008.

Holm, Tom. *The Great Confusion in Indian Affairs: Native Americans and Whites in the Progressive Era.* 1st ed. Austin: University of Texas Press. 2005.

Holm, Tom, ed. *Mechanistic versus Organic Human-Land Relationships: The Navajo-Hopi Joint Use Area Dispute as a Case Study*. Edited by D. Fixico, *Native Views of Indian-White Historical Relations*: Newberry Library. 1989.

Holm, Tom, J. Diane Pearson, and Ben Chavis. Peoplehood: A Model for the Extension of Sovereignty in American Indian Studies. *Wicazo Sa Review* 18 (1). 2003.

Indian Gaming Regulatory Act. 100–497.

Iverson, Peter, and Jennifer Denetdale. *The Navajo, Indians of North America (Heritage ed)*. Philadelphia: Chelsea House Publishers. 2005.

Johnson, Ralph, and Berrie Martinis. Chief Justice Rehnquist and the Indian Cases. *Public Land and Resource Law Review* 16:1–25. 1995.

Johnson, Ralph W. The States Versus Indian Off-Reservation Fishing: A United States Supreme Court Error. *Washington Law Review* 47 (2):207. 1972.

Jorgensen, Miriam, ed. *Rebuilding Native Nations: Strategies for Governance and Development.* Tucson: University of Arizona Press. 2007.

King, Gary, Robert O. Keohane, and Sidney Verba. *Designing Social Inquiry: Scientific Inference in Qualitative Research.* Princeton, N.J.: Princeton University Press. 1994.

Klah, Hasteen, and Mary C. Wheelwright. *Navajo Creation Myth.* New York: AMS Press. 1980.

Lee, Jennifer. Don't Tell Amy Chua: Mexicans Are the Most Successful Immigrants: A study of Los Angeles immigrants finds that when we measure success as progress from generation to generation, Mexican-Americans come out ahead. *Time.* 2014.

Lemont, Eric D. *American Indian Constitutional Reform and the Rebuilding of Native Nations.* 1st ed. Austin: University of Texas Press. 2006.

Lerma, Michael. "Concepts of Indigenousness" *Red Ink.* 2008.

———. Guided by the Mountains: Traditional and Contemporary Approaches to Navajo Governance, American Indian Studies, University of Arizona, Tucson. 2010.

———. Indigeneity and Homeland - Land, History, Ceremony, and Language. *American Indian Culture and Research Journal* 36 (3). 2012.

———. Shocks to the Navajo (Diné) Political System: Resiliency of traditional Diné institutions in the face of colonial interaction (Contact to 1923). *Indigenous Policy Journal* 25 (1):1–20. 2014.

Lomawaima, K. Tsianina. *They Called It Prairie Light: The Story of Chilocco Indian School.* Lincoln: University of Nebraska Press. 1994.

Lomawaima, K. Tsianina, and T. L. McCarty. *"To remain an Indian": lessons in democracy from a century of Native American education, Multicultural education series.* New York: Teachers College Press. 2006.

Lukes, Steven. *Power: A Radical View, Studies in Sociology.* London; New York: Macmillan. 1974.

Mahoney, James. *Colonialism and development: Spanish America in comparative perspective, Cambridge studies in comparative politics.* New York: Cambridge University Press. 2010.

Moreton-Robinson, Aileen. Towards a New Research Agenda? Foucalt, Whiteness, and Indigenous sovereginty. *Journal of Sociology* 42 (4):383–395. 2006.

Morgenthau, Hans J. *Politics Among Nations; The Struggle for Power and Peace.* 1st ed. New York,: A. A. Knopf. 1948.

"Nanit'a Sa'ah Naaghai, Nanit'a Bikeh Hozho," (Living the Order: The Dynamic Cosmic Process of Diné Cosmology), D. H. Begay and N. C. Maryboy, Doctoral Dissertation (1998).

Navajo Treaty of 1868.

Nielsen, Marianne O., and James W. Zion. *Navajo Nation Peacemaking: Living Traditional Justice*. Tucson: University of Arizona Press. 2005.

Peterson, V. Spike. *A Critical Rewriting of Global Political Economy: Integrating Reproductive, Productive, and Virtual Economies, Routledge/RIPE series in global political economy RIPE series in global political economy*. London ; New York: Routledge. 2003.

Porter, Robert Odawi. *Sovereignty, colonialism and the indigenous nations: a reader*. Durham, N.C.: Carolina Academic Press. 2005.

Ragin, Charles C. *The Comparative Method: Moving Beyond Qualitative and Quantitative Strategies*. Berkeley: University of California Press, 1987.

———. *Fuzzy-Set Social Science*. Chicago: University of Chicago Press, 2000.

———. "Set Relations in Social Research: Evaluating Their Consistency and Coverage." *Political Analysis* 14 (2006): 291-310.

———. *Redesigning Social Inquiry: Fuzzy Sets and Beyond*. Chicago: University of Chicago Press. 2008.

Ragin, Charles C., and Howard Saul Becker. *What Is a Case?: Exploring the Foundations of Social Inquiry*. Cambridge England; New York, NY, USA: Cambridge University Press. 1992.

Ragin, Charles C. and Claude Rubinson, "Comparative Methods," in *International Encyclopedia of Political Science*, ed. Bertrand Badie, Dirk Berg-Schlosser, and Leonardo Morlino. (London: Sage, 2011)

Regan, Shawn. Unlocking the Wealth of Indian Nations: Overcoming obstacles to Tribal Energy Development. edited by T. P. a. E. R. Center. Bozeman: Property and Environmental Research Center. 2014.

Richardson, J. L. *Contending Liberalisms in World Politics: Ideology and Power*. Boulder, Colo.: L. Rienner. 2001.

Robertson, Lindsay Gordon. *Conquest by Law: How the Discovery of America Dispossessed Indigenous Peoples of Their Lands*. Oxford; New York: Oxford University Press. 2005.

Sartori, Giovanni. Concept Misformation in Comparative Politics. *American Political Science Review* 64 (4):1033–1053. 1970.

Smith, Noel Lyn. Council combines committees into 4. *Navajo Times*, January 22, 2011.

The State of the Native Nations Conditions under U.S. Policies of Self-Determination. Edited by T. H. P. o. A. I. E. Development: Oxford University Press. 2007.

Taylor, Jonathan B, and Joseph P. Kalt. American Indian on Reservations: A Data Book on Socioeconomic Change Between the 1990 and 2000 Censuses Cambridge: Harvard Project on American Indian Economic Development. 2005.

"Tiis Tsoh Sikaad Chapter." [cited September 12, 2013].

Waltz, Kenneth N. *Theory of International Politics*. 1st ed. Boston, Mass.: McGraw-Hill. 1979.

Wilkins, David. 2008. A Matter of Disrespect. *Indian Country Today*, http://indiancountrytodaymedianetwork.com/ictarchives/2008/04/28/wilkins-a-matter-of-disrespect-79682.

———. *American Indian Sovereignty and the U.S. Supreme Court: The Masking of Justice*. 1st University of Texas Press ed. Austin: University of Texas Press. 1997.

———. *American Indian Politics and the American Political System*. 2nd ed, *The spectrum series, race and ethnicity in national and global politics*. Lanham, Md.: Rowman & Littlefield. 2007.

———. *The Navajo Political Experience*. Fourth edition. ed. 2013.

Wilkins, David E., and K. Tsianina Lomawaima. *Uneven Ground: American Indian Sovereignty and Federal Law*. Norman: University of Oklahoma Press. 2001.

Wilkins, David E., and Heidi Kiiwetinepinesiik Stark. *American Indian Politics and the American Political System*. 3rd ed, *The spectrum series: race and ethnicity in national and global politics*. Lanham, Md.: Rowman & Littlefield. 2011.

Williams, Robert A. *Linking Arms Together: American Indian Treaty Visions of Law and Peace, 1600–1800*. New York: Routledge. 1999.

———. *Like a Loaded Weapon: The Rehnquist Court, Indian Rights, and the Legal History of Racism in America, Indigenous Americas*. Minneapolis, MN: University of Minnesota Press. 2005.

———. *Savage Anxieties: The Invention of Western Civilization*. 1st ed. New York: Palgrave Macmillan, 2012.

Wilson, Shawn. *Research Is Ceremony: Indigenous Research Methods*. Black Point, N.S.: Fernwood Pub. 2008.

Yazzie, Robert, Moroni Benally, Andrew Curley, Nikke Alex, James Singer, and Amber Crotty. Navajo Nation Constitutional Feasibility and Government Reform Project. edited by R. Yazzie. Tsaile: Diné Policy Institute. 2008.

Yazzie, Robert, Avery Denny, Amber Crotty, Dana Eldridge, Moroni Benally, Michael Lerma, and Andrew Curley. Recommendations for Restructuring the Navajo Nation Council. Diné Policy Institute. 2011.

Cases and Court Decisions

Alaska v. Native Village of Venetie, 522 U.S. 520 (1998).
Amoco Production Co. v. Southern Ute Indian Tribe, 526 U.S. 865 (1999).
Arizona Dept. of Revenue v. Blaze, 526 U.S. 32 (1999).
Babbitt v. Youpee, 519 U.S. 234 (1997).
Brendale v. Confederated Yakima Indian Nation, 492 U.S. 408 (1989).
Bryan v. Itasca County, 426 U.S. 373 (1976).
California v. Cabazon Band of Mission Indians, 480 U.S. 202 (1987).
Central Machinery Company v. Arizona Tax Commission, 448 U.S. 160 (1980).
Cotton Petroleum Corporation v. New Mexico, 490 U.S. 163 (1989).
Department of the Interior v. Klamath Water Users Association, No. 99–1871 (2001).
Duro v. Reina, 495 U.S. 676 (1990).
El Paso Natural Gas Company v. Neztsosie, 526 U.S. 473 (1999).
Employment Division, Oregon Department of Natural Resources v. Smith, 494 U.S. 872 (1990).
Ex Parte Crow Dog. U.S. Supreme Court. (1884).
Ex parte KENYON. In Parker, J.: Circuit Court, W.D. Arkansas. (1878).
Idaho v. Coeur d'Alene Tribe of Idaho, 521 U.S. 261 (1997).
Johnson and Graham's Lessee v. William M'Intosh. U.S. Supreme Court. (1823).
Kerr-McGee v. Navajo Tribe, 471 U.S. 195 (1985).
Kiowa Tribe of Oklahoma v. Manufacturing Technologies, Inc., 523 U.S. 751 (1998).
Lyng v. Northwest Cemetery Protection Association, 485 U.S. 439 (1988).
Merrion v. Jicarilla Apache Tribe, 455 U.S. 130 (1982).
Mescalero Apache Tribe v. Jones, 411 U.S. 145 (1973).
Minnesota v. Mille Lacs Band of Chippewa Indians, 526 U.S. 172 (1999).
Moe v. Salish & Kootenai Tribes, 425 U.S. 463 (1976).
Montana v. Blackfeet Tribe, 471 U.S. 759 (1985).
Montana v. Crow Tribe of Indians, 523 U.S. 696 (1998).
Montana v. United States, 450 U.S. 544 (1981).
Morton v. Mancari, 417 U.S. 535 (1974).
National Farmers Union Insurance Companies v. Crow Tribe of Indians, 468 U.S. 1315 (1984).
New Mexico v. Mescalero Apache Tribe, 462 U.S. 324 (1983).
Oklahoma Tax Commission v. Citizen Band Potawatomi Tribe, 498 U.S. 505 (1991).
Oklahoma Tax Commission v. Sac & Fox Nation, 508 U.S. 114 (1993).

Oliphant v. Suquamish Indian Tribe, 435 U.S. 191 (1978).
Puyallup Tribe v. Washington Game Department, 433 U.S. 165 (1977).
Ramah Navajo School Board v. Bureau of Revenue, 458 U.S. 832 (1982).
Rice v. Cayetano, 528 U.S. 495 (2000).
Rice v. Rehner, 463 U.S. 713 (1983).
Seminole Tribe of Florida v. Florida, 517 U.S. 44 (1996).
South Dakota v. Bourland, 508 U.S. 679 (1993).
South Dakota v. Yankton Sioux Tribe, 522 U.S. 329 (1998).
Strate v. A-1 Contractors, 520 U.S. 438 (1997).
Tee-Hit-Ton Indians v. United States. U.S. Supreme Court. 1955.
Three Affiliated Tribes v. Wold Engineering, 467 U.S. 138 (1984).
United States Ex Rel. Standing Bear V. Crook, 25 F.Cas. 695, 697 (1879).
United States v. Antelope, 430 U.S. 641 (1977).
United States v. Kagama. United States Supreme Court. (1886).
United States v. Mazurie, 419 U.S. 544 (1975).
United States v. Wheeler, 435 U.S. 313 (1978).
The United States, Plaintiffs, v. William S. Rogers. In Taney, Chief Justice: Supreme Court of the United States. (1846).
Washington v. Confederated Tribes, 447 U.S. 134 (1980).
White Mountain Apache Tribe v. Bracker, 448 U.S. 136 (1980).
Yakima v. Confederated Tribes, 502 U.S. 251 (1992).

CPSIA information can be obtained
at www.ICGtesting.com
Printed in the USA
BVHW03s1802220318
511306BV00001B/165/P

9 781890 357498